THE THREE CREEDS

THE THREE CREEDS

BY THE RIGHT REV.
EDGAR C. S. GIBSON, D.D.

Lord Bishop of Gloucester

WIPF & STOCK · Eugene, Oregon

Wipf and Stock Publishers
199 W 8th Ave, Suite 3
Eugene, OR 97401

The Three Creeds
By Gibson, Edgar C. S.
ISBN 13: 978-1-5326-5642-2
Publication date 4/23/2018
Previously published by Longmans, Green, and Co., 1908

CONTENTS

CHAPTER I.—OF CREEDS IN GENERAL

	PAGE
§ 1. THE GROUNDS ON WHICH THE REQUIREMENT OF FAITH IS MADE	3
§ 2. THE REQUIREMENT OF OPEN CONFESSION, AND THE CONNECTION OF THE CREED WITH BAPTISM	13
§ 3. THE DEVELOPMENT OF CREEDS	26

CHAPTER II.—THE APOSTLES' CREED

§ 1. THE EARLY HISTORY OF THE APOSTLES' CREED	39
§ 2. THE LATER INSERTIONS IN THE APOSTLES' CREED	60
§ 3. THE USE MADE OF THE APOSTLES' CREED BY THE CHURCH	80
§ 4. THE DOCTRINE OF THE APOSTLES' CREED	86
NOTE A. Authorities for the later additions to the Apostles' Creed	108
NOTE B. An early Metrical Translation of the Apostles' Creed	110

CHAPTER III.—THE NICENE CREED

	PAGE
§ 1. THE COUNCIL OF NICÆA	115
§ 2. THE NICENE CREED FROM NICÆA TO CHALCEDON	138
§ 3. THE NICENE CREED AFTER CHALCEDON	154
§ 4. THE USE OF THE NICENE CREED IN THE SERVICES OF THE CHURCH	166
NOTE C. The English Translation of the Nicene Creed	169
NOTE D. On the Origin of the enlarged Nicene Creed	175
NOTE E. On 1 Cor. xv. 24, and the clause 'Whose kingdom shall have no end'	176

CHAPTER IV.—THE ATHANASIAN CREED

§ 1. THE DATE AND AUTHORSHIP OF THE ATHANASIAN CREED	181
§ 2. THE USE MADE OF THE ATHANASIAN CREED BY THE CHURCH	195
§ 3. EXPOSITION OF THE ATHANASIAN CREED	206
§ 4. THE MONITORY CLAUSES, AND THE CONTROVERSIES RAISED AS TO THE USE OF THE ATHANASIAN CREED	226
NOTE F. Early Authorities for the Athanasian Creed	259
NOTE G. Early English and French Metrical Versions of the Athanasian Creed	270
NOTE H. The English Translation of the Athanasian Creed	278
INDEX	281

CHAPTER I

OF CREEDS IN GENERAL

CHAPTER I

OF CREEDS IN GENERAL

§ 1

The Grounds on which the Requirement of Faith is made

No one can read the New Testament with any care and attention without being struck by the prominence given therein to faith or belief. Our Lord's ministry began with the call to 'repent and believe the Gospel.'[1] Faith was the demand which He habitually made from those who sought His help; and as the reward of faith His mighty works were wrought. 'According to your faith be it unto you.' 'Thy faith hath made thee whole.' 'O woman, great is thy faith: be it unto thee even as thou wilt.' 'If thou canst believe: all things are possible to him that believeth.' 'If ye have faith, and doubt not, ye shall not only do this which is done to the fig tree, but also if ye shall say unto this mountain, Be thou removed, and be thou cast into the sea; it shall be done. And all things,

[1] S. Mark i. 15.

whatsoever ye shall ask in prayer, believing, ye shall receive.'[1] Such passages as these all show the importance attached to faith by our Lord, and in one instance there is a definite demand for what we might almost describe as a creed made by Him. When the blind man whom He had healed in Jerusalem was cast out of the synagogue, Jesus finding him 'said unto him, Dost thou believe on the Son of God? He answered and said, Who is He, Lord, that I might believe on Him? And Jesus said unto him, Thou hast both seen Him, and He it is that talketh with thee. And he said, *Lord, I believe.* And he worshipped Him.'[2] Again and again our Lord Himself attaches promises of spiritual privileges to belief in Him or in His name, as in the great discourses in S. John's Gospel. 'He that cometh to Me shall never hunger; and he that believeth on Me shall never thirst'; or this: 'He that believeth on Me, as the Scripture hath said, out of his belly shall flow rivers of living water';[3] and, if we may trust the conclusion appended to S. Mark's Gospel, to His last charge to 'preach the Gospel to every creature' there was added the promise, 'He that believeth and is baptized shall be saved.'[4]

Accordingly when we turn to the Acts of the Apostles we find that belief or faith appears from the first as the special characteristic which marked the

---

[1] S. Matt. ix. 22, 29; xv. 28; S. Mark ix. 23; S. Matt. xxi. 21, 22.
[2] S. John ix. 35-38.   [3] S. John vi. 35; vii. 38.
[4] [S. Mark] xvi. 16.

OF CREEDS IN GENERAL

followers of Jesus. The Christian community is spoken of as 'all that believed,' or 'the multitude of them that believed.'[1] When fresh accessions are made to the Church, the fact is stated in terms such as these: 'Believers were the more added to the Lord.' 'As many as were ordained to eternal life, believed.' 'A great multitude both of the Jews and also of the Greeks believed.'[2] And when the question is asked of Paul and Silas by the trembling gaoler: 'Sirs, what must I do to be saved?' the answer is at once returned: '*Believe on the Lord Jesus*, and thou shalt be saved, thou and thy house.'[3]

Even more prominent, if possible, is the position given to faith or belief in the Epistles; and St. Paul, with inspired insight, traces the requirement of it back to the Old Testament, finding in the words of the prophet Habakkuk, 'the just shall live by his faith,' the great principle which he worked out so fully in his teaching,[4] and seeing in the case of Abraham, who 'believed God, and it was accounted to him for righteousness,' the first example of justification by faith.[5]

It is obvious that the words 'faith' and 'believe' are not used in all these passages with precisely the same shade of meaning. In some they imply that conviction of the truth of a doctrine or system which leads

---

[1] Acts ii. 44; iv. 32. [2] Acts v. 14; xiii. 48; xiv. 1.
[3] Acts xvi. 30, 31.
[4] Hab. ii. 4. Cf. Rom. i. 17; Gal. iii. 11.
[5] Gen. xv. 6. Cf. Rom. iv. 3; Gal. iii. 6.

to its acceptance. In others they suggest *trust in* a person. Thus a distinction is often drawn between believing a doctrine about Christ and believing *in* Christ. The distinction is a real one, but it is easy to exaggerate it; for the two things are closely connected together, and both are required in Scripture. It was because they believed Him to be the Messiah and the Son of God (*i.e.* believed a doctrine about Him) that the early disciples believed (or trusted) *in* Jesus, and looked for salvation through Him. There is, further, yet another different shade of meaning given to the word 'faith' or 'belief' (for it must always be remembered that there is but one Greek word, $\pi i \sigma \tau \iota s$, to represent both these English words)—a meaning which became very common in later days, and is already found in Holy Scripture. 'The faith' (η $\pi i \sigma \tau \iota s$ with the definite article) sometimes means *the substance of what is believed*, *i.e.* what we might fairly call the Christian Creed, understanding by this phrase not the actual formulary which we know, but its contents or substance. The phrase is so used in the Epistle of S. Jude, who speaks of 'the faith once for all delivered to the saints,' and again a little lower down uses the expression 'your most holy faith.'[1] So in the Acts of the Apostles we read of Elymas the sorcerer seeking to 'turn away the deputy from the faith,'[2] where the word is apparently used with something of the same shade of meaning; and this use of the term becomes increasingly common in the later

---

[1] S. Jude 3, 20.   [2] Acts xiii. 8.

OF CREEDS IN GENERAL

Epistles of S. Paul, who speaks of 'preaching the faith which he once destroyed,' of 'striving for the faith of the Gospel,' 'making shipwreck concerning the faith,' 'falling away from the faith'; of Timothy being 'nourished in the words of the faith and of the good doctrine'; of 'denial of the faith'; of men being 'led astray from the faith,' 'erring concerning the faith,' 'reprobate concerning the faith'; of 'keeping the faith,' and being 'sound in the faith.'[1] All such expressions and phrases are very noteworthy. They clearly imply that the Christian creed or belief was something definite, something which needed to be jealously guarded, something from which men might fall away to their great spiritual loss.

And yet in the present day it requires some courage for a man to stand up and admit that he attaches importance to a definite belief and soundness in the faith. The tendency of much of modern thought is to disparage the value of a definite faith, to belittle the importance of what is sometimes scornfully termed 'credal Christianity.' Any definite belief is apt to be set down as narrow and sectarian; and the familiar lines,

> 'For modes of faith let graceless zealots fight,
> His can't be wrong whose life is in the right,'[2]

would be accepted by many persons as expressing their views and needing no qualification whatever.

[1] See Gal. i. 23; Phil. i. 27; 1 Tim. i. 19; iv. 1, 6; v. 8; vi. 10, 21; 2 Tim. iii. 8; iv. 7; Tit. i. 13.
[2] Pope's *Essay on Man.*

Under these circumstances, it becomes necessary for churchmen to review their position and ask themselves why it is that Holy Scripture lays such stress not only upon the possession of faith (*subjective*), but also upon holding 'the faith' (*objective*); and further, why it is that the Church has from the very first required profession of a definite Creed from all who seek shelter within her fold and are received by baptism into her Communion; why she has, if not from the first, yet from comparatively early times, called for a profession of faith from all Communicants before they draw near in the most sacred service of all, to receive the Holy Communion of the Body and Blood of Christ; and why, lastly, she bids her ministers, when visiting the sick and dying, examine them whether they 'believe as a Christian man should or no.'[1]

There is, of course, an element of truth in Alexander Pope's lines quoted above. It does not really matter what a man *says* that he believes, if that is all. True belief is not a mere matter of words; practice may, and often does, belie profession. 'To have faith in a doctrine,' it has been truly said, 'is to believe, and not to make-believe.' Moreover, men are often better than their Creed, and even after faith in a definite Creed has been lost, the effect of past belief may still

---

[1] '*Then shall the minister exhort the sick person after this form, or other like.* . . . Therefore I shall rehearse to you the Articles of our Faith, that you may know whether you do believe as a Christian man should or no.'—*The Order for the Visitation of the Sick.*

be seen in the life; while tradition and Christian environment may influence the conduct of many who would disown the Christian faith. But though this holds good to some extent, yet in the long-run and on a wide scale it will be found that belief affects conduct far more profoundly, and that Creed and character correspond far more closely, than men in general recognise. Some striking testimonies to this may here be cited. The late Bishop Westcott says that 'all experience goes to show that conduct in the long-run corresponds with belief.' The Christian bishop does not stand alone in such an assertion. Thomas Carlyle is no less emphatic: 'When belief waxes uncertain, practice becomes unsound.' Nor has any one expressed the truth more forcibly and picturesquely than Emerson in his fine saying: 'A man's action is but the picture-book of his Creed.'[1] These sayings are absolutely true; but in order to recognise their truth we must realise what belief really means, and that much which passes in the world for belief is not worthy of the name. Unless belief manifests itself in conduct it is unreal. 'No belief,' says Professor Bain, 'is real unless it guide our actions.' With equal emphasis Professor Clifford asserts that 'preparedness to act upon what we affirm is the sole, the genuine, the unmistakable criterion of belief.'[2]

---

[1] These three citations are all given in the Rev. A. W. Robinson, *The Church Catechism Explained*, p. 37.

[2] Cited in Page Roberts, *Liberalism in Religion*, p. 78.

The truth of these sayings may easily be tested in matters not connected with religion; and it will be found that they hold good equally in regard to religious faith. Do you want to know whether belief affects conduct? You may apply a very simple test by putting a pistol to your neighbour's head. If he believes it to be unloaded, he may smile at your act as a piece of harmless folly; but if he believes it to be loaded, you will soon find to your cost that his belief guides his actions. He will knock up the pistol at once, and you will soon find yourself stretched on the floor, or carried off to gaol as a dangerous person.

Again, a man tells you that he believes in homeopathy. You accept his statement without question at the moment. He *says* he does, and that is enough for you until the occasion arises for him to put his belief into practice. His wife or child is struck down by some disease. At once you inquire who is the medical practitioner for whom he sends. If he be a homeopath, his action is the picture-book of his creed, and illustrates his belief. If, however, you find that it is not the homeopath who is called in and entrusted with the care of the sick person, you can scarcely help questioning the reality of his faith. Or take the case of the famous German pessimist who denounced life as not worth living. 'Schopenhauer was bound by his own principles to seize the first opportunity that fairly offered of " shuffling off this mortal coil." . . . The cholera came to Berlin. Here was a door to *Nirvana*—cessation of existence—open to him. He packed his portmanteau like the veriest optimist, and found in safer quarters renewed pleasure in the activity of denouncing all activity as pain.'[1]

Tried by Professor Clifford's test the faith of the homeopath and of the philosopher was lacking in the sole criterion that could have established its genuineness. And in common fairness we must be prepared to have the same test applied to religious belief. It is a severe one, but Christians ought not to shrink from it. In days when men were called to suffer for their Creed it was the test which was universally employed; and it was easy for the world to learn that the Christian character was bound up with the Christian Creed. The evidence was brought before men in such a way that they could not help seeing it. That they are so slow to realise it to-day is partly due to the fact already noticed, that Christian ideas remain in the air and continue to affect those who have ceased to believe, and that environment and tradition count for much in influencing conduct. But unhappily it is due still more to the feeble character of much that is called belief, and to the fact that with many it is a profession and nothing more. This it is which more than anything else blinds men's eyes to the truth, and leads to the popular depreciation of faith and dogma. Let Christians only remember that 'preparedness to act upon what we affirm is the sole, the genuine, the unmistakable criterion of belief,' and let them live accordingly, and the world will soon come to see that belief in the

[1] Archbishop Thomson, *Word, Work, and Will*, p. 222.

revelation of the Gospel is the real groundwork of the Christian character, and that the two cannot be separated. If the belief goes, the character falls with it.

In the ancient Church there was a charge given to a 'reader' when he was set apart for his office, which has still lingered on among us and is familiar to many in a slightly altered form as a prayer for use in the vestry with the choir. This brings out well the connection between creed and conduct. 'Vide ut quod ore cantas, corde credas, et quod corde credis operibus comprobes.' With us the charge has become a prayer, and it is one which every Christian should make his own. 'Grant, O Lord, that what we say with our lips we may believe in our hearts, and what we believe in our hearts we may show forth in our lives through Jesus Christ our Lord.'[1]

[1] The charge is found in Canon 10 of the 'fourth Council of Carthage'; a series of canons which probably belongs in reality to a Gallican source, not later than the sixth century. Almost the same phrase is found as early as the fourth century in the writings of Niceta of Remesiana, *De Psalmodiae Bono* (*ed*. Burn, p. 67).

§ 2

The Requirement of Open Confession, and the Connection of the Creed with Baptism

THE quotation at the close of the last section brings out the fact that between belief and practice there is something else required, viz. confession with the lips. This, as well as belief, is often insisted on in the New Testament. The primary passage is that in the Gospel, where our Lord Himself directly requires open confession or acknowledgment of Him to be made by His followers. 'Every one who shall confess Me before men, him will I also confess before My Father which is in heaven. But whosoever shall deny Me before men, him will I also deny before My Father which is in heaven.'[1] This passage does not stand alone. S. Paul also, in a remarkable passage, couples together the necessity of faith and such open confession. 'If thou shalt confess with thy mouth Jesus as Lord, and shalt believe in thy heart that God raised Him from the dead, thou shalt be saved: for with the heart man believeth unto righteousness, and with the mouth confession is made unto salvation.'[2] S. John also, evidently with a view to false teaching that was

[1] S. Matt. x. 32, 33. [2] Rom. x. 9, 10.

already current concerning the nature of our Lord's humanity, says: 'Every spirit which confesseth that Jesus Christ is come in the flesh is of God: and every spirit which confesseth not Jesus is not of God'; and again, a little lower down in the same chapter: 'Whosoever shall confess that Jesus is the Son of God, God abideth in him and he in God.'[1]

It is true, as has already been pointed out, that words are not everything, and 'what we say with our lips' does not necessarily represent 'what we believe in our hearts'; but still the spoken confession is something to appeal to, and, broadly speaking, the public profession is in many cases the best, and sometimes the only, testimony that can be given to the reality of the belief to which it gives expression, especially if it be made as a solemn act, and in a case where no worldly advantage can be looked for from it. It forms something to appeal to afterwards. It not only makes an impression upon others, but it also steadies and strengthens the confessor's own faith and purpose. It is a taking of sides. A man who has made his public confession of faith has committed himself, and is stronger for such an act. He has come out into the open, and given a pledge of the sincerity of his faith. An interesting and striking example of the value of such open profession is given by the story which S. Augustine relates in his *Confessions* of the conversion of the famous Roman rhetorician Victorinus. This man had for some time studied the Scriptures

[1] 1 S. John iv. 2, 3, 15.

in secret, and used to say privately to the Christian priest Simplician, whom he knew well, that he was already a Christian. To this Simplician replied: 'I shall not believe it, nor shall I reckon you among Christians, until I see you in the Church of Christ.' Victorinus laughed and rejoined, 'So then walls make a Christian.' 'Often,' says Augustine, 'he used to affirm that he was already a Christian. Often Simplician made the same answer. Often his jest about the walls was repeated. He was afraid to offend his friends, who were proud demon-worshippers.' So things went on for a time, but at length

'By reading and reflection he gained strength; he feared to be denied by Christ before the holy angels, if he should fear to confess Him before men; he saw that he would be guilty of a great sin if he was ashamed of the sacraments of the humility of Thy Word, and not ashamed of the godless worship of those proud demons, whereof he had been a proud worshipper and participant; he was disgusted with vanity, and blushed for the truth; and so, quite suddenly and unexpectedly, he said to Simplician, "Let us go to church. I want to become a Christian." Simplician went with him scarce able to contain himself for joy. He received the first sacraments of instruction, and not long afterwards gave in his name that he might receive the baptism of regeneration, to the great wonder of Rome and the great joy of the Church. . . . Finally, when the hour arrived for making the public profession of faith, which at Rome is made from a platform in full sight of the faithful, in a set form of words said by heart, the presbyters would have given Victorinus leave to make his profession in private, this being not unusual in the case of persons who had reasons for shrinking from the ordeal; but he deliberately chose to profess his salvation in the sight of the holy congregation. For there was no salvation in the rhetoric which he had taught; yet he had professed that openly. . . . And so, when he mounted the platform to deliver his profession, all who knew him uttered his name with a cry of delight. And who was there that knew him not? And so a whisper was heard running all round that jubilant assembly, "Victorinus! Victorinus!" Sudden was the sound of exultation, when they saw him; sudden was the hush of attention, that they might hear. He repeated the true faith with unfaltering confidence, and all would have clasped him to their hearts, yea, they did clasp him to their hearts with the arms of love and joy.'[1]

The incident well illustrates the importance and value of the requirement of open confession with the lips as well as of belief in the heart. It shows what it means, both to the man who makes it and to those who hear it. Accordingly it is no wonder that from the first the Christian Church laid stress on the necessity of it. Indeed, we find in various parts of the Epistles indications that in very early days forms of

---

[1] The passage is slightly abridged from S. Augustine's *Confessions*, viii. 2.

OF CREEDS IN GENERAL 17

confession of belief began to be, as it were, crystallised, and to take definite shape. Thus in 1 Corinthians xv. S. Paul speaks of handing on to the Corinthians that which he had previously 'received' from others, and his words almost give the impression that he was reciting or alluding to a formula that he had learnt by heart. For having reminded them 'in what words' he had preached the Gospel to them, he proceeds to say: 'I delivered unto you first of all that which I also received, how that Christ died for our sins according to the Scriptures, and that He was buried, and that He hath been raised again the third day according to the Scriptures.'[1] Still earlier in the same Epistle he writes: 'For though there be that are called gods, whether in heaven or on earth; as there are gods many and lords many; yet to us there is *one God, the Father*, of whom are all things, and we unto Him; and *one Lord, Jesus Christ*, through whom are all things, and we through Him,'[2] where some writers have detected a similar reference to some formulary. Elsewhere in writing to Timothy he gives what appears to be a citation from an early Christian hymn, in which some of the Articles of the Church's faith are put together and summarised:[3]

> 'He who was manifested in the flesh,
> Justified in the spirit,
> Seen of angels,
> Preached among the nations,
> Believed on in the world,
> Received up in glory';

---

[1] 1 Cor. xv. 1-4.   [2] 1 Cor. viii. 6.   [3] 1 Tim. iii. 16.

while the references to 'the words of the faith,' 'the pattern of sound words,' and the 'deposit' which Timothy was to guard as a precious treasure have been thought to allude to some kind of summary of the faith or early form of Creed.[1]

Thus there is ample evidence in the New Testament, not only of the importance which the Apostolic Church attached to a definite belief, and the open confession of it, but also of the fact that the confession was at least tending to take a fixed form, and to be embodied in something like a formulary. There were various occasions on which such might prove useful; but there was one on which it would be pre-eminently required. It was in Baptism that a person was admitted to the Church, and thus definitely took a side, and declared himself a Christian. On this occasion some public acknowledgment of his acceptance of the Christian faith, however simple, was not only natural but almost a necessity; and there can be no doubt that it was required from the first. An allusion to this has been traced by commentators, such as Bishop Westcott and the present Dean of Westminster, in S. Paul's words in Ephesians v. 26: 'Christ loved the Church, and gave Himself up for it, that He might sanctify it, having cleansed it by the washing of water *with the word* ($\dot{\epsilon}\nu$ $\dot{\rho}\acute{\eta}\mu\alpha\tau\iota$).' In this Bishop Westcott sees a definite reference to the initiatory sacrament of Baptism, 'accompanied by a confession of the Christian

[1] 1 Tim. vi. 20; 2 Tim. i. 13, 14.

Faith.'[1] The Dean of Westminster also writes as follows: 'The "word" that is here spoken of as accompanying " the washing of water" is plainly some solemn mention of " the name of the Lord Jesus," in which they "were washed" from their former sins. The candidate for baptism confessed his faith in the Name: the rite of baptism was administered in the Name. The actual phrase which is here used is vague: literally translated it is " in a word ": that is to say, accompanied by a solemn word or formula, which expressed the intention of baptiser and baptised, and thus gave its spiritual meaning to " the washing of water." The purpose of Christ was accordingly that He might hallow His Bride by the cleansing waters of a sacrament in which, in response to her confession, His Name was laid upon her.'[2]

Another possible allusion to the primitive confession of faith is found in 1 S. Peter iii. 21, where the 'answer' or rather 'interrogation' of a good conscience is spoken of in connection with Baptism; and this may perhaps refer to the question asked of candidates as to their belief, and the answer returned by them. Indeed, according to the received text, we have an actual example of such a confession in the very earliest days of all, in the story of the Baptism of the Ethiopian eunuch by Philip: 'As they went on their way, they came unto a certain water: and the eunuch said, See, here is water; what doth hinder me to be baptized?

---

[1] *The Epistle to the Ephesians*, p. 84.
[2] *S. Paul's Epistle to the Ephesians*, p. 125.

And Philip said, If thou believest with all thine heart, thou mayest. And he answered and said, *I believe that Jesus Christ is the Son of God.*'[1] The latter part of this, however, is not found in some of the best MSS., and is generally regarded as an interpolation. It is consequently omitted altogether from the Revised Version of the New Testament. But even if we cannot appeal to it as part of Canonical Scripture, it may nevertheless be cited as a very early witness to the practice of the Church, for we know that it had actually found its way into the text of the Acts of the Apostles some time before the last quarter of the second century, since Irenæus, Bishop of Lyons in Gaul, actually read it in his copy of the Acts, and quoted it as if it were Scripture about the year 180 A.D.[2]

It is on account of this connection with Baptism that Creeds have assumed the form that is common to them all in every part of the Church. Our Lord's command shortly before His Ascension[3] was to 'go, and make disciples of all the nations, baptizing them in (or *into*) the name of

(1) The Father,
(2) The Son,
(3) The Holy Ghost.'

Naturally, then, if any profession of belief was to be required from the recipient of baptism, it would be one

---

[1] Acts viii. 36, 37.
[2] See Irenæus, *Adv. Hær.* III. xii. 10.
[3] S. Matt. xxviii. 19.

of belief in the Father, the Son, and the Holy Ghost; and accordingly it is round the threefold Name that the three paragraphs of the Creed have grown up. It is possible that at first nothing more may have been demanded than the simplest and shortest formula: 'I believe in God the Father, and in the Son, and in the Holy Ghost,' or even, as some have thought, from a consideration of some of the passages of Scripture cited above, of belief in Jesus Christ as Lord; but of this we cannot speak with certainty; and if it were so there is no doubt that the form was very soon amplified. Questions were sure to arise which when once asked required an answer; and this answer would be embodied in the Creed, and thus additions would be made after each Name, explaining to some extent what was involved in the belief in each case. Thus Tertullian, writing in Africa towards the close of the second century, in describing Christian Baptism uses the following expression: 'We are then three times immersed, *making a somewhat fuller answer than the Lord appointed in the Gospel.*'[1] This obviously points to some expansion or amplification of the Creed. The precise reasons for this amplification will be considered later on, together with the character of the additions made. What it is desired to emphasise here is the close connection between the Creed and holy Baptism, and the fact that its form is due to that connection. Indeed, so close was the association that for a considerable period the use of the Creed in public was confined

[1] Tertullian, *De Corona militis*, cap. iii.

to this service and the preparation for it. The custom of the Church, as we can clearly trace it in the fourth century, and as it probably existed also in earlier times, was this: the solemn administration of Baptism was ordinarily restricted to the seasons of Easter, and (less frequently) Pentecost, and Epiphany. The catechumens were required to undergo a lengthy and elaborate preparation, something like that given among us to candidates for confirmation. In the course of this preparation, some time before the actual Baptism, the Creed was taught to them, and carefully explained clause by clause in an address or sermon by one of the presbyters. The catechumens were required to commit it to memory, and when the day of Baptism arrived and they were assembled in church, they were interrogated as to their faith, and were required to make answer in the words of the Creed which had been delivered to them. These two ceremonies were known as the *traditio* (*i.e.* delivery), and *redditio* (*i.e.* the giving back) *symboli*[1] (*i.e.* the Creed); and this *symbolum* or Creed was henceforth preserved in the memory, as a convenient summary of the articles of faith, to be treasured as a constant reminder, but to be regarded as a secret belonging to the initiated, a 'watchword,' by ignorance of which heretics might be detected; and in order that it might not be known to such, it was jealously guarded and not committed to paper; nor was it used in any other service of the Church. The following

[1] For the meaning of this term see below, p. 44.

OF CREEDS IN GENERAL 23

extract from a sermon actually delivered by S. Augustine, Bishop of Hippo, at the delivery of the Creed, may serve to illustrate the position given to it and the use made of it in early ages.

'Receive, my children, the rule of faith which is called the Creed, and when you have received it write it in your hearts, and say it to yourselves every day. Before you go to bed, before you leave your room, arm yourselves with your Creed. Nobody writes the Creed so that it may be read, but for saying it over with yourselves, lest forgetfulness should obliterate what diligent instruction has delivered to you, let your memory be your book. What you are going to hear, that you are to believe; and what you shall have believed, that you will also repeat aloud. For the Apostle says, "With the heart man believeth unto righteousness, and with the mouth confession is made unto salvation." For this confession to which the Apostle refers is the Creed which you are presently to say over to yourselves, and to repeat aloud.'[1]

This ceremony of the *traditio* and *redditio symboli* was, then, a part of the preparation for Baptism. But over and above the recitation of the full form of the Creed required in it, there were *interrogations* addressed to the catechumens at the time of their immersion or immediately before it; and these contained—in some instances, at least—a shorter form of Creed out of which the fuller one was probably developed. Thus at Jerusalem, in the fourth century, although a much

[1] *Sermo ad Catech.* § 1.

fuller form of Creed was delivered beforehand to the catechumens in the course of their preparatory instruction, yet at the time of the actual Baptism we gather from the lectures of S. Cyril of Jerusalem that each candidate was simply asked whether he believed in the name of the Father and of the Son and of the Holy Ghost, and that he was taught to say immediately after he had renounced the devil, 'I believe in the Father, and the Son, and the Holy Ghost, and in one baptism of repentance.'[1] Similarly at a considerably later date we find that at Rome the following short interrogatory Creed was still in use:—

> 'Dost thou believe in God the Father Almighty?—I believe.
> Dost thou believe in Jesus Christ, His only Son, our Lord, Who was born and suffered?—I believe.
> Dost thou believe also in the Holy Ghost, the Holy Church, forgiveness of sins, resurrection of the flesh?—I believe.'[2]

Elsewhere the baptismal interrogations appear to have been fuller, and corresponded more closely to the Creed in the developed form used in the preparation of the candidates. Thus in the so-called 'Canons of Hippolytus,' which probably belong to the third century (250-300), or possibly the end of the second, and which seem to be either Roman or Alexandrian, the priest questions the catechumen as follows:—

[1] S. Cyril, *Cat. Lect.*, xix. 9, xx. 4.
[2] *The Gelasian Sacramentary*, p. 86.

OF CREEDS IN GENERAL

'Dost thou believe in God the Father Almighty?—
The catechumen answers: I do believe.

Then he dips him for the first time in the water, keeping his hand placed upon his head.

A second time he questions him in these words:

Dost thou believe in Jesus Christ, the Son of God, Whom Mary the Virgin bore of the Holy Ghost [Who came to save the race of men], Who was crucified [for us] under Pontius Pilate, Who died, and rose again the third day from the dead, and ascended into heaven, and sitteth at the right hand of the Father, and shall come to judge the quick and the dead?

He answers: I do believe.

And he dips him a second time in the water.

Then he questions him a third time:

Dost thou believe in the Holy Ghost, [the Paraclete, proceeding from the Father and the Son]?

He answers: I do believe.

And the third time he dips him in the water.'[1]

These different forms indicate very clearly how close was the connection of the Creed with the sacrament of Baptism, and illustrate the manner in which the more fully developed form gradually grew up out of the original baptismal formula and the threefold name.

[1] *The Canons of Hippolytus* (*ed.* Achelis), p. 96.

§ 3

The Development of Creeds

THE Church's Creeds, then, were gradually developed out of the baptismal formula, fresh clauses being added from time to time to expand the profession of belief required in each Person of the Godhead—Father, Son, and Holy Ghost. Something more, however, should be said as to the causes which led to this development. These causes were apparently two in number. First, there was the natural desire for clearness and precision, which would lead almost insensibly to additions being made in the course of catechetical instruction, and from this there would be a tendency for them to find their way into the text of the Creed employed in this instruction, and repeated before the Baptism in the manner described above. Thus the simple expression of belief in the Father, the Son, and the Holy Ghost, required some amplification if it was to be rendered intelligible to converts new to the faith. What, for instance, was meant by belief in 'the Son'? Who is He, and what is to be thought of Him? 'The Son' would naturally be explained as referring to Him who is called in Scripture God's 'only' or 'only begotten' Son, and an identification of Him with the historic 'Jesus' of the Gospels and 'Jesus Christ our Lord' of the Epistles would naturally follow. So the clause would be made to run 'and in Jesus Christ His only Son our Lord.' In the same way it would be felt that in the course of catechetical instruction an outline of the main facts concerning the earthly life and manifestation of Jesus Christ would be a necessity, and thus a considerable number of statements regarding His birth, crucifixion, resurrection, and ascension would be introduced quite simply and naturally without any more precise reason than the desire to instruct the candidates in the elements of the faith. This was almost certainly the main cause of the growth of Creeds in the early days of the Church.

But, besides this, a second cause was at work, for there is no doubt that the rise of false teaching brought home to the Church from the first the necessity of emphasising certain articles of the Creed, and that words and phrases were introduced with the express purpose of guarding against the intrusion of those who held heretical views. That this danger was present and had to be guarded against even before the close of the apostolic age is evidenced by the emphasis which S. John lays on the *reality* of the human nature which our Lord took at the Incarnation. 'Every spirit that confesseth that Jesus Christ is *come in the flesh* is of God.'[1] Even in his days it is clear that there was false teaching on the Incarnation, and that it was found necessary to guard against the Docetic

[1] 1 S. John iv. 2.

heresy, or the view that our Lord had not really 'come in the flesh,' but that the humanity was a mere appearance or phantom, and that therefore there had been no true suffering or death, and therefore no real resurrection. In the early part of the second century this error was a formidable one; and consequently we find that Ignatius of Antioch (*c.* 115), in summing up the articles of the faith, attaches the greatest weight to the reality of the Incarnation, the Passion, and the Resurrection. In writing to the Church of Tralles he gives the following charge :—

'Be ye deaf, when any man speaketh to you apart from Jesus Christ, Who was of the race of David, Who was the Son of Mary, Who was *truly* born and ate and drank, was *truly* persecuted under Pontius Pilate, was *truly* crucified and died in the sight of those in heaven and those on earth and those under the earth; Who, moreover, was *truly* raised from the dead, His Father having raised Him, Who in the like fashion will so raise us also who believe on Him—His Father, I say, will raise us—in Christ Jesus, apart from Whom we have no true life.'[1]

This passage does not stand alone; similar ones are found in the Epistles of Ignatius to the Magnesians and Ephesians, as well as in that to the Church of Smyrna, in which he writes as follows :—

'Fully persuaded as touching our Lord that He is *truly* of the race of David according to the flesh, but Son of God by the Divine will and power, *truly* born

[1] *Ad Trall.* 9, 10.

of a virgin and baptized by John that all righteousness might be fulfilled by Him, *truly* nailed up in the flesh for our sakes under Pontius Pilate and Herod the Tetrarch . . . that He might set up an ensign unto all the ages through His resurrection, for His saints and faithful people, whether among Jews or among Gentiles, in one body of His Church. For He suffered all these things for our sakes [that we might be saved]; and He suffered *truly*, as also He raised Himself *truly*; not as certain unbelievers say, that He suffered in semblance, being themselves mere semblance.'[1]

These and similar passages show us how short summaries of the faith were arising and taking shape in formula-like sentences; while they also indicate how particular clauses might need enlarging and emphasising if erroneous beliefs were to be excluded.

Another example may be given with reference to the first article in the Creed: 'I believe in God the Father.' The Gnostics of the first and second centuries in many cases drew a distinction between the Supreme God and the Demiurge or Creator to whose work they attributed the existence of the world. They imagined also a number of intermediate beings, through whom the gulf between the Infinite and the universe was bridged over. Under these circumstances it became necessary for the Church in admitting members to insist not only on the unity of the Divine Nature, but also on the fact that the Supreme

[1] *Ad Smyrn.*, 1, 2; cf. *Ad Magn.*, 11, and *Ad Eph.*, 7, 18, 20.

God was the Creator of all things, and indeed—to guard against possible evasion—that He was the Creator not only of heaven and earth, but of *all things visible and invisible.* Consequently, instead of the simple statement of belief in 'the Father,' in Whose name the Lord had commanded that men should be baptized, an expression of belief was required 'in one God, the Father Almighty (or *All-sovereign*), Maker of heaven and earth and of all things visible and invisible.'

It is probable also that the definite statement of belief in 'the resurrection of the flesh' was added to the Creed with a view to exclude the Docetic Gnostics of the second century, in whose systems this doctrine was denied or explained away.

Similarly, though at a later date, under the influence of heresy, other portions of the Creed were enlarged. In the fourth century this cause of amplification became more marked than ever, and, as will be shown later on, the very full statement of our Lord's essential Godhead which we now read in the Nicene Creed was deliberately inserted with the object of excluding Arianism from obtaining a footing in the Church; and subsequently an ampler statement concerning the Person of the Holy Spirit than had previously been required was placed in the third paragraph of the Creed, to guard against the recognition of those who denied the Divinity or Personality of the Third Person of the Blessed Trinity.

It will readily be understood that these causes for

the enlargement of the Creed did not operate equally and at the same time in all parts of the Church; and thus even if all Creeds spring ultimately from one archetype (which as we shall see later on, is possible, though not certainly established), local variations would very soon arise. A clause or word would find its way into the Creed in one place owing to local circumstances, or to something which we might almost call an accident, but it would not necessarily be received elsewhere. Heresies would be formidable in one country which were unknown in another. Our knowledge of early Creeds is very fragmentary, and often we can only speak doubtfully of their exact words and the range of their contents; but when we come to the fourth century we have much fuller information, and we are able to say without hesitation that in that century, and to some extent in the two following ones, the Creeds of different countries and districts, as Rome, North Italy, Africa, Gaul, Spain, Jerusalem, and Antioch, varied in several details from each other. We can see also that at that time, amid much variation, there were two clearly marked types of Creed, which we may call Eastern and Western: the Creeds, *e.g.* of Jerusalem and Antioch, are closely connected with each other, while those of the Western Church fall into a distinct group, there being a strong family likeness between those of Rome, North Italy, Africa, Gaul, and Spain.

Broadly speaking, it is the fact that heresy was much more liable to arise in the speculative East than in the practical West, and hence the Eastern Creeds as a rule are fuller and more elaborate. Of the Creeds that are still in use among us, the Nicene is in its origin an Eastern Creed, the Apostles' a Western one. These may, therefore, stand as representatives of the two types, and a reference to them will easily enable the reader to note the main distinctions between the two classes. In the Apostles' Creed none of the clauses are amplified and elaborated as the corresponding ones often are in the Nicene. The first merely has 'I believe in God the Father Almighty, Maker of heaven and earth,' and these last words 'Maker of heaven and earth' were not inserted into it until a very late date, the seventh or eighth century; till then it was simply 'I believe in God the Father Almighty.' In the second paragraph, after the mention of 'Jesus Christ' as God's 'only Son, our Lord,' the Creed proceeds immediately to the fact of the Incarnation, and gives the briefest summary of the main facts of our Lord's earthly life, mentioning after the Ascension His session at the right hand of God, and return to judgment.

Once more, in the third paragraph there is a bare statement of belief 'in the Holy Ghost,' from which the Creed proceeds at once to the concluding articles, 'the Holy Catholic Church,' etc. Turning now to the Nicene Creed, we notice that each paragraph has been amplified with the evident purpose of guarding against misunderstanding, and of making it plain *what* the exact belief of the Church is. In the first paragraph 'one' is inserted before God, and the reference to the work of creation is fuller and is found much earlier than in the West. 'Maker of heaven and earth and of all things visible and invisible.' In the second article there is a full and complete statement of our Lord's Divinity: 'And in one Lord Jesus Christ, the only begotten Son of God, begotten of His Father before all worlds, God of God, Light of Light, Very God of very God, Begotten not made, Being of one substance with the Father, By Whom all things were made.' To all this there is nothing corresponding in the Apostles' Creed or in Western Creeds generally. Again, in the third paragraph there is a clear statement on the divinity of the Holy Ghost: 'I believe in the Holy Ghost, the Lord and Giver of life, Who proceedeth from the Father [and the Son], Who with the Father and the Son together is worshipped and glorified, Who spake by the prophets.' How these particular additions came to be made will be explained later; for the present it is sufficient to notice generally that they are characteristically Eastern features. Nor is this all, for a careful reading will show further that, while the Apostles' Creed of the Western type confines itself severely to the briefest notice of historical facts, the Nicene or Eastern Creed concerns itself also with the 'ideas' of Christianity and sets itself to explain the reason of the facts and to give a fuller account of them. Thus it gives—what is wholly wanting in the Apostles' Creed—a reason for the Incarnation and the Passion. It is not merely 'Who came down from heaven,' but '*Who for us men and for our salvation came down from heaven.*' It is not simply 'was crucified,' but 'was crucified *also for us*.' Again, it is not only the bare fact of the Resurrection that is stated, but its conformity with the Scriptures, *i.e.* in all probability the Scriptures of the *Old* Testament, as the phrase must necessarily mean in 1 Cor. xv. 4: 'And that He hath been raised on the third day according to the Scriptures'—which is obviously the original source whence were drawn these words in the Creed: 'the third day He rose again according to the Scriptures.' The words, then, mean not merely that Christ rose from the dead as is historically described in the Gospels, but that the Resurrection took place in fulfilment of God's purpose as declared beforehand by the prophets, 'according to the Scriptures' of the Old Testament. Once more, when Christian Baptism is mentioned, its purpose or meaning is at once pointed out: 'I acknowledge one Baptism *for the remission of sins.*' Every one of these phrases and expressions that have been now pointed out is wanting in the Apostles' Creed, and none of them occur, save very exceptionally, in Western Creeds, which as a rule give no explanation of the facts, with one single exception. In the article on Christ's return hereafter, the reason for it is given, 'From thence He shall come'—why?—'*to judge both the quick and the dead*.' Very characteristic is it of the intensely practical West that this thought of judgment to come should from the first find a prominent place in its Creed, and that this should be the single article in which it unites with the Eastern Church in giving a reason for the statement made.

The Eastern Creeds, then, are generally longer and more elaborate than the Western ones, but, on the other hand, there are two articles which ultimately found their way into the Creed of the whole of Western Christendom which (whatever their origin) were never generally adopted in the East, viz.: 'He descended into hell' and 'the communion of saints.' There are also other minor differences between the two types of Creeds, but those given above are the principal ones, and there is no need to enter into greater detail here.

It may be added that whereas this considerable variety of detail that has been mentioned as existing in the Creeds of different branches of the Church in the fourth century lingered on to a much later date, yet by degrees the Apostles' Creed superseded all other forms as the baptismal Creed of the Western Church, while in the East the Nicene Creed took the place of local forms, and came ultimately to be the sole Creed recognised for use in Baptism as well as in the service of Holy Communion.

CHAPTER II

THE APOSTLES' CREED

CHAPTER II

THE APOSTLES' CREED

§ 1

The Early History of the Creed

THE Apostles' Creed, as we know it, is the work not of one man or of one age. It is the ultimate form taken by the baptismal Creed of the Western Church, and in the precise form in which we are familiar with it it is almost certainly the latest of the three Creeds, though, as we shall see, its substance is of very early date. It is a purely Latin Creed, being unknown in the Greek Church to-day. In tracing out its history, and showing how it arrived at its present form, it will be convenient to take as our starting-point the commentary of Rufinus in the fourth century. Rufinus was a presbyter of Aquileia in North Italy, who, at the request of one Laurentius, of whom we know nothing save that he was a bishop, wrote a Commentary upon the Creed about the year 390. From this we learn not only what was the exact form of the baptismal Creed at that time, but what was believed as to its origin in the fourth century. The following extract will make this last point clear:—

'Our forefathers have handed down to us the tradition that, after the Lord's Ascension, when, through the coming of the Holy Ghost, tongues of flame had settled upon each of the Apostles, that they might speak diverse languages, so that no race however foreign, no tongue however barbarous, might be inaccessible to them or beyond their reach, they were commanded by the Lord to go severally to the several nations to preach the word. Being on the eve therefore of departing from one another, they first mutually agreed upon a standard of their future preaching, lest haply, when separate, they might in any instance vary in the statements which they should make to those whom they should invite to believe in Christ. Being all therefore met together, and being filled with the Holy Ghost, they compose, as we have said, this brief formulary of their future preaching, each contributing his several sentence to one common summary (*in unum conferendo quod sentiebat unusquisque*); and they ordain that the rule thus framed shall be given to those who believe.

'To this formulary for many and most sufficient reasons they gave the name of Symbol. For Symbol (Σύμβολον) in Greek answers to both *Indicium* (a sign or token) and *Collatio* (a joint contribution made by several) in Latin. For this the Apostles did in these words, each contributing his several sentence. It is called *Indicium* or *Signum*, a sign or token, because at

that time, as the Apostle Paul says, and as is related
in the Acts of the Apostles, many of the vagabond
Jews, pretending to be apostles of Christ, went about
preaching for gain's sake, or their belly's sake, naming
the name of Christ indeed, but not delivering their
message according to the exact traditional lines. The
Apostles therefore prescribed this formulary as a sign
or token by which he who preached Christ truly,
according to the Apostolic rule, might be recognised.
Finally, they say that in civil wars, since the armour
on both sides is alike, and the language the same, and
the custom and mode of warfare the same, each general,
to guard against treachery, is wont to deliver to his
soldiers a distinct symbol or watchword—in Latin
signum or *indicium*—so that, if one is met with, of
whom it is doubtful to which side he belongs, being
asked for the symbol (watchword), he discloses whether
he is friend or foe. And for this reason, the tradition
continues, the Creed is not written on paper or parchment, but is retained in the hearts of the faithful, that
it may be certain that no one has learnt it by reading,
as is sometimes the case with unbelievers, but by tradition from the Apostles.

'The Apostles, therefore, as we have said, being
about to separate in order to preach the Gospel, settled
upon this sign or token of their agreement in the faith;
and, unlike the sons of Noah, who, when they were
about to separate from one another, built a tower
of baked bricks and pitch, whose top might reach to
heaven, they raised a monument of faith, which might

withstand the enemy, composed of living stones and pearls of the Lord, such that neither winds might overthrow it, nor floods undermine it, nor the force of storms and tempests shake it. Right justly, then, were the one, when, on the eve of separation, they builded a tower of pride, condemned to the confusion of tongues, so that no one might understand his neighbour's speech; while the others, who were building a tower of faith, were endowed with the knowledge and understanding of all languages; so that the former might prove a sign and token of sin, the latter of faith.'[1]

This passage is very important as proving that towards the close of the fourth century the Creed was believed to have been deliberately drawn up by the Apostles before their separation; and that it was also believed to be their joint composition, to which each of the twelve contributed his sentence. Very similar language is used in a sermon ascribed with much probability to St. Ambrose.[2] Later writers, as is so often the case with traditions, know more than earlier ones, and are able to assign without hesitation his particular sentence to each of the twelve. It is not uncommon in mediæval sermons and addresses to find the Creed thus portioned out. To give but one instance, in a sermon that has been wrongly ascribed to S. Augustine, we read as follows:—

'On the tenth day after the Ascension, when the disciples were gathered together for fear of the Jews,

---

[1] Rufinus, *Com. in Symb. Apost.*, § 2 (Heurtley's translation).
[2] See Caspari, *Quellen*, ii. 48; *Alte und Neue Quellen*, 196.

the Lord sent the promised Paraclete. And when He came, the Apostles, inflamed like burning iron, and filled with the knowledge of all tongues, composed the Creed. Peter said: *I believe in God the Father Almighty, Maker of heaven and earth.* Andrew said: *And in Jesus Christ, His only Son, our Lord.* James said: *Who was conceived by the Holy Ghost, born of the Virgin Mary.* John said: *Suffered under Pontius Pilate, was crucified, dead, and buried.* Thomas said: *He descended into hell, the third day He rose again from the dead.* James said: *He ascended into heaven, He sitteth at the right hand of God the Father Almighty.* Philip said: *From thence He shall come to judge both the quick and the dead.* Bartholomew said: *I believe in the Holy Ghost.* Matthew said: *The Holy Catholic Church: the communion of saints.* Simon said: *The forgiveness of sins.* Thaddeus said: *The resurrection of the flesh.* Matthias said: *The life everlasting.*'[1]

This tradition need not detain us long. In its later form it is manifestly false. Not only are the several articles of the Creed differently distributed among the twelve Apostles in different documents, but we have historical evidence that some of them were only inserted in the Creed centuries later than the days of those Apostles to whom tradition has assigned them. Nor is it really possible to believe that even in its earlier and simpler form the tradition represents the facts of the case. Had there been such common action on the

[1] Ps. Aug., *Serm.* ccxli., *Opera*, v. (*App.*), 395, 396; cf. *Serm.* ccxl. *ib.* 394, 395.

part of the Apostles, S. Luke could scarcely have passed it over without some notice in his summary of the history in the Acts of the Apostles, and we should almost certainly have found reference to it in earlier writers than Rufinus. It must be noticed also that Rufinus is undoubtedly wrong in connecting the name *Symbolum* with the tradition that it was a joint composition. His mistake is due to imperfect knowledge of Greek and a confusion of two distinct Greek words, Σύμβολον, which means a token or watchword, and Συμβολή, which means a joint contribution. This latter Greek word, however, is never used of the Creed, and there can be no doubt that the name Σύμβολον, in its Latin form *Symbolum*, was given to the Creed as early as the third century as being the watchword of the Christian soldier, according to the alternative view stated by Rufinus.

The tradition as given above lasted throughout the Middle Ages, but after the revival of learning it was speedily seen that it could not be maintained. Laurentius Valla and Erasmus were apparently the first to question it. In spite of this, however, in the Catechism of the Council of Trent, published by order of Pope Pius V. in 1566, it is boldly said that 'the holy apostles, the greater leaders and teachers of the faith, inspired by the Holy Ghost, have divided [it] into the twelve articles of the Creed. For when they had received a command from the Lord to go forth into the whole world, acting as His ambassadors, and preach the Gospel to every creature, they thought fit to compose a form of Christian faith, to wit, that all might think and speak the same thing, and that amongst those whom they should have called to the unity of the faith no schisms should exist, but that they should be perfect in the same mind, and in the same judgment.'[1] Nearly twenty years earlier Cranmer, with truer historic insight, had admitted that its authorship was uncertain, for so early as 1548 he wrote that 'though the articles thereof are firmly and steadfastly to be believed of every Christian man, as articles sufficiently proved by Scripture, yet that they were gathered together by the twelve Apostles, and specially that every one of the Apostles made one article, as painters show that they did, cannot be proved by Scripture, ne is it not necessary to be believed for our salvation. And though it were but a small offence in the people to believe that it were an article necessary to be believed for our salvation, because the clergy, which be the lanterns and leaders unto the people, do instruct them that it is so; and it is neither against the law of God nor the law of reason but that it may be so; yet it is a great offence to the clergy to affirm for certain the thing that is to themselves uncertain; and therefore it would be reformed for eschewing of offences unto the clergy.'[2] In accordance with this, when the first Prayer Book of Edward VI. was published in the following year, Cranmer was careful to avoid using the name 'The Apostles' Creed,' and spoke of it

---

[1] *Catechism of the Council of Trent*, Part I. cap. i. q. 2.
[2] Cranmer, *Remains and Letters*, p. 515.

simply as 'the Creed,' and in the XLII. Articles of 1553 it is described as 'that which is commonly called the Apostles' Creed.'[1]

This was perhaps excess of caution and scrupulosity, for even if the Creed cannot claim to have been drawn up by the Apostles, or to be strictly speaking their work, its title may very reasonably be defended. It is the Apostles' Creed in the sense that it contains a summary of the doctrine which the Apostles preached, and that many of the phrases embodied in it became, so to speak, stereotyped in the common form of Apostolic preaching to which the New Testament bears witness. We have already seen that there are traces of something very like formularies of faith in the New Testament, and such expressions as the following seem to have become accepted phrases in the days of the Apostles: 'One God the Father,' 'Jesus Christ,' 'His Son,' 'His only begotten Son,' or 'His only Son,' 'Our Lord,' or 'One Lord,' 'under Pontius Pilate,' 'was buried,' 'rose again the third day,' 'sitteth at the right hand of God,' 'to judge the quick and the dead.'[2] It

[1] Not till 1662 was the title, *The Apostles' Creed*, given a place in the rubrics of the Prayer Book.

[2] See *e.g.* 1 Cor. viii. 6, 'One God the Father . . . and one Lord Jesus Christ'; 1 S. John iv. 9, 14, 15; cf. S. John iii. 16, 18; 'His only begotten Son,' etc. ; 1 S. Tim. vi. 13, 'Who before Pontius Pilate witnessed a good confession'; 1 Cor. xv. 4, 'How that He was buried, and that He rose again the third day according to the Scriptures'; Col. iii. 1, 'Where Christ sitteth at the right hand of God.' Cf. Rom. viii. 34; Eph. i. 20; Heb. i. 3, viii. 1, x. 12, xii. 2 ; 1 S. Pet. iii. 22 ; 2 S. Tim. iv. 1, 'who shall judge the quick and the dead'; cf. 1 S. Pet. iv. 5.

is possible, therefore, that the title was originally given to it as being in this sense the Apostolic Creed, and that when this had passed into common use its origin was forgotten, and the name gave rise to the tradition, the formation of which would have been assisted by the misunderstanding of the name *Symbolum* into which Rufinus and others fell.[1]

After the introduction on the origin of the Creed, Rufinus proceeds to comment upon the several Articles in due order, carefully pointing out wherein the Creed of the Roman Church differed from that of his own Church of Aquileia, and (in some cases) from those of the Eastern Churches; telling us also that whereas in other Churches some additions had been made on account of heresies, none had been made in the Church of Rome, partly because no heresy had its origin there, and partly because owing to the great publicity there given to the recitation of the Creed before Baptism, any addition was at once detected and not permitted. We are consequently in a position to say what was the exact form of the Roman Creed in the last quarter of the fourth century. It then consisted of the following articles :—

1. I believe in God the Father Almighty ;
2. And in Christ Jesus, His only Son, our Lord,

[1] Another possible explanation of the name is that the Creed of the Roman Church was originally known as the Apostolic Creed, because that Church of Rome was the only Apostolic See in the West. But this does not appear so probable as the view stated in the text.

3. Who was born of (*de*) the Holy Ghost, of (*ex*) the Virgin Mary,
4. Was crucified under Pontius Pilate, and was buried,
5. Rose again from the dead the third day,
6. Ascended into heaven,
    Sitteth on the right hand of the Father,
7. From thence He shall come to judge the quick and the dead;
8. And in the Holy Ghost,
9. The Holy Church,
10. The forgiveness of sins.
11. The resurrection of the flesh.

Some fifty years earlier we have another authority for the Roman Creed, which confirms what Rufinus tells us of it. In 341 Marcellus, Bishop of Ancyra, who had taken a prominent part in the Arian controversy, and had through Arian influence been deposed from his see and banished, was in Rome. On leaving he addressed a letter to Julius, Bishop of Rome, in defence of his orthodoxy, to which he appended his Creed, speaking of it apparently as the faith which he had been taught by his forefathers in God out of the holy Scriptures, and which he himself had been accustomed to preach in the Church of God. The letter of Marcellus, together with the Creed, is preserved in the work of Epiphanius,[1] a Greek writer, and it is not possible to be quite certain whether Greek is the

[1] Epiphanius, *Hær.*, lxxii.

original language of the Creed, which is acknowledged to be that of the Roman Church, and not an Eastern Creed or a private composition of Marcellus. On the whole, the probability appears to be that Marcellus was really using an original Greek text which had come down from the earlier days when the Roman Church was a Greek-speaking community. However this may be, the Creed which he gives is verbally identical with that given by Rufinus, except that in the text as given by Epiphanius the title 'The Father' is wanting in the first article, and at the close there is added another article, 'the life everlasting.' It is generally thought that these two differences are due to the blunders of Epiphanius, or the copyists of his book, and that the form given by Rufinus is the correct one. Anyhow, the agreement between the two is so close that they may be treated as practically identical. This gives us a fixed point from which to work in considering the history of the Creed. We know for certain the form it took before the middle of the fourth century. There, at least, we are on sure ground; and starting from this we may ask the following questions:—

(1) How much earlier than Marcellus can the old Roman Creed be traced, and when, and how did it originate?

(2) When, where, and why were the additions made which brought it into the form in which it is familiar to us?

(1) With regard to the former of these questions,

recent writers have been able to show that there are allusions to the very words of the Roman Creed in representative writers of the third century, *e.g.* Felix, Bishop of Rome, 269-274; Dionysius, Bishop of Rome, *c.* 259, as well as Novatian, a presbyter of the Roman Church about the same time. Even earlier it is thought that traces of an acquaintance with the same form may be found in the writings of the African presbyter Tertullian, *c.* 200 A.D.; and if so, we must hold that it had passed from Rome to Africa before the close of the second century. An apparent indication of knowledge of it in the writings of the heretic Marcion carries it back to the middle of that century, and it is now generally agreed that it cannot have been composed later than 150. Harnack puts it between 140 and 150, while other good authorities, as Kattenbusch, hold that its composition must be dated still earlier, viz. a little before or after the year 100. We shall thus be on safe ground if we claim for the form an origin in sub-apostolic days, when the leaders of the Church were men who had actually known some of the Apostles, and had lived familiarly with their immediate successors.

The experts, then, are nearly agreed as to the approximate date of the Creed, but on two points connected with its origin they are more sharply divided. (*a*) Some are disposed to think that it was a gradual compilation, and that it cannot be assigned to any one author, since it ' grew up,' as it were, by the crystallisation of floating formulæ in use in the Church.

Others, and their opinion appears to the present writer the more probable one, hold that it is definitely the work of a single hand, being deliberately composed to meet a felt want of the Church, and that its birthplace was Rome. The question cannot be considered as finally settled, as names of weight can be pleaded on either side, and there seems to be no need to enter on a discussion of the matter here. (*b*) A further question which is much debated is this: Is this old Roman Creed the parent of all other forms of Creed, or was there another type constructed on similar lines, but with certain characteristic features of its own, which was also current in the early centuries, emanating perhaps from Antioch or Ephesus, and possibly carried with him to the West by Irenæus? It is at least remarkable that, besides the general differences of character previously indicated, many of the Eastern Creeds of the fourth century and (so far as we can trace them) even earlier, have certain phrases which have either never, or in some cases only in very late days, found a place in the Roman Creed, such as '*one* God,' '*Maker of heaven and earth*,' '*one* Lord,' '*suffered*,' 'shall come *again with* (or *in*) *glory*'; and that some of these are found in the rule of faith as given by Irenæus, in words which suggest that he is actually quoting phrases from his Creed. Once more, there appears to be no need to discuss the question here, as it must be regarded as one that is still *sub judice*. All that need be said is that if the Roman Creed is really the parent of all others, it must have been introduced into the East at a very early date, possibly by Polycarp, after his visit to Rome in the days of Anicetus, c. 150 A.D. To the present writer, however, the differences between the two types appear to be so marked, and to be manifest at so early a date, that he is disposed to hold that the types are really distinct, and that both must have had their origin in some simpler form, of which they are independent developments on somewhat parallel lines. This is perhaps as far as we can go in answering the questions which are raised concerning the origin and date of the old Roman Creed, of which our form of the Apostles' Creed is a later development. We now turn to the consideration of the second group of questions concerning it.

(2) When, where, and why were the additions made which brought it into the form in which it is familiar to us?

A reference to the Roman Creed, as given above on pp. 47, 48, will show the reader that the following are the additions which have been introduced into it since the days of Rufinus:—

1. Maker of heaven and earth.
2. Conceived.
3. Suffered.
4. Dead.
5. He descended into hell.
6. God . . . Almighty.
7. Catholic.

8. The Communion of Saints.
9. The life everlasting.

We now know that almost every one of these words and articles had been already adopted in some Churches before the time at which Rufinus wrote, although they had not then found their way into the Roman Creed, which, as he expressly tells us, had remained free from later insertions. Thus we find from his Commentary that the clause 'He descended into hell' was already contained in the Creed of the Church of Aquileia, although, as he says, 'it was not added in the Creed of the Roman Church, nor in that of the Eastern Churches.' We know further from two passages in S. Cyprian's letters that, so early as the middle of the third century, the Creed of the African Church contained the clause on 'the life everlasting,'[1] which (or something equivalent to it) is also found in Eastern Creeds of the fourth century. These also sometimes contain the words 'Maker of heaven and earth,' 'suffered,' 'dead,' 'Catholic.' There remains the word 'conceived,' and the article on 'the Communion of Saints,' as well as the words 'God ... Almighty' in the sixth article,—words which are obviously of no special importance in this connection, as really adding nothing to the substance of the Creed, for they are already contained in the first article.

Until quite recently it was believed that the article on the Communion of Saints was not found anywhere

[1] S. Cyprian, Epp. lxix., lxx.

until the fifth century, when it is met with in more than one Gallican Creed; and it was regarded as a special peculiarity of the Western Creed, and thought to be unknown in the East. Recent research has, however, established the fact that it is considerably older than was imagined, and that it may actually have an Eastern origin. It is contained in the Creed of Niceta, Bishop of Remesiana in Dacia, which certainly belongs to the fourth century, and may perhaps be dated about the year 375. It is also contained in a recently discovered document known as the 'fides Hieronymi,' *the faith of S. Jerome*, which there are good grounds for thinking may be a genuine work of the saint whose name it bears. This very interesting Creed, which, however, is a private profession of faith, and not a baptismal Creed, not only contains 'the Communion of Saints,' but also furnishes another early example of the clause ' He descended into hell,' and is the earliest known Creed in which the conception is mentioned separately from the birth: '*Conceived* by the Holy Ghost, born of the Virgin Mary.' In one of his letters S. Jerome mentions a formulary that he had sent to S. Cyril of Jerusalem, and it has been suggested that this is the very document of which he speaks. If so, it will belong to the year 377 or thereabouts, and as S. Jerome had recently been in Pontus, Bithynia, Galatia, Cappadocia, and Cilicia before settling in Syria, it is thought that he may have found the article on the Communion of Saints existing in some Eastern Creed somewhere in Asia Minor, as quite independently traces of its possible existence there have been discovered; and that he thence adopted it in his own profession of faith.[1] Of this clause more must be said hereafter. For our present purpose it is sufficient to note that it was already in existence in the fourth century, like the other clauses noted above. Thus they were none of them novelties when they subsequently found their way into the Roman Creed. Most of them are common in Creeds given by Gallican writers of the fifth century, and are found in early service-books of the same church. Consequently it is generally believed that the Apostles' Creed as we know it, is a Gallican recension of the old Roman Creed, proceeding perhaps from the monastery of Lerins, a centre of great activity in the fifth century. Dr. A. E. Burn, however, who has made a special study of the subject, is disposed to think that it may

[1] The theory is due to Dom. Morin, *Sanctorum Communionem* (Macon, 1904). The 'faith' itself runs as follows: 'I believe in one God the Father Almighty, Maker of things visible and invisible. I believe in one Lord Jesus Christ, the Son of God, born of God, God of God, Light of Light, Almighty of Almighty, true God of true God, born before the ages, not made, by Whom all things were made in heaven and in earth, Who for our salvation descended from heaven, was conceived of the Holy Ghost, born of the Virgin Mary, suffered by suffering under Pontius Pilate, under Herod the King, crucified, dead, descended into hell, trod down the sting of death, rose again the third day, appeared to the Apostles. After this, He ascended into heaven, sitteth at the right hand of God the Father, thence shall come to judge the quick and the dead. And I believe in the Holy Ghost, God not unbegotten nor begotten, not created nor made, but coeternal with the Father and the Son. I believe [in] remission of sins, in the holy Catholic Church, Communion of Saints, resurrection of the flesh unto eternal life. Amen,'

have been at Rome itself that the additions were made, and that they spread from thence to other parts of the Western Church.[1] However this may be, it is remarkable that we nowhere meet with the Creed in the exact form in which it is now used by us, as by the Church of Rome, until towards the middle of the eighth century. The earliest writer who gives it *totidem verbis* as we have it is Pirminius or Priminius, a bishop who laboured in France and Germany during the first half of the eighth century (720-750). In a work of his entitled *Scarapsus*, he transcribes the Creed in full, giving it in the very words in which it is now current throughout the West,[2] and assigning each article to one or other of the Apostles. But even later than this there were variations in the forms used in some places, and it was only gradually that the longer form superseded the older Roman Creed everywhere. On the Continent this was largely due to the influence of Charlemagne, so that it would appear that from about 800 A.D. its use became general. In England the use of the older form lingered some time longer. It had probably been brought to our shores by Augustine, and there are clear traces of its use in the ninth century, though the fuller form was also employed, and from the date of the Norman Conquest it is probable that the English Church fell into line and adopted the

[1] *The Apostles' Creed* (1906), p. 51 ; cf. the same writer's *Introduction* (1899), cap. ix.

[2] It should perhaps be stated that whereas the current text has *ad inferos* in the article on the descent into hell, the text of Pirminius has *ad inferna*.

THE APOSTLES' CREED

exclusive use of the Creed, which by that time had become the accepted one of the whole of the Western Church. Yet even so, it is curious to find that there still remains in our Prayer Book at least one trace of a slightly different form, of the use of which there are indications in Ireland and France in early days. The wording of the interrogative Creed contained in the Baptismal Services and the Visitation of the Sick differs in several points from that which stands in the order for Mattins and Evensong. This will be at once apparent when the two forms are placed side by side:—

THE CREED AS CONTAINED IN THE ORDER FOR MATTINS AND EVENSONG, AND IN THE CHURCH CATECHISM.	THE CREED AS CONTAINED IN THE BAPTISMAL SERVICES, AND THE ORDER FOR THE VISITATION OF THE SICK.
I believe in God the Father Almighty, Maker of heaven and earth ;	Dost thou believe in God the Father Almighty, Maker of heaven and earth ?
And in Jesus Christ His only Son our Lord,	And in Jesus Christ His *only begotten* Son our Lord ?
Who was conceived by the Holy Ghost,	And that He was conceived by the Holy Ghost ;
Born of the Virgin Mary,	Born of the Virgin Mary ;
Suffered under Pontius Pilate,	That He suffered under Pontius Pilate,
Was crucified, dead, and buried,	Was crucified, dead, and buried ;
He descended into hell ;	That He *went down* into hell,
The third day He rose again *from the dead*,	And also did rise again the third day ;
He ascended into heaven,	That He ascended into heaven,
And sitteth on the right hand of God the Father Almighty ;	And sitteth *at* the right hand of God the Father Almighty ;

From thence He shall come to judge the quick and the dead.	And from thence shall come *again at the end of the world*, to judge the quick and the dead?
I believe in the Holy Ghost;	And dost thou believe in the Holy Ghost?
The holy Catholic Church;	The holy Catholic Church;
The Communion of Saints;	The Communion of Saints;
The Forgiveness of sins;	The *Remission* of sins;
The Resurrection of the body,	The Resurrection of the *flesh*;
And the life everlasting. Amen.	And everlasting life *after death*?

Some of the differences are obviously mere variations of translation, as 'went down' for 'descended,' 'Remission' for 'Forgiveness,' and 'Flesh' (a more accurate rendering of the Latin *carnis*) for 'Body.' But there are others which cannot be accounted for in this way. 'Only begotten' for 'only' is probably a mere variety of translation, as the Latin *unicus* is the recognised equivalent of the Greek μονογενής, but it may *possibly* point to a difference of text in the creed translated, as in some Gallican Creeds we find *unigenitum* for *unicum*.[1] The omission of the words 'from the dead' may, again, be due to similar influence, as they are wanting in a certain number of Gallican Creeds.[2] The insertion of 'after death' in the last article comes immediately from the old English baptismal service, in which, according to the Sarum Manual, a short interrogative Creed was used, in the following form:—

[1] See Hahn, *Bibliothek der Symbole*, pp. 75, 77, 79.
[2] *Ib.*, pp. 71, 73, 77, 80.

'Dost thou believe in God the Father Almighty, Maker of heaven and earth?

Dost thou also believe in Jesus Christ His only Son, our Lord [who was] born and suffered?

Dost thou believe also in the Holy Ghost, the holy Catholic Church, the Communion of Saints, the forgiveness of sins, the resurrection of the flesh, and everlasting life *after death*?'[1]

This, too, is probably due ultimately to Gallican influences, as there are traces of the occurrence of the words *post mortem* in a few Gallican Creeds, as well as in the very curious Irish Creed contained in the famous manuscript of the seventh century, known as the Bangor Antiphonary.[2] 'Again,' in the clause on the return to judgment, may be taken from the form of examination of the sick in the old English services, where we have the word '*iterumque* venturum ad judicandum vivos et mortuos,'[3] but what is the origin of the words 'at the end of the world' it is not possible to say. No explanation of their appearance seems to be forthcoming, and the precise origin of the English form of Creed which appears for the first time in the ministration of public Baptism in the Prayer Book of 1549 remains among the unsolved problems connected with Cranmer's revision of that service.[4]

[1] See Maskell, *Monumenta Ritualia*, vol. i. (2nd ed.) p. 23.
[2] Hahn, pp. 74, 80, 85.   [3] Maskell, *op. cit.* p. 92.
[4] For other unexplained signs of Gallican influence in this service see Frere and Proctor, *A New History of the Book of Common Prayer*, p. 571.

§ 2

The Later Insertions in the Creed

The later additions to the old Roman Creed require a fuller notice than has yet been given of them, in order that the reader may understand their meaning, and the reasons for their introduction into the Creed; and to these we may now return. They may conveniently be divided into three groups :—

(1) The words 'conceived,' 'suffered,' 'dead,' 'God . . . Almighty,' are quite obviously natural amplifications, made perhaps for the sake of completeness, or half-unconsciously introduced from the catechetical instruction given to catechumens. It is impossible to attach any special significance to their presence or absence, save that wherever they are found they mark a comparatively late type of creed; and in this connection it is interesting to notice that 'conceived,' 'dead,' and 'God . . . Almighty,' as well as 'He descended into hell,' and 'the Communion of Saints,' are all to this day absent from the Nicene Creed, even in its enlarged form; and that it thus preserves the more ancient type of Creed. In the same group may also be placed the words 'the life everlasting,' the omission

THE APOSTLES' CREED 61

of which from the old Roman Creed is harder to account for than is their insertion into its later form.

(2) In the second group we may place the phrase 'Maker of heaven and earth' and the word 'Catholic,' as a more special significance may attach to them. Mention has already been made of the fact that in very early days the truth that the God of the Christians was also Maker of heaven and earth was insisted on, and prominence was given to it in opposition to Gnostic theories of a distinction between the Supreme God and the Demiurge or Creator. So in the recently discovered Apology of Aristides (c. 120) emphasis is laid on the fact that Christians 'know and believe in God, *the Maker of heaven and earth.*'[1] Justin Martyr (c. 140) lays stress on the same fact,[2] as does Irenæus (c. 180) in more than one passage where he gives what he calls 'the rule of faith,' saying that the Church has 'received from the Apostles and their disciples the faith in One God, the Father Almighty, *Maker of heaven and earth*, the sea, and all that in them is.'[3] In all these passages it is now generally recognised that allusion is made to the actual words of a Creed, and, even if this cannot be laid down as absolutely certain, there is no question that these words, 'Maker of heaven and earth,' found a place in the Creeds of the Eastern Church in very early days. There is therefore good reason to think that they were first

---

[1] *Apol. Arist.*, cap. xv.; see *Texts and Studies*, vol. i. p. 25, where there is a reconstruction of the creed of Aristides.
[2] Justin Martyr, *Apol.* I. xiii.   [3] Irenæus, I. ii.

inserted with the direct object of guarding against the Gnostic heresy. Whether there was any special reason for adding them in later days to the baptismal Creed of the Western Church, it is harder to determine. Some early writers, as Novatian, had considered that they were substantially contained in the word 'Almighty,' or *All Sovereign* (*Omnipotens*), *i.e.* the Maker as well as the Ruler of all things, and after the disappearance of Gnosticism, which was always more prevalent in the East than in the West, there would be no special need for amplification of the thought. Probably, then, this phrase, like those in the first group, was merely added for general reasons, as a natural amplification, and conceivably to make the baptismal Creed conform more closely to the Nicene. But it remains a possibility that there may have been some special reason, no longer evident to us, for the addition, which was one of the very latest to be made, being rarely found in Western Creeds before the eighth century.

The word 'Catholic,' as an epithet of the Church, is also contained in the Creeds of the Eastern Church so far back as we can trace them, but in this case the evidence only takes us back to the fourth century, for there is scarcely anything to show us what was the wording of the third division of the Creed in the East before that date. But in very early days it was usual to speak of the Church as *Catholic*. The word in itself merely means *general* or *universal*. It is so employed, for instance, by Justin Martyr, who speaks of 'the catholic (*i.e.* general) resurrection.' As applied to the Church, the earliest instance of its use is found in one of the epistles of Ignatius at the very beginning of the second century. Writing to the Church of Smyrna, Ignatius says that 'wheresoever is Jesus Christ, there is the Catholic Church,' where, as Bishop Lightfoot points out,[1] he means the universal Church as opposed to a particular body of Christians. Very soon, however, it came to acquire a more technical sense, and men spoke of the Church as 'Catholic,' to mark its distinction from the heretical sects, which were partial, scattered, localised, and isolated. There was thus a secondary shade of meaning superadded to the original one; it signified not only *universality*, but also *orthodoxy*. It is so used even before the close of the second century in the writings of Clement of Alexandria, and in the Muratorian fragment on the canon of Scripture, in which we are told of certain heretical writings that they 'cannot be received in the Catholic Church.' In later days this use became very common. In the acts of the martyr Pionius, who suffered in the persecution of Decius, A.D. 250, the magistrate is represented as asking him, 'Who are you?' to which the answer was returned 'a Christian.' 'Of what Church?' was the next question: 'Of the Church Catholic,' the reply. So Pacian, Bishop of Barcelona, said of himself, '"Christian" is my name, "Catholic" my surname; the latter distinguishes me from others who bear the same

[1] *Apost. Fathers*, Part II. vol. ii. p. 310.

name, but are not of the same family.'[1] No positive evidence is forthcoming to show whether, when the word was first given a place in the Eastern Creeds, this secondary sense was attached to it; but to judge from the very early date to which this meaning of the word can be traced, there can be little doubt that it was intended, as well as that of 'universal.' And certainly, when the use of it passed over to the West, and it began to make its way into Western Creeds, this meaning was so fixed that it would necessarily be given to it. Indeed S. Augustine, in explaining the words of the Creed of the African Church to catechumens, explains the phrase 'the holy Church' by means of it: 'the holy Church, that is the Catholic Church, for both heretics and schismatics call their congregations Churches.'[2] Whether there was any particular occasion which called for the introduction of the word we cannot say. Possibly, like the other additions mentioned above, it slipped into a place in the Western Creeds from its very familiarity. But, whether this were so or not, Dr. Swete is undoubtedly right in saying that 'it may readily be admitted that this secondary meaning was present to the thoughts of the generation which defined the Holy Church of the Western Creed to be "catholic." Possibly it was the exclusiveness of the term quite as much as its comprehensiveness which commended it to the post-Augustinian Church.' '*Catholicam*, as understood in the

---

[1] See Swete, *The Apostles' Creed*, p. 79.
[2] *De Fide et Symbolo*, § 21.

THE APOSTLES' CREED 65

fifth century, was exclusive as well as comprehensive ; it embraced all Christian communities which held fast by the Apostolic doctrine and discipline, but shut the door against those who rejected either. Neither the Arian nor the Donatist could claim to belong to a Church which was defined as Catholic.'[1]

(3) The third group consists of the two complete clauses, ' He descended into hell,' and ' the Communion of Saints.' Obviously neither of these can have slipped in half accidentally, owing to the fact that they were current phrases, as may have happened with all the other later additions just considered. In the case of these two clauses, whatever may have been the motives for it, their insertion must have been a deliberate act. Each of them must now be considered separately.

(a) ' He descended into hell.' In order to understand this properly, the reader must begin by clearing his mind from any idea that ' hell ' in the Creed means the place of final punishment to which impenitent sinners are to be banished at the last day. For this the regular term in Scripture is Gehenna, or the Gehenna of fire ; and neither the Greek *Hades* nor the Latin *Inferi* or *Inferna* are properly used for it. It is these latter terms, together with ' the lower parts of the earth,' or ' the parts beneath the earth,' which are ordinarily used where our Lord's descent into hell is referred to either in Scripture or in ecclesiastical writings, and they do not of themselves suggest the ideas of torment associated with Gehenna, and so

[1] Swete, p. 80.

unfortunately called up in many minds by the English 'hell' where it occurs in the Creed. It is there the representative of the Latin *Inferi* or *Inferna* (the equivalent of the Greek *Hades*), and is a purely neutral term, meaning the place of departed spirits—in Hebrew *Sheol*, which was conceived of as being beneath the earth. In itself it implies nothing of the condition of the souls there, whether they are at rest or in suffering: the expression *descendere ad inferos* or *inferna* is a fairly common one in the Latin version of the Old Testament, being the translation of the Hebrew phrase 'to go down into Sheol,' used when a person's death is spoken of.[1] The exact phrase is nowhere used in Scripture of our Lord, though there is abundant testimony to the fact of which it speaks, which is indeed involved of necessity in the conception of Christ's death as a real one. The body was laid in the grave, and the soul or human spirit, being separated from it, was *ipso facto* in the place of departed spirits, *i.e.* in Hebrew phraseology 'descended into hell.' To this reference is made by S. Peter in his sermon on the day of Pentecost, in which he quotes the words of Psalm xvi., 'Thou wilt not leave my soul in hell, neither wilt Thou suffer Thine holy one to see corruption,' and applies them to Christ, 'that neither was He left in hell, nor did His flesh see corruption.'[2] To this S. Paul also probably refers in the Epistle to

---

[1] See *e.g.* Gen. xxxvii. 35; Job vii. 9; xxi. 13; Ps. liv. (lv.) 16; cxiii. (cxv.) 17; cxxxviii. (cxxxix.) 8.

[2] Acts ii. 24 *seq*.

THE APOSTLES' CREED 67

the Ephesians, where he says 'Now that He ascended, what is it but that He also descended first into the lower parts of the earth.'[1] We may also connect with it our Lord's promise to the penitent thief, 'To-day shalt thou be with Me in Paradise.'[2] Besides these there is the difficult passage in 1 S. Pet. iii. concerning the preaching to the spirits in prison. This is not the place for a full discussion of the meaning of this passage. It will be sufficient to say that no interpretation can satisfy the obvious meaning of the words, which does not take it of something which took place in the interval between our Lord's death and resurrection, and that it appears to indicate that the object of His descent into hell was not only to fulfil the conditions of death (as we might have supposed had it not been for this passage), but that there was a further object, viz. to 'preach unto the spirits in prison, which aforetime were disobedient, when the long-suffering of God waited in the days of Noah.'[3] There is no thought of those who have actually heard the Gospel preached and have refused it. S. Peter is speaking of those who had had no chance of hearing the Gospel preached to them on earth. He mentions one generation alone, 'those who were disobedient in the days of Noah,' but it is possible that the preaching was not limited to these, and that an appeal was then made not merely to the antediluvians, but generally to those who had been given no opportunity of hearing the Gospel in this life. We cannot speak with

[1] Eph. iv. 9.   [2] S. Luke xxiii. 43.   [3] 1 S. Pet. iii. 18 *seq.*

certainty on this point, for Scripture is silent as to any but that one generation. But that others were included among those to whom the Gospel was then preached, and that they were made sharers of Christ's resurrection, was certainly the strong belief of the Church in very early days. It is remarkable how constantly we meet with references to it in writers not only of the third and fourth centuries, but even of the second. Not to lay stress on the fact that it occupies a prominent place in some of the apocryphal Gospels, as the recently discovered 'Gospel of Peter' and the 'Gospel of Nicodemus,' it should be noticed that Ignatius of Antioch bears witness to it at the very beginning of the second century. 'Even the prophets,' he writes to the Magnesians, 'being His disciples, were expecting Him as their Teacher, through the Spirit. And for this cause He, whom they rightly awaited, when He came, raised them from the dead.'[1] Irenæus hands on a tradition which he tells us he had received from a certain presbyter 'who had heard it from those who had seen the apostles, and from those who had been their disciples,' that 'the Lord descended to the places beneath the earth, preaching His advent there also, and declaring remission of sins received by those who believe in Him. But all those believed in Him whose hope was set on Him—that is, who foretold His advent and submitted to His dispensations, just men, and prophets, and patriarchs.'[2] Besides this, both Irenæus and Justin Martyr refer to the following pas-

[1] Ignatius, *Ad. Magn.* ix.   [2] Irenæus, *Adv. Hær.* IV. xlii.

THE APOSTLES' CREED 69

sage, which comes from some unknown source, but which the Jews were supposed to have cut out from either Isaiah or Jeremiah: 'The Lord God remembered His dead people of Israel who lay in the graves; and descended to preach to them His own salvation.'[1] There is no need to quote later testimonies, though a continuous stream of them might easily be given. Those already cited are sufficient to show how firmly fixed this belief was in the mind of the early Christians, and how prominent a place the descent into hell took in their thoughts. But it is certain that the belief found no expression in the earliest Creeds. It has already been mentioned that the first baptismal Creed of certain date to contain it is that of Aquileia as commented on by Rufinus,[2] and that about the same date, or a little earlier, we find in the *Fides Hieronymi*: 'descended into hell, trod down the sting of death.' Even earlier it occurs in three Arian Creeds accepted at the Councils of Ariminum, Nicé, and Constantinople in 359 and 360.[3] Before this we meet with no trace of it, and we are left to conjecture in trying to account for its insertion.

Taking the Arian Creeds as the earliest to contain it, it has been suggested that its appearance in them may be due to the desire to make a rather ostentatious disavowal of any sympathy with the rising heresy of

[1] Justin Martyr, *Dialogue with Trypho*, lxxii.; Irenæus, III. xxii.; IV. xxxvi., lv.
[2] Rufinus, c. xviii.
[3] See Hahn, *Bibliothek der Symbole*, 204-209.

Apollinarianism. The Apollinarian heresy denied to our Lord the possession of a true human soul or spirit, and consequently in combating it the descent into hell appeared specially important, for it could refer to nothing but the human spirit. It is conceivable that this gave the occasion for its insertion, but it is by no means certain.[1] Dr. Swete thinks that in the Creed of Aquileia the clause must be considerably older than the time of Rufinus, and is inclined to assign it to the beginning of the third century, or even the end of the second, thinking that it may have been added to guard against a Docetic view of our Lord's humanity.[2] Dr. Sanday is of opinion that it was not directed against any special heresy, but that 'just in some particular locality or in the mind of some influential individual the doctrine of the descent . . . was so naturally associated with the burial that the mention of the one naturally called up the other, and that so in some one church the two together found a place in the baptismal Creed, and from thence passed into the Creeds of other Churches.'[3] So Harnack says: ' I am disposed to believe that what led to the acceptance of this part of the Creed was less any anti-Apollinarian interest, or any definite theory as to the condition of the souls in the kingdom of the dead, than the endeavour to give as complete an account as possible of

---

[1] This was the view of the late Dr. Heurtley. See *Harmonia Symbolica*, p. 134.

[2] *The Apostles' Creed*, p. 61.

[3] *Journal of Theological Studies*, iii. 16.

the history of Christ's passion and His glory.'[1] In favour of this is the fact that Rufinus, the first writer to comment upon it as it stands in the Creed, attaches no special anti-heretical significance to it, but simply connects the clause closely with the thought of the burial, saying that though not contained in the Creeds of other Churches, it seems to be implied, when it is said that He ' was buried.'[2] It is also remarkable to find that forty years earlier (c. 348) Cyril of Jerusalem in commenting on the Creed of his church (which did *not* contain the clause), introduces the doctrine of the descent under the head of the burial, and writes fully concerning it and its object, saying that 'He descended into the realms beneath the earth that He might thence ransom the righteous.'[3] It is perhaps impossible to arrive at any very definite conclusion, but on the whole the view which Dr. Sanday has put forward appears to the present writer the most probable. The clause certainly completes and amplifies the idea of ' was buried,' by stating what happened to the human spirit of the Lord during the interval between His death and resurrection. It is silent as to the object of the descent, but from the evidence given above it is at least probable that there was present to the minds of those who first inserted it, the thought not only of the fulfilment of the conditions of death, but also of the preaching to the spirits in prison and the ransoming of the souls there detained. It is not *necessary* to

---

[1] *The Apostles' Creed*, p. 87.   [2] *In Symbolum*, xviii.
[3] S. Cyril, *Catech.* iv. 11.

72   THE THREE CREEDS

interpret it as including this thought, but there is, of course, ample evidence that in later times it was so taken. One single example may be given. In the course of an instruction on the faith, delivered to a sick man, according to the ancient use of the Church of England, the priest was charged to instruct him that it was necessary to his salvation that he should believe the various articles of the faith, including this: 'The true descent of Christ into hell in the spirit, for the harrowing of hell (*ad spoliationem tartari*) while the body rested in the grave.'[1]

(*b*) 'The Communion of Saints.' The early history of this clause has been already given, and we have seen that it was certainly in existence in the last quarter of the fourth century,[2] and that it probably had an Eastern origin. These facts have an important bearing on the questions of the meaning of the clause, and the reason for its insertion in the Creed, on which something must now be said.

With regard to the meaning of the words there have been various theories. To begin with, the Latin *Sanctorum Communionem* and the Greek [τῶν] ἁγίων [τὴν] κοινωνίαν are not free from ambiguity, as the genitives may be either masculine or neuter, either 'holy persons' or 'holy things.' There is evidence that in comparatively early days the latter view of the meaning of the clause was sometimes taken, and that it was interpreted to refer to the sacraments. This view

---

[1] See Maskell, *Mon. Rit.*, i. (ed. 2) 91 ; cf. iii. 253.
[2] See above, p. 54.

appears to be given in a curious old English paraphrase of the Creed found in a MS. of the fifteenth century, where we read : ' I byleve also in holy chirch ordrynge us. I byleve in the sacrament of Goddis flesche and his blood that he shed on the blessid rood tre for me and for alle mankind.'[1] It is also contained in the metrical English version of the Apostles' Creed contained in the *Lay Folk's Mass Book* (thirteenth century) :—

> 'Well I trow in tho holi gost
> And holi kirc that is so gode;
> And so I trow that housel es
> bothe flesshe and blode.'[2]

Again, in a Norman-French translation of the Creed, belonging to the twelfth century, the words are actually rendered *La communion des saintes choses*. The interpretation is also mentioned as a possible one by a few earlier theological writers, and in an anonymous sermon attributed to the sixth century the clause is said to teach that we ought to communicate every Sunday.[3] The view that the word *sanctorum* is neuter has been recently revived, and it has been suggested that the primary intention of the words may have been to append a reference to the sacraments to the mention of the Church (just as in the Nicene Creed there is the mention of the ' one Baptism for the remission of sins ' immediately after the clause on the one Holy Catholic

---

[1] Maskell, *Mon. Rit.*, iii. (ed. 2) 253.
[2] Simmons, *The Lay Folk's Mass Book*, p. 20 ; cf. p. 225.
[3] See Swete, *The Apostles' Creed*, p. 82, and Burn, *The Apostles' Creed*, p. 95.

and Apostolic Church), and that the article was intended to witness to the efficacy of the Sacraments. 'I believe in the communion of the holy things,' *i.e.* not merely 'I believe that Sacraments exist,' but 'I believe that in the Sacraments I am made a partaker of holy things,' viz. of the blessings which the Sacraments not only typify, but also convey. There is a certain attractiveness in this view, but the weight of authority is decidedly against it. It only appears sporadically, and the main stream of traditional interpretation, which certainly goes back to the fourth century, takes *sanctorum* as masculine—holy persons, not holy things.[1]

We may, then, with a fair amount of confidence take the English translation, ' the Communion of Saints,' as accurate, but even so the precise meaning of the words and their original intention are not immediately obvious. Are 'the saints,' as so often in the New Testament, those living on earth, or are they, as so often in later ecclesiastical language, those at rest, or are thoughts of both the living and departed combined in the phrase ? Various answers have been returned to these questions in accordance as one or other of the following interpretations have been adopted.

(1) It has been thought that the first insertion of the words was connected with the cultus of the saints

---

[1] It has indeed been suggested that the phrase was purposely left indefinite in order that the masculine and neuter might be combined in interpreting it. But the suggestion has really nothing to recommend it.

departed, as if the phrase meant 'communion with the martyrs and chosen saints,' and that they passed into the Creeds of the several Churches of the West as a safeguard against the teaching of Vigilantius, a presbyter who in the early years of the fifth century protested strongly against the growing tendency to saint worship. In favour of this view it has been urged that the clause appears prominently in Gallican Creeds of the fifth century, and that certain Gallican writers take the words as referring to the blessed dead and the regard to be paid to them. Thus Faustus of Riez (who died about 492) writes :—

'Let us believe in *the communion of saints*, not as though they shared the prerogatives of God, but for the honour of God; let us do homage to the fear and love of God manifested in them; they are worthy of our veneration, inasmuch as by their contempt for death they induce in us a spirit of devotion to God and of eager longing for the life to come.'

Far more extravagantly an unnamed later writer exclaims of the clause, that it

'Shuts the mouth of those who blasphemously refuse to honour the ashes of the saints and friends of God, and who do not hold that the glorious memory of the blessed martyrs is to be cherished by doing honour to their tombs; such persons are false to their Creed, and have given the lie to the promise which they made to God at the font.'

This is to *read into* the words a great deal which is not there. Had they really been added with the intention here attributed to them, we should expect them to be far clearer and better calculated to express the thought. Moreover, since the article has been traced to an Eastern source and to a date considerably earlier than the days of Vigilantius, there is no longer room for doubt that this interpretation is merely an afterthought and does not express the original idea of the words.

(2) A second view put forward is that the clause was added as a protest against the Donatists, the 'Puritans' of the fourth and fifth centuries. 'The Donatists,' writes Dr. Swete, 'declaimed against a church in which a "*communio malorum*," or joint participation in sacraments of the evil and the good, was not only permitted but enforced. "What communion," they asked with S. Paul, "hath light with darkness?" Augustine replied that though in the Catholic Church the evil were mingled with the good, and the Church was to that extent a mixed body, there was within her a true *communio sanctorum*, in which the evil have no part, and which is not impaired by their presence. The conception is therefore Augustinian, yet it did not claim a place in the African Creed, or perhaps in any Creed, until after Augustine's death.'[1]

But the phrase *Communio sanctorum* scarcely occurs in Augustine. It is found once in one of his sermons,[2] but apparently it occurs nowhere in any of his treatises against the Donatists. It certainly was not a household

[1] *The Apostles' Creed*, p. 83.   [2] *Serm.* lii. 6, vol. v. p. 304.

THE APOSTLES' CREED 77

word with him, as *communio bonorum* was, and had the clause originally contained an anti-Donatist reference, we should expect that it would have first appeared in Africa, where alone Donatism was a power ; nor does it appear, standing alone, to be sufficiently clear to be of any service in the controversy ; indeed, it might even have been claimed by the Donatists as exactly expressing their views ; and it was as a matter of fact actually used by them.[1] Then, further, we now know that it is in all probability older than Donatism, and that it first appears in quarters to which Donatism never spread.

(3) A third view is that of the learned Benedictine, Dom. Morin, who has made a special study of the clause, throwing considerable light on its date and origin.[2] He gives good reason for thinking that, though we do not actually meet with it in any Creed till the last quarter of the fourth century, it was then already of some antiquity ; and suggests that it originated in the third century when S. Cyprian of Carthage and Firmilian of Cæsarea were resisting the Novatianists and Montanists, being probably first inserted in Asia in order to guard against admitting into the Church persons who had been baptized by heretics and schismatics. The holy Catholic Church was a 'Communion of Saints,' and could not therefore admit such. This

[1] It occurs in the decree of the Donatist Council of Cabarsussum against Pirminian, quoted by Augustine, *Enarr. in Psalm*, xxxvi. Serm. 2, vol. ii. 279, and also in the Letter of the Donatists to Flavius Marcellinus, in Aug. *Op.* vol. ix., App. 65.

[2] *Sanctorum Communionem* ; Macon, 1904.

view is perhaps the most probable yet suggested, but it wants further verification.

(4) The traditional interpretation of the clause which takes it of the union of the faithful, living and departed, in Christ, is found as early as the fourth century, and must at any rate have been present to the minds of those who introduced it into the Western Creeds in the fifth century. It is expressed by Niceta of Remesiana, the earliest writer to comment upon the clause yet discovered:—

'What is the church but the congregation of all saints? For from the beginning of the world, patriarchs, as Abraham, Isaac, and Jacob, prophets, apostles, martyrs, and all other just men who have been, are, or shall be, are one church, because sanctified by one faith and life, marked by one Spirit, they constitute one body, of which Christ is declared to be the head. And I say yet more. Even angels and the powers on high are joined together in this one church, according to the apostle's teaching, that " in Christ all things are reconciled, not only the things on earth, but also those in heaven." Believe, therefore, that in this one church you will attain to the *communion of saints.*'[1]

With this comprehensive view we may for the present rest content. It has, as has been said, become traditional; and this section may well be closed with the expression of it in the early English form of the Visitation of the Sick, where, in close connection with

[1] Niceta of Remesiana, *De Symbolo*, c. 10.

the instruction already referred to as giving the mediæval interpretation of the descent into hell, the priest is required to address the sick man on the articles of his belief as follows:—

'Dearest brother, dost thou believe in . . . the communion of saints; that is, that all men who live in charity are partakers of all the gifts of grace which are dispensed in the Church, and that all who have fellowship with the just here in the life of grace, have fellowship with them in glory?'[1]

[1] Maskell, *Mon. Rit.*, i. 92.

§ 3

The Use made of the Creed by the Church

UP to this point nothing has been said of the use of the Apostles' Creed except in connection with Baptism and the preparation for it. Of this, as we find it in the fourth century, a sufficient account has been given. But it is obvious that as the custom of Infant Baptism spread, the *traditio* and *redditio symboli* lost all their significance so far as the children baptized were concerned; and unless these were to be allowed to grow up in ignorance of the faith, means would have to be taken to instruct them in its elements *after* Baptism. The value of the Apostles' Creed for this purpose was soon recognised, and before long it and the Lord's Prayer (to which much later the Ten Commandments were added) came to be regarded as the things which a Christian ought to know and believe to his soul's health, and the clergy were required not merely to be well acquainted with these forms themselves, but diligently to teach them to their flocks in the vulgar tongue. So in Bede's letter to Egbert, Archbishop of York (A.D. 734), he earnestly advises that all should know by heart in their own

THE APOSTLES' CREED 81

tongue 'the Catholic faith which is contained in the Apostles' Creed, and the Lord's Prayer which the holy Gospel teaches us,' and says that with this object he has procured their translation into English.[1] A few years later the Council of Clovesho (A.D. 747) passed a canon on the subject requiring the clergy diligently to teach the Creed to their people, that they may understand what they ought to believe and hope. It is also to be taught to children, and to those who stand as sponsors in baptism.[2] Again, in the Canons of Ælfric (c. 957) we have this charge: 'The Mass-priest, on Sundays and Mass-days, shall speak the sense of the Gospel to the people in English, and of the *Pater Noster* and the Creed, as often as he can, for the inciting of the people to know their belief, and retaining their Christianity';[3] while the following canon of Edgar's reign (c. 960) shows the earnestness of the endeavour made that the people might become familiar with it: 'That every man learn to be expert at *Pater Noster et Credo*, as he desires to lie in holy ground, or to be esteemed worthy of the Housel; for he who refuseth to learn that is not a good Christian, and he cannot of right undertake for others at baptism, nor at the bishop's hands. Let him who knows it not first learn it.'[4]

It was the same on the Continent, and numerous

---

[1] See Haddan and Stubbs, *Councils and Eccl. Documents*, iii. 316.
[2] *Ibid.*, 366.   [3] Johnson's *English Eccl. Canons*, i. 397.
[4] *Ibid.*, 416.

testimonies might be cited from capitulars and canons to prove the importance attached to the familiarising of the people generally with the words of the Creed in their own language, more especially in connection with the revival of learning and religion under Charlemagne. Indeed, the knowledge of the Creed and Lord's Prayer was sometimes enforced under pains and penalties, and it was directed that men who had failed to learn them should be put on bread and water, while women were to be flogged or starved![1]

It is about the same period, *i.e.* in the ninth century, that we first come across the use of the Creed in the Hour Services. It apparently found no place in these when Isidore wrote in the seventh century, but it was introduced into the office of Prime between his time and the ninth century, and in this office it has retained its place ever since, being also at some subsequent date introduced into Compline, and given a place in the introduction to Mattins. In this position it was said privately as part of the preparation; and where it occurred in Prime and Compline, the custom was for it also to be said privately up to the last two articles, which were repeated aloud; the reason for this, as given by Durandus, being that 'with the heart man believeth unto righteousness, and with the mouth confession is made unto salvation.'[2]

This Creed was emphatically the people's Creed, being

---

[1] See Swainson, *Nicene and Apostles' Creeds*, p. 184.

[2] Durandus, *Rationale*, V. v. 11.

THE APOSTLES' CREED

intended for all Christians alike. Naturally it found a place, together with the Lord's Prayer and the Ten Commandments, in the Primer, and being thus constantly kept before the laity, it was far more familiar to the majority of them throughout the Middle Ages than the Nicene Creed which was recited in Latin at Mass. Consequently we find that it was sometimes suggested to the laity that they might profitably repeat to themselves the Apostles' Creed while the longer form was being sung or recited by the priest; and it is in order to facilitate this that the metrical version of the Apostles' Creed already referred to in the previous section is given in the *Lay Folk's Mass Book*.[1] It was, of course, from the Hour Services of the Mediæval Church that it passed into Mattins and Evensong in the English Prayer Book; and the use made of it in the Catechism as well as in the directions of the Baptismal service to sponsors are entirely in the spirit of the Mediæval Church. In the Visitation of the Sick, according to the Sarum use, questions on the lines of the Apostles' Creed were asked of the sick man, but the actual form itself was not ordinarily used. When, however, the service was put forth in English in the first Prayer Book of Edward VI. in 1549, the direction was given that in examining the sick man the priest should 'rehearse the articles of the faith,' and it has remained the rule of the English Church ever since that assent to the Apostles' Creed should be

[1] See above, p. 73. This metrical version is given in full as an appendix to this chapter.

the sole test of faith required from the sick. It is thus the case that this Creed is the only formulary of faith to which a formal assent is ever asked from the laity of the Church of England. The position of the Nicene Creed in the Communion Service clearly gives it an immense weight of authority, and it is difficult to understand how any one who could not heartily assent to it could expect to be admitted to Communion; but it cannot be said that the Church ever requires subscription or a formal declaration of assent to be made to it as a condition of Communion. To the Apostles' Creed a definite act of assent is required as a condition of Baptism. This, too, is the final test proposed, when the hour of death draws near, that the sick man remains sound in the faith.

A word may be added here on the custom of turning to the East at the recitation of the Creed, now so generally adopted. Curiously enough, the custom does not appear to be a really ancient one. It has no rubrical authority, neither has it any pre-Reformation precedent. According to Mr. Frere, 'it was begun in Caroline times, partly in imitation of the practice of the Jews, who always turned their faces in the direction of Jerusalem, toward the mercy-seat of the holy temple, when they prayed, and partly in imitation of the early Christian ceremonies of Baptism, in which it was usual for the catechumens to renounce the devil with their faces to the West, and then turn to the East to make their covenant with Christ: the East, or region of the rising sun, being the source of light. Hence the turning towards the East became associated with Christian worship generally from early times, but not till quite recently in any special sense with the daily recitation of the Creed.'[1]

[1] *A New History of the Book of Common Prayer*, p. 391.

§ 4

The Doctrine of the Creed

WE have seen that our Apostles' Creed is an enlarged form of the old Roman Creed, and that the Roman Creed can be traced back quite certainly to the second century, and with great probability to the very earliest years of it. It might well have been thought that this early date would have been sufficient guarantee of the fact that we have in it a true summary of Apostolic doctrine, and that the faith of the Church in the earliest days was that which, as we are taught in the Church Catechism, we 'chiefly learn' in these articles of our belief, viz., first, belief in 'God the Father, Who made me and all the world; secondly, in God the Son, Who hath redeemed me and all mankind; and thirdly, in God the Holy Ghost, Who sanctifieth me and all the elect people of God.'

Unhappily, we can no longer assume that these things are admitted by everybody. A different interpretation has recently been placed upon the words of the Creed, and allegations have been made concerning it, without some notice of which this book would seem to be incomplete.

(1) It is said that the Creed was not composed with the meaning which we have learned to attach to its words; that it was originally a 'Unitarian' Creed, and that only in later ages was the doctrine of the Eternal Trinity read into the names Father, Son, and Holy Ghost, which are employed in it. Thus Harnack boldly says: 'Whoever introduces the doctrine of the Three Persons of the Godhead into the Creed, explains it contrary to its original meaning, and alters its true sense'; he holds further that such an alteration was only 'demanded of all Christians from the end of the fourth century onward.'[1]

(2) It is also said that, early as it is, its composition represents a change from primitive Christianity, and marks a stage in the growth of dogma which has ended by transforming the character of Christianity. 'It belongs,' says McGiffert, 'even in its earliest form, to the age when the catholic spirit was beginning to displace the primitive spirit, and when the interest in sound doctrine was beginning to crowd out the interest in the evangelisation and salvation of the world. It is primarily a doctrinal and polemical creed, not an evangelistic or missionary symbol.'[2]

These allegations have been seriously made, and cannot be altogether passed over in silence.

(1) The former of them raises the grave question, Is the Apostles' Creed really a Trinitarian formula?—in

[1] *Das apostolische Glaubensbekenntniss* (1892), translated in the *Nineteenth Century*, July 1893, art. xiv.
[2] *The Apostles' Creed* (1902), p. 33.

other words, in what sense were the titles 'the Father,' 'His only Son,' and 'the Holy Ghost' first placed in it? The assertion now made is that 'the Father' means Father of the universe, *i.e.* simply Creator and Ruler of all things, and thus that in it there is no thought of 'the Father' as the first Person in the Blessed Trinity; that 'His only Son' merely refers to the historic figure Jesus Christ, and not to the Eternal Word or Son, the second Person in the Trinity; and that the Holy Spirit is merely conceived of as an influence or gift, and not as the third Person in the Trinity.

In answer to this it must first be pointed out that the Creed cannot possibly be understood without a reference to its origin in connection with baptism. It is no accident that it is drawn up in three distinct paragraphs, each of which in some later forms is prefaced, as the first of the three invariably is, by the words 'I believe.' These three paragraphs correspond to the three Divine titles employed by our Lord when, as we believe, He came and said to His disciples: 'All authority hath been given unto Me in heaven and on earth. Go ye, therefore, and make disciples of all the nations, baptizing them into [or *in*] the name of the Father and of the Son and of the Holy Ghost: teaching them to observe all things whatsoever I commanded you: and lo, I am with you alway, even unto the end of the world.'[1] Whether these words were intended

[1] S. Matt. xxviii. 18-20. This is not the place in which to enter upon a discussion of the authenticity of this charge. Reference may, however, be made to the very able article by the present Bishop of

to prescribe the use of a particular baptismal formula, or whether they unfold the spiritual meaning of the sacrament thus instituted, need not be considered here. There is no room for doubt, since the discovery of the *Teaching of the Twelve Apostles*, that the actual formula was employed in very early days; and in either case the significance of the titles must be the same; nor is it possible to doubt what that significance is. We have only to substitute titles which are not Divine or not personal, to realise that it is inconceivable that 'the Son' and 'the Holy Ghost' can be other than Divine Persons. How, for instance, could we imagine such a command as this to be given: 'Baptise in the name of the Father, and of S. Paul, and of the Divine Providence'? Such a question scarcely needs an answer. Such a combination is wholly inconceivable. No titles but Divine ones could be associated with the name of the Eternal Father. Again, the titles Father and Son are personal ones: they would be misleading did they not imply the distinct Personality of those to whom they are given; and if two of the names are personal, surely the third must be personal also. Thus we find wrapped up, as it were, in this great commission so solemnly given just before the Ascension,—the commission which sent forth the Church on her work of winning the world—the full doctrine of the Holy

Ely, in the *Journal of Theological Studies*, vi. 481, in which it is shown, among other things, that there is not the slightest reason for questioning the integrity of the text, and that there is no reason to doubt that in it we have the substance of words actually spoken by our Lord.

Trinity as in later days formulated in technical and precise terms by the Church. It is out of this command that the Apostles' Creed is developed; and if the command is Trinitarian, the Creed must be Trinitarian also. The words 'Father,' 'His only Son,' 'the Holy Ghost,' must be given the same meaning in it, which they bear in our Lord's charge in the Gospels.

To this it must be added that there is ample evidence independently of the Creed that from the very first the faith of the Church was such that it can only be described as Trinitarian, even though the use of the term had not yet arisen. Such a benediction as that with which S. Paul closes the Second Epistle to the Corinthians is deeply significant: 'The grace of our Lord Jesus Christ, and the Love of God, and the communion of the Holy Ghost, be with you all.' It cannot be explained away; and when we find that such language is echoed in later writers, and that S. Clement of Rome, the first of the Apostolic Fathers, in writing to the Corinthian Church (c. A.D. 96) exclaims: 'As God liveth, and the Lord Jesus Christ liveth, and the Holy Ghost, who are the faith and hope of the elect,'[1] we feel that the chain which connects the belief and language of the later Church with the days of the Apostles themselves is complete.

This may serve as a general answer to the first allegation made concerning the Creed. But it may be developed more fully in regard to each of the three Blessed Persons mentioned in it.

---

[1] Clem. Rom. *Ad Cor.*, cap. lviii.

(a) *I believe in God the Father Almighty.*—So, we have seen reason to believe, ran the first article of the old Roman Creed, from which it is now sought to exclude all reference to the deeper meaning of 'Father,' confining it to the thought of God as the Father of all things in the sense of Creator and Ruler, in spite of the admitted fact that the deeper meaning is already found in the New Testament. It is, for instance, quite impossible to exclude it from such a passage as S. Matthew xi. 25-27. 'At that season Jesus answered and said, I thank Thee, O Father, Lord of heaven and earth, that Thou didst hide these things from the wise and understanding, and didst reveal them unto babes: yea, Father, for so it was well-pleasing in Thy sight. All things have been delivered unto Me of My Father: and no one knoweth the Son, save the Father; neither doth any know the Father, save the Son, and he to whomsoever the Son willeth to reveal Him'; and if it is found in the Gospels, why should it be excluded from the Creed? It may be frankly admitted that the sense of Creator and Ruler is sometimes given to the title by writers of the second century, and that special stress is laid by them on God's sovereignty over all things; and that in any case this thought is not absent from the Creed. It is certainly expressed in the word 'Almighty,' or rather 'All-sovereign,' for the Latin *Omnipotens* is the equivalent of the Greek παντοκράτωρ, a nobler word than παντοδύναμος— 'All-sovereign' rather than 'All-powerful,' for the word expresses the idea of exercised dominion rather than abstract might.[1] But, as Dr. Swete has forcibly pointed out, the very men who, in the second century and the age to which the formation of the Creed belongs, speak of God's fatherly relation to nature, speak also of His special relation to Jesus Christ and the members of His Church, so that even if there were nothing further to urge, it would be 'purely arbitrary to say that the deeper meaning of the word was probably absent from the mind of the author of the Creed.' But this is not all that can be urged, for 'I believe in God the Father' is followed by 'and in Jesus Christ His only Son,' and in view of this fact 'it is more than arbitrary' to exclude the deeper meaning, for it is impossible to believe that the one term 'Father' has no reference to the other 'His Son.'[2]

(b) So also when we turn to this second article, '*and in Christ Jesus, His only Son*,' it is impossible to exclude what has been called a 'backward reference' to the first article. The titles 'Father' and 'Son' in such close connection must mutually imply and refer to each other. It must be remembered, too, that the word 'only' in the English version of the Creed represents the Latin *unicus*, and that this again is the equivalent of the Greek Μονογένης, 'only begotten,'[3] which regularly stands in this place in

---

[1] Cf. Westcott's *Historic Faith*, p. 36.

[2] Swete, *The Apostles' Creed*, pp. 22, 23.

[3] In a few Latin Creeds *unigenitus* actually stands in the place of *unicus*.

Eastern Creeds, and is the word used in the old Roman Creed as given by Marcellus. This term is, of course, a Scriptural one, and expresses the unique character of our Lord's Sonship. The use of it in S. John's writings, from which there is no reasonable room for doubt that the Church adopted it, is absolutely inconsistent with any limitation of the idea of Sonship to the historic manifestation of Christ on earth, and points directly to a pre-existent and eternal Sonship. 'No man hath seen God at any time; the only begotten Son, Which is in the bosom of the Father, He hath declared Him.' 'God so loved the world, that He gave His only begotten Son, that whosoever believeth on Him should not perish, but have eternal life. For God sent not the Son into the world to judge the world; but that the world should be saved through Him. He that believeth on Him is not judged: he that believeth not hath been judged already, because he hath not believed on the name of the only begotten Son of God.'[1] When once it is grasped that 'only' and *unicus* are the Western equivalents of 'only begotten,' their full force is at once obvious, and the character of the Sonship of which they speak cannot be in doubt. To weaken it down to the Sonship of the historic manifestation through the Incarnation is out of the question; and if, as seems clear in spite of efforts to prove the contrary, *unicus* or μονογένης stood in the old Roman Creed from the first, there is no room for doubt that it was intended

[1] S. John i. 18; iii. 16 *seq.*

94 THE THREE CREEDS

to express the eternal Sonship of Christ, of the acknowledgment of which by representative writers of the second century there is ample evidence, independently of the existence of the Creed. Thus, as Dr. Swete points out, Justin Martyr says of our Lord, 'He was the only begotten of the Father of the universe, inasmuch as He was after a peculiar manner produced from the Father as His Word and Power.' Rather earlier Aristides says, 'the Son of God most high is confessed . . . as having come down from heaven,' while in the Epistles of Ignatius we have 'frequent references to a Sonship which lies beyond the limit of time. "Jesus Christ . . . came forth from one Father"; is "both of Mary and of God," " of the family of David according to the flesh, Son of God by [the Divine] Will and Power"; was "with the Father before the world was."'[1] All these writers belong to the first half of the second century, that is, to the period to which the formation of the Creed is supposed to belong, and their witness to the faith of the Church at that date is clear. Early Christian writers and thinkers had not yet attained to the precision of later theologians, but substantially their belief was identical with that of the Nicene Fathers, and that belief is what they expressed in the simple phrase of the primitive creed, 'His only Son.'

(c) Coming now to the third paragraph of the Creed, we are told that the Church of the second century was unaware of the doctrine of the Personality

[1] Swete, *op. cit.*, p. 27.

of the Holy Spirit, and that the words 'and in the Holy Ghost' when first placed in the Creed can only have been intended to express belief in the Holy Spirit as a gift or power. In this statement there appears to be grave exaggeration. It is quite true, indeed, that we do not find so much attention given to the doctrine of the Holy Spirit in the second century as was given to it in the last half of the fourth, when the Divinity of the Third Person of the Blessed Trinity was denied by many of the Arians and the Macedonians. It is true also that it was this denial which led to the formal statements and definitions on the subject which the Church of that age was compelled to make. But these statements and definitions did not create or give rise to any new belief. They were only made in order to protect the faith which had been implicit ever since the earliest days. The language of many passages of Holy Scripture would be inexplicable and misleading if the Spirit was merely an attribute, influence, gift, or operation. Nothing short of a belief in what we have learned to call His distinct Personality will explain the terms in which our Lord speaks of Him as 'another Comforter,' and in which both He and His apostles ascribe personal attributes and actions to Him.[1] Consequently, when we pass from Scripture to the writings of the early fathers, we find that, although the

[1] For a full statement of this, reference may perhaps be permitted to the author's *Thirty-nine Articles of the Church of England, explained with an Introduction*, p. 201 *seq*.

doctrine is not dogmatically stated, there are a number of passages (such as that in S. Clement of Rome already cited [1]) which *imply*, if they do not directly affirm, the doctrine which the later Church defined. 'The Catholic doctrine of the Deity of the Holy Ghost,' it has been truly said, 'found a place from the first in the life and worship of the Church; in her worship because in her life. Yet the dogmatic expression of this truth will be sought in vain among the outpourings of Christian devotion. Until heresy attacked one by one the treasures of the traditional Creed, they were held firmly indeed, yet with a scarcely conscious grasp: the faithful were content to believe and to adore.' [2]

If this is so, we have no right whatever to limit the idea of the words in the Creed to the thought of the Spirit as a gift; for we may feel sure that when the unknown author of it, after having expressed his belief in 'God the Father' and in 'His only Son,' added 'and in the Holy Ghost,' even though he might not have been fully able to define in words his meaning, he nevertheless intended to express his belief in the Holy Spirit as revealed in Scripture, and to claim for him a 'personal Life which is not absolutely identified with the Life of the Father, and yet is understood to be Divine.' [3]

---

[1] See above, p. 90.
[2] Swete, *On the Early History of the Doctrine of the Holy Spirit*, p. 8.
[3] Swete, *The Apostles' Creed*, p. 32.

(2) The second allegation given above which requires consideration was this: Granted that the Creed is an early work, yet its composition represents a change from primitive Christianity, and marks a stage in the growth of dogma which has ended by changing the character of Christianity.

A contrast is often drawn between primitive Christianity with the teaching of Christ on the one hand, and what is called dogmatic Christianity on the other. The latter is said by Harnack to be 'in its conception and execution a work of the Greek spirit on the soil of the Gospel.' Even by 200 A.D., we are told, the living faith is transformed into a creed to be believed.[1] In answer to this we may reply with Dr. Sanday, that 'the antithesis which is drawn between the Christian faith propagated through Christ and demanding assent to a series of propositions about Him, is unreal,' and 'the contrast between the first age and a hundred years later is not so sensational as Harnack's words might lead us to suppose.'[2] As a matter of fact, a living faith in Christ cannot be separated from a Creed to be believed about Him. The real question is, 'What think ye of Christ?' for questions are inevitably raised by much of His teaching with regard to the personality of the Speaker. To these questions we cannot shut our eyes, nor can we rightly ignore the interpretation given to Christ's teaching by His followers. It must be frankly

[1] Harnack's *Outlines of the History of Dogma*, p. 5, and *What is Christianity?* p. 192 seq.
[2] *Lecture on Harnack's What is Christianity?* p. 18.

asserted that 'dogma' is implied in our Lord's statements concerning Himself, and that the Christianity of the Apostolic age, while primarily (as Christianity is still) a life to be lived, involved also (as it does still) a very definite and 'dogmatic' belief, and not merely a vague sentiment, which it is only possible to maintain by ignoring inconvenient questions. This is the first point to be established, and in establishing it we may point to our Lord's own claims, even those made at the very beginning of His ministry, in the Sermon on the Mount, which is so often and so unfairly contrasted with the Church's 'Creed.' Such tremendous claims as those involved in the following utterances cannot be overlooked:—

'Think not that I came to destroy the law or the prophets: I came not to destroy, but to fulfil. . . . Ye have heard that it was said to them of old time, Thou shalt not kill; and whosoever shall kill shall be in danger of the judgment: but I say unto you, that every one who is angry with his brother shall be in danger of the judgment; and whosoever shall say to his brother, Raca, shall be in danger of the council; and whosoever shall say, Thou fool, shall be in danger of the hell of fire. . . . Ye have heard that it was said, Thou shalt not commit adultery; but I say unto you, that every one that looketh on a woman to lust after her hath committed adultery with her already in his heart. . . . Again, ye have heard that it was said to them of old time, Thou shalt not forswear thyself, but shall perform unto the Lord thine oaths: but I say unto you, swear not at all.'—(S. Matthew v. 17-34.)

And again:—

'Not every one that saith unto Me, Lord, Lord, shall enter into the kingdom of heaven ; but he that doeth the will of My Father which is in heaven. Many will say to Me in that day, Lord, Lord, did we not prophesy by Thy name, and by Thy name cast out devils, and by Thy name do many mighty works ? And then will I profess unto them, I never knew you: depart from Me, ye that work iniquity.'—(S. Matthew vii. 21-23.)

It is the same all through the ministry. Christ claims to be greater than Solomon, greater than the Temple. His service takes precedence of all others, and supersedes the claims of the closest natural and earthly ties. He speaks of Himself throughout as 'the Son of Man,' and sets before His disciples that wondrous scene 'when the Son of Man shall come in His glory and all the angels with Him, and shall sit on the throne of His glory: and before Him shall be gathered all nations.' It is He who then divides them 'as the shepherd separateth the sheep from the goats,' and sets some on the right hand and some on the left. It is He who pronounces the sentence, summoning those on the right hand to inherit the kingdom prepared for them, and dismissing those on the left 'into the eternal fire which is prepared for the devil and his angels.' 'And these shall go away into eternal punishment: but the righteous into eternal life.'—

(S. Matthew xxv. 31-46.) He makes the claim that He alone 'knows the Father,' and can reveal Him to men; and—perhaps the most tremendous claim of all —He claims to give rest to wearied humanity. 'Come unto Me, all ye that labour and are heavy laden, and I will give you rest. Take My yoke upon you and learn of Me; for I am meek and lowly in heart: and ye shall find rest for your souls. For My yoke is easy, and My burden is light.'—(S. Matthew xi. 28-30.)

All these and many more utterances which might be cited suggest questions concerning the person of the Speaker which cannot lightly be put aside, questions which imperatively demand an answer, since the moral character of the Speaker is involved; and the Church from the first has had no doubt about the answer. It is because the Speaker is God's 'only Son' that His teaching can be trusted, and His claims can be justified. So once more, when we turn from the Gospels to the Epistles, we are brought face to face with the fact that these questions were raised in the very earliest days, and that no uncertain answer was returned to them. It would be hard to conceive of more dogmatic utterances than these, which are contained in S. Paul's Epistles:—

'Of whom is Christ as concerning the flesh, who is over all, God blessed for ever.'—(Romans ix. 5.)

'Christ Jesus: Who, being in the form of God, counted it not a prize to be on an equality with God, but emptied Himself, taking the form of a servant, being made in the likeness of men; and being found in fashion as a man, He humbled himself, becoming obedient even unto death, yea, the death of the cross.'—(Phil. ii. 5-8.)

'Giving thanks unto the Father, Who . . . translated us into the kingdom of the Son of His love ; in Whom we have our redemption, the forgiveness of our sins : Who is the image of the invisible God, the firstborn of all creation ; for in Him were all things created, in the heavens and upon the earth, things visible and things invisible, whether thrones or dominions or principalities or powers ; all things have been created through Him, and unto Him ; and He is before all things, and in Him all things consist. And He is the head of the body, the Church: Who is the beginning, the firstborn from the dead ; that in all things He might have the pre-eminence.'—(Col. i. 12-18.)

Such passages should give rise to serious reflection. They show decisively how the Church of the Apostolic age answered the question, 'What think ye of Christ ?' and furnish a complete justification for the statements made in the Church's Creed of later days, showing us what was understood in the first century to be what S. Jude calls 'the faith once for all delivered to the saints,' for which men are to ' contend earnestly.' [1]

We deny, then, altogether that the formation of the Apostles' Creed represents a change from primitive Christianity, or that it marks a stage in the growth of dogma which has ended by changing the character of

[1] S. Jude 3.

Christianity. That there is a sense in which it marks a stage in the growth or development of dogma may be readily admitted. But it must be explained what is meant by the phrase. There are two senses in which the term development may be spoken of. It may mean development by addition, or it may mean development by explanation. The two are quite distinct; and it is in the latter sense only that a development of the Church's Creed can be really admitted. It will be shown later on in connection with the Nicene Creed that what was done at Nicæa was not to extend the area of the faith, or to 'vote a new honour to Jesus Christ' which He had not possessed before, but to explain in the philosophical language of the fourth century the position which God's 'only Son' had from the beginning occupied in the belief of Christendom. And if this is true of the Nicene Creed, it is most certainly true also that there is no 'addition' to the faith in the simpler formulary of the Apostles' Creed. What those who first formulated it did was to bring together in a short compass, in all probability for missionary and catechetical purposes rather than with any special polemical intent, the main beliefs of the Church; and by thus formulating them there is no doubt that a forward step was taken in giving coherence and clearness to those beliefs. So far, and in this sense, there was even in the Apostles' Creed some development. In later days there was more, for it became necessary to enlarge these simple statements because of the denials of false teachers which threatened the loss of the faith. Additions were then made to the Creed, not really by way of attempt to *explain* the mysteries of the faith, but rather to protect them in all their largeness and grandeur from the negations of rationalising explanations. The reader may be glad to have in support of this statement the following striking testimony from Mr. A. J. Balfour's volume on the *Foundations of Belief*:—

'Whatever opinion the reader may entertain of the decisions at which the Church arrived on the doctrine of the Trinity, it is at least clear that they were not in the nature of explanations. They were, in fact, precisely the reverse. They were the negation of explanations. The various heresies which it combated were, broadly speaking, all endeavours to bring the mystery as far as possible into harmony with contemporary speculations, Gnostic, Neo-Platonic, or Rationalising, to relieve it from this or that difficulty: in short, to do something towards "explaining" it. The Church held that all such explanations or partial explanations inflicted irremediable impoverishment on the idea of the Godhead which was essentially involved in the Christian revelation. They insisted on preserving that idea in all its inexplicable fullness; and so it has come about that while such simplifications as those of the Arians, for example, are so alien and impossible to modern modes of thought that if they had been incorporated with Christianity they must have destroyed it, the doctrine of Christ's Divinity still gives reality and life to the worship of millions of pious souls, who are wholly ignorant both of the controversy to which they owe its preservation, and of the technicalities which its discussion has involved.'[1]

We may now advance a step further, and, having admitted that the formation of the Creed marks a stage of development in the *expression* of the faith rather than of growth in the faith itself, we may acknowledge further that the language of creeds and formularies can never be wholly adequate to express the full significance of the truths which they enshrine. No one age can completely apprehend the fullness of the truths as set forth in them. It cannot have been entirely apprehended by those who drew them up. Their language is true. It endures and will endure; but subsequent ages are often able to see more deeply into their meaning. To quote Mr. Balfour once more:—

'If their meaning could be exhausted by one generation they would be false for the next. It is because they can be charged with richer and richer content as our knowledge slowly grows to a fuller harmony with the Infinite Reality, that they may be counted among the most precious of our inalienable possessions.'[2]

It would be easy to illustrate this in detail from almost any article of the Apostles' Creed from the first to the last. Our conception of the meaning of the word 'God,' and of all that is involved in belief in a Personal God Who is 'the Father,' 'All-Sovereign,' 'Maker of heaven and earth,' has been infinitely enlarged since the words were put together in which

[1] *Foundations of Belief*, p. 279. [2] *Ibid.*, p. 278.

that belief is expressed. And so with the words towards the end of the Creed in which we express our belief in 'the resurrection of the body,' or, as it is more literally, 'the flesh' (*carnis*). A more spiritual view of the nature of the resurrection body may be ours than was that of those who placed this article in the Creed, as with the experience of the ages we have come to see deeper into the heart of the Scriptural truth which they were endeavouring to safeguard and express.[1] There need be no hesitation on the part of any who believe in the Divine guidance of the Church by the Holy Spirit in admitting this. A thoughtful writer can speak thus of Shakespeare: 'When a subtile critic has detected some recondite beauty in Shakespeare, the vulgar are fain to cry that Shakespeare did not mean it. Well! what of that? If it be there, his genius meant it. This is the very mark whereby to know a true poet. There will always be a number of beauties in his works, which he never meant to put into them';[2] and if this is so, then surely in a similar way the Christian need never shrink from acknowledg-

[1] On this article see Swete, *The Apostles' Creed*, p. 89, where its original meaning is fully discussed.

[2] Hare, *Guesses at Truth*, p. 196. Cf. Westcott: 'We have all found, I suppose, that study, reflection, experience, reveal new teachings in a masterpiece. In meditating on it, fresh and unexpected thoughts flash upon us. When this is so there is one question which may be dismissed without the least compunction: "Did the artist mean all this?" The question is wholly irrelevant. The seer is not dependent on conscious effort. The thought need not precede the vision. He saw, and has recorded for our service what he saw.'— *Lessons from Work*, p. 445.

ing that there are depths of meaning in the Creed, which its compilers were not conscious of putting into it, and he will thank God reverently for the insight which has come with the ages, and which enables him to see them.

But, lastly, this deeper apprehension of the inner meaning of the Creed must not be confused with what is really a very different thing from it, viz. the exchange or substitution of one meaning for another. If, for instance, the view that the Creed was originally a Unitarian one could be established, it would be impossible on the principles stated above to justify the Church's appropriation of it as a Trinitarian formulary. It would be no genuine case of a deeper insight into the meaning of the words. It would be the substitution of one meaning for another—almost a jugglery with words. In the same way with regard to the birth of our Lord from the Virgin Mary: certain writers have contended that it is immaterial whether the statement of the Creed is literally true or not. They have claimed to subscribe the Creed, though disbelieving or doubting the literal truth of the words 'born of the Virgin Mary,' thinking that it is possible somehow to interpret them metaphorically. But this, again, is to exchange one meaning for another, since no metaphorical explanation of the words can possibly be accepted as if it were implicitly contained in the original statement. The statement is obviously literal; even the name of the Virgin is introduced; and unless the literal interpretation be accepted, the article can only be regarded as untrue. Very much the same must be said in regard to the article on our Lord's resurrection : 'The third day He rose again from the dead.' There may be ample room for clearing our conceptions of the nature of the glorified body with which Christ rose, and thus for seeing more deeply into the meaning of the statement; but the definite note of time, 'the third day,' shows that it is a historic fact which is spoken of, and that to interpret the clause as speaking merely of a continuance of spiritual life after the crucifixion, and to deny in any sense that the tomb was empty and the body raised from the dead, would be to exchange one meaning for another, substituting for what the Creed says something which really demands a wholly different form of words to express it. So much it seemed well to say, in order to guard against misconception. There is no need to pursue the subject further. This is not the place to discuss the very important question of the ethics of subscription. That is outside the writer's province. It may, however, be added that the lessons of history should not be disregarded. The Church to-day has much to learn from the controversies on subscription in the eighteenth century ; and the robust common sense of Waterland's treatises on the subject, which destroyed the claims of the Arian clergy to a right to subscribe the Church's formularies, whenever they could *in any sense* reconcile them with Scripture, is not without its value in questions that are sometimes raised to-day.

NOTE A

AUTHORITIES FOR THE LATER ADDITIONS TO THE CREED

THE following note will give the reader some idea of the way in which the articles not contained in the old Roman Creed of the fourth century, gradually spread throughout the Western Church.

1. *Maker of heaven and earth.* This, or something equivalent to it, is generally found in *Eastern* Creeds from the earliest date to which they can be traced. It is also contained in the 'rule of faith' as given by Irenæus (c. 180). The earliest known baptismal Creed of the West to contain it is that given by Niceta of Remesiana in Dacia, c. 375. It is given in an African Creed (Fulgentius of Ruspe) at the end of the fifth or beginning of the sixth century; but is not found in the Creeds of a number of representative writers, chiefly Gallican, of the fifth and sixth centuries; it was probably the latest article to be generally adopted. It is found in the Gallican service-books of about A.D. 700, and then in Pirminius (730).

2. *Conceived.* This is first found in the *Fides Hieronymi* (c. 377), which, it must be remembered, is a private Creed, not a baptismal one. It was adopted in Gaul from the beginning of the fifth century, being found in the Creed as given by a number of representative writers (Phœbadius of Agen, c. 400; Faustus of Riez, 430; Cæsarius of Arles and Cyprian of Toulon, c. 500; and later ones). Outside Gaul its earliest appearance is in the Bangor Antiphonary, an Irish service-book of the seventh century.

3. *Suffered.* Found in the *Fides Hieronymi* and in the baptismal Creed of Niceta. From the fifth century onwards we meet with it in Creeds of Africa (Augustine, who died in 430,

THE APOSTLES' CREED 109

and Fulgentius of Ruspe, c. 500); Spain (Priscillian, c. 400, and Martin of Bracara, d. 580); Gaul (Phœbadius of Agen (?), Victricius of Rouen, c. 430, Faustus of Riez, Cæsarius of Arles, and later writers); Britain (Pelagius, c. 400, and the Bangor Antiphonary).

4. *Dead.* The *Fides Hieronymi* and Niceta. Rarely in Gaul from the fifth century (Cæsarius of Arles, and Gallican service-books). Elsewhere not till much later.

5. *He descended into hell.* The *Fides Hieronymi* and Niceta. Found at Aquileia at the end of the fourth century (Rufinus, 390); in Gaul from the sixth (Cæsarius of Arles, Venantius Fortunatus, c. 550, and Gallican service-books); Spain from the sixth century (Martin of Bracara (?)); Britain in the seventh (Bangor Antiphonary).

6. *God . . . Almighty.* The former of these words is found in the *Fides Hieronymi* and in a few early Creeds, such as those of Victricius of Rouen (Gaul) and Pelagius (Britain). The full form, 'God the Father Almighty,' seems to appear first in Spain at the end of the fourth century (Priscillian and Ildefonsus of Toledo, seventh century). In Gaul it is possibly contained in the Creed of Faustus of Riez, and is found in some of the Gallican service-books of the seventh century, but was not established till comparatively late. In Africa it is found at the end of the fifth or beginning of the sixth century (Fulgentius of Ruspe).

7. *Catholic.* The *Fides Hieronymi* and Niceta. Found in Gaul from the fifth century (Faustus of Riez, Cæsarius of Arles, and Gallican service-books); Spain from the sixth (Martin of Bracara, Ildefonsus of Toledo); Britain, seventh century (Bangor Antiphonary).

8. *Communion of Saints.* The *Fides Hieronymi* and Niceta. Found in Gaul from the fifth century (Faustus of Riez, Cæsarius of Arles, and service-books). Spain from the sixth (Martin of Bracara, Ildefonsus of Toledo).

9. *Life everlasting.* This stood in the African Creed certainly since the middle of the third century, being more than once quoted as part of the Creed by S. Cyprian (c. 250). It is also

110   THE THREE CREEDS

given by Augustine and Fulgentius of Ruspe. Elsewhere we
meet with it first in the *Fides Hieronymi* and Niceta. It is found
very occasionally in Gaul in the fifth century (viz. Faustus of
Riez and Cæsarius of Arles); in Spain from the sixth (Martin
of Bracara and Ildefonsus of Toledo); in Britain from the fifth
(Pelagius and the Bangor Antiphonary).

It must be understood that our knowledge is very incomplete,
and that the introduction of the several clauses into the Creeds
of the different Churches of the West may have been some time
earlier than the date of the first writer who happens to give
them. The authorities for the various statements made in this
note will be found in Burn, *Introduction to the Creeds*, and
Hahn, *Bibliothek der Symbole*.

NOTE B

AN EARLY METRICAL TRANSLATION OF THE CREED

THE following is the old English metrical version of the
Apostles' Creed referred to above on pp. 73 and 83.

> I trow in God, fader of might,
>   That alle has wroght,
> Heven and erthe, day and night,
>   And alle of noght.
> And in Ihesu that God's Son is
>   Al-onely,
> Bothe God and mon, Lord endles,
>   In him trow I ;
> Thurgh mekenes of tho holy gast,
>   That was so milde,
> He lyght in Mary mayden chast,
>   Be-come a childe ;
> Under pounce pilat pyned he was,
>   Us forto save,
> Done on cros and deed he was,
>   Layde in his grave ;

THE APOSTLES' CREED

Tho soul of him went into helle,
    Tho sothe to say;
Up he rose in flesshe and felle
    Tho thryd day;
He stegh till heven with woundis wide,
    Thurgh his pouste;
Now sittes opon his fader right syde,
    In mageste;
Thethin shal he come us alle to deme
    In his manhede,
Qwyk and ded, alle that has ben
    In Adam sede,
Wel I trow in tho holi gost,
    And holi kirc that is so gode;
And so I trow that housel es
    Bothe flesshe and blode;
Of my synnes, forgyfnes,
    If I wil mende;
Up-risyng als-so of my flesshe,
    And lyf with-outen ende.

See Simmons, *The Lay Folk's Mass-Book*, p. 20. Other old English (prose) translations may be seen in Maskell, *Monumenta Ritualia*, vol. iii. (ed. 2) p. 251.

CHAPTER III

THE NICENE CREED

CHAPTER III

THE NICENE CREED

§ 1

The Council of Nicæa

THE Nicene Creed as we know and use it is not verbally identical with that which was actually drawn up at Nicæa, but it is so closely connected with it that its name may well be justified. It is 'Nicene' in the sense that it contains the great formula which was then inserted in the Creed, and that it guards and maintains the faith which was then defined against Arianism. In order, therefore, to understand and appreciate it, it is necessary to start with a brief account of the rise of the Arian heresy, and of the proceedings at the Council of Nicæa.

The Arian heresy was first propounded about the year 319, when Arius, a presbyter of Alexandria, who had been trained in the school of Lucian of Antioch, charged his bishop Alexander with teaching Sabellianism, or the denial of the eternal distinction of the Persons in the Godhead. Sabellianism, which had been a real danger to the Church in the third century, had maintained that the distinction between the Father and the Son was merely a distinction in appearance or character, some teachers going so far as to assert that it was actually the Father who suffered on the Cross in the character of the Son. As a body or sect Sabellians were never formidable, but as a tendency or mode of thought Sabellianism was constantly reappearing, and there is no reason to doubt that Arius was sincere in his dread of it. But unhappily, in his opposition to it he was led to formulate the heresy which has ever since been associated with his name, the essence of which consists in the denial of the true Godhead of the Son. As Sabellianism 'confounded the Persons,' confusing the Father with the Son, so Arianism 'divided the substance,' separating the nature of the Father and the Son, and teaching that the Son was not of the same essence with the Father. Not content with attacking the teaching of Alexander, he propounded his own views positively, maintaining that if Christ was the Son, there must have been a period when He did not exist, and that the term 'begotten' referred to the period when He began to be, whereas the Church, guided by the teaching of Holy Scripture, and especially of S. John, held that the term generation signified not an event which once took place, but an eternal fact in the Divine nature. This had been expressed by so early a writer as Origen (who died in 253) in the phrase 'the Saviour is ever begotten,' from which the Church has adopted the term 'eternal generation.' It must be remembered that 'the Son' is not the only title used in Holy Scripture, but that the title 'Word' (*Logos*) is also applied to the same Person; and that this most emphatically proclaims the eternity of Him to Whom it is given, for it is impossible to conceive the Father as ever having existed without that eternal 'Thought' or 'Reason' (*Logos*), of Whom S. John says that He 'was in the beginning with God,' and that He 'was God.'[1] It was this that Arius failed to grasp. In a sense he allowed the Son to be called God and worshipped. He asserted that all other creatures were made by Him, but, refusing to allow Him to be one with the Supreme God, he was driven in the last resort to maintain that He was a creature, though not as one of the creatures. He thus introduced a sort of intermediate being between God and creation; and by his admission that this being was to be worshipped he reintroduced idolatry or the worship of a creature (even though the most exalted of creatures) into the Church. This, briefly, is the heresy the rise of which startled the Church in the early years of the fourth century. The excitement raised by it was intense. The subject was discussed everywhere at Alexandria and in its neighbourhood. In the streets, in the shops, in the markets, theological questions were propounded and eagerly and hotly contested. Arius was not without sympathisers in high places in the Church, and when condemned at Alexandria he found supporters in

[1] S. John i. 1, 2.

Palestine; and it was soon obvious that the storm aroused would not quickly subside. The controversy came to the ears of Constantine, who was now sole master of the Roman Empire, and after some ineffectual attempts to stop it, he determined to refer it to a council of bishops representing the whole Catholic Church throughout the world. Accordingly at his command there was summoned the first General Council, which met at Nicæa, in Bithynia, in the year 325. The main business of this Council was the consideration of Arianism. There were other subjects also referred to it, but of these there is no need to take any notice here.

The number of bishops who met together was large; it is traditionally given as 318, and was certainly over 250. The great majority, as was natural, came from the East, but the West was not without its representatives, of whom the most important was Hosius, Bishop of Cordova, the friend and adviser of Constantine, who had previously visited Alexandria with a letter from the Emperor, and was therefore well acquainted with the true character of the question at issue. There seems to have been a general agreement that the opportunity should be taken to put forth a Creed which might represent the universal belief of the Church, and be accepted by all bishops as a test of orthodoxy. This was really a new thing. Till now different Churches had possessed their own baptismal Creeds, differing in various minor points from one another—though the substance of the faith was iden-

THE NICENE CREED 119

tical everywhere. What was now proposed was something more complete and formal, a theological Creed for the bishops of the universal Church. It was, however, soon manifest that the bishops were not all agreed among themselves. In fact, they were sharply divided, and we may mark out three groups among them. (1) *The Arians*. The party that was in full sympathy with the teaching of Arius appears to have comprised about seventeen bishops, of whom the leader was the determined and unscrupulous Eusebius of Nicomedia. (2) *The Anti-Arians*. This again was but a small party, for at the opening of the Council the great body of the bishops hardly understood the question at issue. Those who had really grasped the position and understood the issues involved were only about twenty in number, their leaders being Alexander, Bishop of Alexandria (who was attended by his deacon, Athanasius), Hosius of Cordova, and Marcellus of Ancyra. (3) Between these two parties there was a large middle party of more than two hundred bishops, some of whom had but very slight grasp of the question, while others appear to have been more or less in sympathy with Arius, and others were simply for maintaining things as they were. This party, of which Eusebius, Bishop of Cæsarea, was the ablest, may be fairly termed the party of Conservatives.

It would appear that comparatively early in the proceedings a profession of faith was put forward for acceptance by Eusebius of Nicomedia. This has not come down to us, but it must have been a thorough-going Arian formulary, for it was at once torn up and denounced as blasphemy. Its production probably did much to open the eyes of some of the conservatives to the true character of the teaching of Arius, and thus to prepare their minds for the adoption of some more definite formulary. After the rejection of the Creed proposed by Eusebius of Nicomedia, his namesake of Cæsarea came forward, and proposed to the Council a formulary which he tells us was the baptismal Creed of his Church of Cæsarea, and which was declared to be good and unexceptionable. The Creed ran as follows:—

'We believe in One God, the Father Almighty, Maker of all things visible and invisible. And in One Lord Jesus Christ, the Word of God, God of God, Light of Light, Life of Life, the only begotten Son, before all worlds begotten of the Father, by Whom also all things were made; Who for our salvation was made flesh, and lived among men, and suffered, and rose again the third day, and ascended to the Father, and will come again in glory to judge the quick and the dead. And we believe also in one Holy Ghost.'

This Creed was perfectly satisfactory so far as it went; but it failed to meet the question that was really before the Council. It will be noticed that the clauses on the Person of the pre-Incarnate Christ are almost wholly in the very words of Scripture. *One Lord Jesus Christ* comes from 1 Cor. viii. 6: 'To us there is . . . one Lord Jesus Christ.' *The Word of God* is taken from Rev. xix. 1: 'His name is called the

THE NICENE CREED 121

Word of God.' *God of* (or *proceeding from*, ἐκ) *God, Light of* (or *proceeding from*, ἐκ) *Light, Life of* (or *proceeding from*, ἐκ) *Life*, though not found *totidem verbis* in Scripture, are obviously suggested by the opening phrases of S. John's Gospel: 'In the beginning was the Word, and the Word was with God, and the Word was God.... In Him was Life, and the Life was the Light of men.' *The only begotten Son* is from S. John iii. 16: 'God so loved the world that He gave His only begotten Son.' *Before all worlds* comes practically, though not quite verbally, from Col. i. 15, 'He is before all things,' and Heb. i. 2, 'By Whom also He made the worlds.' *Begotten of the Father* is from 1 John v. 18, 'He that is begotten of God'; and *By Whom also all things were made* is quoted directly from S. John i. 3, 'All things were made by Him.'

The creed of Eusebius, then, was thoroughly Scriptural, and the question may be asked, Why was it not accepted as sufficient? To this the answer is that the very fact that it adhered so closely to the phrases of Scripture rendered it inadequate, for the question before the Council was not as to the acceptance of the language of Scripture, but as to its meaning and the interpretation to be put upon it. The creed of Eusebius did little or nothing to settle this; and the behaviour of the Arians at the Council showed that the mere repetition of phrases picked out of Scripture, however exalted the language contained in them, would never serve to protect the Church against the heresy she was seeking to exclude. At an early session it appears, from what Athanasius says, that the bishops had been anxious, in order to 'do away with the irreligious phrases of the Arians, to use instead the acknowledged words of the Scriptures, that the Son is not from nothing but "from God," and is "Word" and "Wisdom," and not "creature" or "work"'; but Eusebius of Nicomedia and those who followed his lead could accept these phrases without difficulty, 'understanding the phrase "from God" as belonging to us, as if in respect to it the Word of God differed nothing from us, and that, because it is written "There is one God from whom are all things"; and again, "All things are from God."'[1] Again, Athanasius, who was himself present at the Council, and therefore an eyewitness of what he describes, tells us that, 'When the bishops said that the Word must be described as the True Power and Image of the Father, in all things exact and like the Father, and as unalterable, and as always, and as in Him without division, Eusebius and his fellows endured indeed, as not daring to contradict, being put to shame by the arguments which were urged against them; but withal they were caught whispering to each other, and winking with their eyes, that "like" and "always," and "power" and "in Him," were, as before, common to us and the Son, and that there was no difficulty in agreeing to these. As to "like," they said that it was written of us, "Man is the image and glory of God." "Always,"

[1] Athanasius, *De Decretis*, § 19.

THE NICENE CREED 123

that it is written, "For we which live are always"; "in Him," "In Him we live and move and have our being"; "unalterable," that it is written, "Nothing shall separate us from the love of Christ"; as to "power," that the caterpillar and the locust are called "power" and "great power," and that it is often said of the people, for instance, "all the power of the Lord came out of the land of Egypt."'[1]

While, however, the Arians showed in this way that they were prepared to accept Scriptural phrases, which they could interpret in a non-natural sense, they also made it clear that they could never accept any formula which proclaimed in such a way that it could not be evaded the essential Divinity of the Son of God. Their spokesman, Eusebius of Nicomedia, in the course of the discussion had used the phrase, 'I will never confess that the Son is of the "*ousia*" of the Father.' The admission was fatal to the cause he championed. It brought the matter to a clear issue. The Greek word *ousia* is not very happily translated by us *substance*, as this latter word, in its popular sense, suggests something material. What is meant by it is rather *essence* or *nature*. So also the adjective *Homoousios* is unfortunately rendered '*Being of one substance with*,' or (as in some well-known hymns) '*Consubstantial*,' for these terms are open to the same misconception. They are, however, firmly fixed, and it would be useless to attempt to alter them. All that can be done is to explain their meaning, and free them from materialistic

[1] Athanasius, *De Decretis*, § 20.

associations, making it clear that they are intended to protect the belief in the true Godhead or Divine nature of the Second Person of the Holy Trinity by the assertion that He is of one essence or nature with the Father. It was this that Eusebius of Nicomedia declared that he could never admit, and by this declaration, as we shall presently see, he probably suggested the use of the term which has since become the distinctive symbol of the Catholic faith.

In the face of such evasions as those described above, it was clearly impossible for the Church to be content with a Creed that merely repeated phrases of Scripture without explaining the sense in which they were to be understood. It is most important that this should be thoroughly realised, since the idea which was current in the fourth century is found still to linger in some quarters, that if a man consents to the terms of Holy Scripture nothing more should be asked of him. The Arian controversy really settled this question for the Church once for all, and convinced her that definitions were necessary. There has never been any desire on the part of the Church to multiply definitions. Indeed, she has been slow to make them; and it is only as they have been forced upon her by the negations and evasions of heresy that she has formulated them. In the case before us it was apparently felt by the great body of bishops that some addition to the Creed of Cæsarea was a necessity; and, according to Eusebius, the Emperor himself advised all present to agree to it, with the insertion of the single term 'Being of one substance (with the Father),' to explain what was meant by 'begotten' or 'only begotten.' If the Emperor was really the first to propose the use of this famous term (*Homoousios*), the Church has reason to be grateful to him, for it was confessedly the one term which the Arians could not explain away. But it can hardly have been his own idea, and there can be little doubt that it must first have been suggested to him by his friend and adviser Hosius, who had himself investigated the question of Arianism at its birthplace, and knew what was really involved in it. The term, however, was not accepted without hesitation. There were real objections to it which were felt by some, and which required to be answered. Four such may be mentioned here:—

(1) It was a philosophical term, and might be taken to imply the existence of some Divine 'substance' or essence, distinct from God, of which the Persons of the Godhead equally partook, being alike made sharers of it.

This difficulty was met by its being made quite clear that the use of the phrase was not intended to imply anything of the kind. It was merely meant to protect the real and essential Divinity of the Son. It may, however, have been partly because of this objection that the Fathers felt that further explanation was necessary, and that the bare insertion of the word *Homoousios* was insufficient.

(2) It was asserted that the term had been rejected in the third century at the Council of Antioch,

A.D. 268, when the teaching of Paul of Samosata was condemned; and thus the bishops who advocated it were contradicting the teaching of the Early Church. To this it was replied that, if it really was rejected at Antioch (which was not quite certain), it was because Paul had falsely argued for its philosophical meaning, and that therefore its acceptance at Antioch would have involved a false belief, whereas, in the sense in which it was now taken, it protected the true faith.

(3) The term was said to be of a Sabellian tendency, and thus to lead to a confusion between the Persons of the Father and the Son, as if 'Ousia' or Substance bore the meaning of Person or Subsistence. There was some ground for this, as the technical phraseology of the Church had not yet been, so to speak, stereotyped, and some writers had spoken as if there was more than one 'Ousia' in the Godhead, taking the word in the sense of 'Person.' The difficulty was, however, met by careful explanation of the sense in which the term was now used, and by the gradual adoption of a different Greek word, 'Hypostasis,' to express the distinction of Persons in the Godhead.

(4) The term was said to be a novelty, and not found in Scripture. This objection has been to some extent dealt with above. It is true that the term was not in Scripture, but in it, as Athanasius says, the bishops 'concentrated the sense of Scripture.' Moreover, it was not really such a novelty as it was asserted to be, for precedents could be cited for its use by earlier writers of unquestioned orthodoxy.

These were the principal objections raised at the time and afterwards, and the answers which were returned to them. But it would seem that the discussions showed that the insertion of the word *Homoousios* alone would be insufficient. Indeed, it might be misleading, and fail altogether to protect the Church's faith in the eternal and coequal Godhead of the Son together with His eternal generation from the Father, which was the full truth which the bishops desired to guard. Accordingly the Creed of Cæsarea was thoroughly overhauled, and various other changes were made in it to which perhaps the Creeds of Antioch and Jerusalem contributed. As finally accepted and promulgated by the Council, the Creed of Nicæa ran as follows, the clauses in italics being those already found in the Creed of Cæsarea as presented by Eusebius :—

> *We believe in One God, the Father Almighty, maker of all things visible and invisible.*
> *And in one Lord Jesus Christ,* the Son of God, *only begotten* of the Father—that is, of the substance of the Father—*God of God, Light of Light,* Very God of Very God ; *Begotten,* not made ; Being of one substance with the Father ; *By whom all things were made,* both that are in heaven, and that are in earth ; *Who* for us men, and *for our salvation,* came down, and *was incarnate,* and was made man ; *suffered, and rose again the third day* ; *ascended* into heaven ; is coming *to judge the quick and dead.*
> *And in the Holy Ghost,*

To this creed was appended the following condemnation of Arian errors :—

> But those who say 'Once He was not,' and 'Before He was begotten He was not,' and 'He came into existence out of what was not,' or 'That the Son of God was of a different hypostasis or ousia,' or 'That He was made,' or 'is changeable or mutable,' these the Catholic Church anathematises.

It will be seen that the changes in and additions to the Creed proposed by Eusebius were considerable, and the object of most of them is not difficult to understand. The title 'Son' was put prominently forward instead of 'Word.' To this no objection would be raised by Arius; but as the whole question was really of the nature of the Sonship, it might well be thought advisable to let this title have the principal place rather than the term 'Word,' which standing alone might not suggest Personality. Next, it was found necessary to explain the word 'only begotten,' as in itself it was open to Arian evasions, Eusebius of Nicomedia in particular having emphatically insisted that it did not involve the participation in the nature or essence of the Father. Thus to the clause 'only begotten of the Father' was added the explanation 'that is of the substance (*ousia*) of the Father,' an explanation which had the further advantage of guarding against erroneous inferences from the subsequent use of the term *Homoousios*. Instead of the Eusebian phrases 'Light of Light, the Firstborn of all creation,' was inserted an emphatic proclamation of the true Godhead of the Son in the words 'Very God of Very God,' *i.e.* true—*verus*, ἀληθινός—God proceeding from (ἐκ) true God. For 'begotten of God before all worlds' was substituted 'begotten, not made,' the two terms which the Arians had confused being thus sharply distinguished. Next comes the insertion of the crucial term *Homoousios*, 'being of one substance with the Father,' on which it may be well to repeat that the original is, of course, free from all those material associations which, in popular use, cling to the English word 'Substance.' What it really means is that the Son is one in essence or nature with the Father, the earlier phrase 'that is of (or from) the substance (or essence or nature) of the Father' having already expressed the belief that the Father is the source of the Godhead of the Son, and having thus guarded against any possible misuse of *Homoousios*, as if it implied the existence of an abstract Godhead, behind the Persons of the Father and the Son, of which both equally partook. To the next clause, 'By Whom all things were made,' were appended the words 'both that are in heaven or that are in earth.' Whether there was any special reason for this addition does not appear, but it may have been thought desirable to add the words because of the Arian contention that the Son was Himself a creature, though not as one of the creatures. In regard to this clause it is well to notice that the English preposition in the phrase 'By Whom all things were made,' is not altogether free from ambiguity, for it fails to bring out what is quite clear in the original, that the Son is spoken of as the *mediate* agent in creation, *through* (διὰ) Whom all things were made. The Creed in reality carefully follows the language of Holy Scripture, where the preposition διὰ (*through*) is regularly employed to express the mediatorial work of the Son in creation. As stated in the first paragraph of the Creed, God the Father is 'Maker of heaven and earth, and of all things visible and invisible,' but it was *through* the agency of the Eternal Word or Son that creation was effected. 'All things were made by (or *through*) Him, . . . the world was made by (or *through*) Him,' says S. John; 'All things were created by (or *through*) Him,' says S. Paul, and it is of Him that the writer of the Epistle to the Hebrews speaks when He says 'By (or *through*) Whom He (God the Father) made the worlds.'[1] All this is lost to the English reader, owing to the looseness with which the preposition 'by' is used; but the precise shade of meaning is one which it is most important to notice, in order that we may enter fully into the teaching of Holy Scripture and the Church's Creed.

The remaining changes made in the Creed of Eusebius are concerned not with the nature of the pre-Incarnate Christ, but with His Incarnation. They are less significant than those just commented on, and it is not easy to see any precise reason for their introduction. The addition of the words 'for us men' and 'came down' can hardly be said to add really new

[1] S. John i. 3, 10; Col. i. 16; Heb. i. 2.

thoughts to the briefer form 'Who for our salvation was incarnate'; but the substitution of the words 'and was made man' for 'and lived among men' may have been made to guard against a possible misconception of the term 'was incarnate'—literally 'was made flesh'; for it is possible that even so early as Nicæa some among the Arians advanced the theory which afterwards became very prominent among them, that it was only the flesh, and not the human spirit or soul, which Christ took at His Incarnation. Such a view would be guarded against by the insertion of the supplementary clause with its wider language. He not only 'was made flesh' (or 'incarnate'), but also 'was made man.' Why the changes which follow were made it is impossible to say. No particular reason has ever been suggested for the substitution of 'into heaven' for 'to the Father' in the clause which speaks of the Ascension; and it is curious that instead of the words 'shall come again in glory to judge the quick and dead' the briefer form should have been preferred, 'is coming to judge the quick and dead.' No explanation is offered of this, which can scarcely have been deliberate, but must have been the result of some accident. It is remarkable also that both the forms of Creed which we are considering should end so abruptly with the words 'I believe in the Holy Ghost,' and that there should be nothing in either as to the Church, the remission of sins, or the resurrection and eternal life. We know from other sources that clauses on these subjects were found in very early days in the baptismal Creeds of the several Churches both in East and West, and it seems impossible that they can really have been wanting in the baptismal Creed of the Church of Cæsarea. We can, therefore, only suppose that Eusebius merely cited so much of that Creed as was necessary in view of the question then raised, and that the bishops in putting forth their new formulary, which was designed not as a baptismal Creed, but rather as a test of orthodoxy for bishops, were content to stop short with the brief mention of belief in the Holy Ghost, because no question had yet been raised on the subject. This is the explanation offered towards the close of the century by S. Basil,[1] and it appears to be a reasonable one. The Creed which they put forth was not intended in any way to be a substitute for the baptismal formulary, and they might well think that there was no need for them to speak of the matters contained in the last section of that, as they were not concerned with them. In the same way we find that various Creeds put forth subsequently by the Councils of the fourth century as substitutes for the Nicene faith all stop short at the same point, and obviously for the same reason.

Such, then, was the Creed as agreed to at Nicæa. From what has been said, it will be clear to the reader that the assent of the bishops to the very full state-

---

[1] S. Basil, Ep. lxxviii. (*al.* cxxv.): 'The doctrine of the Spirit is merely mentioned, as needing no elaboration, because at the time of the Council no question was raised, and the opinion on this subject in the hearts of the faithful was exposed to no attack.'

ment of the Creed on the nature of the pre-Incarnate Christ marks a stage in the history of the Church. By promulgating so full and complete a statement and requiring it as a test of orthodoxy, the Church proclaimed aloud to the world her belief in the true Godhead of Jesus Christ, God's only Son. And it has been freely asserted that by so doing she made new demands on her members, and advanced beyond the doctrine of Scripture in the belief which she now imposed upon them. The answer to this has been to some extent anticipated in what has been said above with regard to the Apostles' Creed. It was there shown that it was impossible to separate the teaching of Christ from the Person of Christ; that questions as to His nature were inevitably raised by His utterances; and that the language of the Apostles is such that it is impossible to doubt their belief that He Who was manifested on earth was indeed one with the Father, and Himself God. From the days of the Apostles onwards it would be easy to compile a catena of representative writers whose words bear witness to the belief of the Church in our Lord's Divinity. Even the heathen knew how the Christians regarded Him, for Pliny in his well-known letter to the Emperor Trajan, at the very beginning of the second century, writes of the Christians as meeting together on a stated day and singing a hymn to Christ as God (or *as a God*). Ignatius of Antioch, the immediate follower of S. John, again and again uses language about which there can be no mistake. It may be well to collect some examples from his epistles, since coming from so early a date, and from a writer so closely connected with the Apostles, they furnish evidence of exceptional value. Writing, then, to the Ephesians, about the year 115, he uses such expressions as these: 'The will of the Father, and of Jesus Christ our God,' 'having your hearts kindled in the blood of God,' 'God in man,' 'our God Jesus Christ,' 'God appeared in the likeness of man.' To the Magnesians: 'One God Who manifested Himself through Jesus Christ His Son, Who is the Word that proceeded from silence.' To the Romans: 'Faith and love towards Jesus Christ our God,' 'our God Jesus Christ being in the Father,' 'permit me to be an imitator of the passion of my God.' To Polycarp: 'I bid you farewell always in our God Jesus Christ.'[1] There is no mistaking language such as this. The belief of Ignatius was identical with the belief of the Nicene fathers. Nor does Ignatius stand alone. When towards the close of the second century one Artemon began to teach that Christ was a mere man, his doctrine was at once denounced as a 'God-denying apostasy,' and appeal was made to the evidence of earlier writers as well as to the worship of the Church in hymns and doxologies, as showing what had been the faith of the Church from the beginning.[2] Again, the fact that such a heresy as Sabellianism could arise, identifying our Lord with the

---

[1] Ignatius, *ad Eph.*, 1, 7, 18, 19; *ad Magn.*, 8; *ad Rom.*, 1, 3, 6; *ad Polyc.*, 8.

[2] Eusebius, V. xxviii.

THE NICENE CREED 135

Person of God the Father, testifies most emphatically to the Church's belief in His Godhead, while at the same time it supplies evidence of the difficulty which the Church had to face in reconciling this belief with the doctrine, so jealously to be guarded, of the Divine unity. It naturally required time and much patient thought for the full bearings of the Scriptural statements in their relation to one another to be clearly seen, for precision of expression to be arrived at, and for the best terms to be selected to state what was almost beyond the power of words to express; and consequently we need feel no surprise if in some of the ante-Nicene fathers we meet with language and phraseology which the mature judgment of the later Church has rejected as inadequate or misleading. But in the main there is really no room for doubt that the Church from the very first accepted the doctrine of Christ's Divinity, and (as she showed by her rejection of Sabellianism) of His personal distinction from the Father. Thus when in the early years of the fourth century the question arose between the Arians and the Catholic party in the Church, Is Jesus Christ truly God? and this was answered in the negative by the Arians, it was Arianism and not the Nicene faith which was the novelty. It was because it was a novelty that it so shocked its opponents, as being inconsistent with the traditional belief of the Church which had come down from the earliest days, and was based on the teaching of holy Scripture. To that traditional belief the Nicene Creed gave greater clearness and precision of statement. It was necessary to do this, if error was to be excluded; but there was nothing new in the faith as thus stated, except its terminology. That may have been new—though it was not altogether such a novelty as was alleged—but the new terms borrowed from Greek dialectics were only adopted in order to protect the old faith. Whatever development there was, was development by way of explanation, not development by way of addition. It was saying a thing in a new way, not saying a new thing. The belief of the Church was really the same before and after Nicæa, only after Nicæa it was held with a deeper insight into its full bearings, and a clearer perception of the relation of its different parts to one another. What actually happened at Nicæa has never been better expressed than by Dr. Liddon in a famous passage of his Bampton Lectures, with the citation of which this section may be appropriately closed :—

'When the question was raised whether Jesus Christ was or was not " of one substance with " the Father, it became clear that of two courses one must be adopted. Either an affirmative answer must be given, or the teaching of the Apostles themselves must be explained away. As a matter of fact, the Nicene fathers only affirmed, in the philosophical language of the fourth century, what our Lord and the Apostles had taught in the popular dialects of the first. If, then, the Nicene Council developed, it was a development by explanation. It was a development which placed the intrinsically unchangeable dogma, committed to the guardianship of the Church, in its true relation to the new intellectual world that had grown up around Christians in the fourth century. Whatever vacillations of thought might have been experienced here or there, whatever doubtful expressions might have escaped from theologians of the intervening period, no real doubt could be raised as to the meaning of the original teachers of Christianity, or as to the true drift and main current of the continuous traditional belief of the Church. The Nicene divines interpreted in a new language the belief of their first fathers in the faith. They did not enlarge it; they vehemently protested that they were simply preserving and handing on what they had received. The very pith of their objection to Arianism was its novelty: it was false because it was of recent origin. They themselves were forced to say what they meant by their Creed, and they said it. Their explanation added to the sum of authoritative ecclesiastical language, but it did not add to the number of articles in the Christian faith: the area of the Creed was not enlarged. The Nicene Council did not vote a new honour to Jesus Christ which He had not before possessed: it defined more clearly the original and unalterable bases of that supreme place which from the days of the Apostles He had held in the thought and heart, in the speculative and active life, of Christendom.'[1]

[1] *Bampton Lectures*, p. 429.

§ 2

The Nicene Creed from Nicæa to Chalcedon

THE Creed of Nicæa was ultimately accepted by all the bishops present at the Council except two, but there were several who only signed under pressure, and with mental reservations ; and the bishops had scarcely separated before a determined effort was made to undo the work of the Council. It was soon manifest that the battle was not yet won, and long, weary years of struggle and controversy were to elapse before the faith as proclaimed in the Creed was firmly established as the faith of Christendom. Into the general history of the controversy there is no need to enter here, for in spite of all efforts to dislodge the term 'Homoousios' (*being of one substance*) from its place in the Creed, the defenders of it, and notably Athanasius, clung firmly to it as absolutely necessary to guard the true faith, and as being the one term which the Arians could not explain away. By the different parties into which the Arians were split up in the years that followed the Council various substitutes were proposed, ranging from the bald expression 'unlike,' through the vague 'like,' up to 'Homoiousios' or 'of like substance,' the term which came nearer than any other to 'Homoousios,' the word chosen to safeguard the true faith—indeed so close did it come as to give rise to Gibbon's famous sneer against 'the furious contests which the difference of a single diphthong excited between the Homoousians and the Homoiousians'[1]—a sneer which may be fairly met by pointing out that it might as reasonably be said that between the *Creatour* (for so the word was formerly spelt) and the *creature* there was but the difference of a single letter. In the course of the controversy, however, many of those who had originally been connected with the party of the Homoiousians or semi-Arians, as S. Basil and S. Cyril of Jerusalem, came gradually to understand the true meaning of the term 'Homoousios,' and as they understood it better, to overcome their objections to it, so that gradually during the latter half of the fourth century the semi-Arian party was broken up, and, while some drifted further away from the orthodox faith and were merged in the Arians, others were absorbed by the Catholic party, and accepted the full faith as established at Nicæa. The result of this was that in many places the local baptismal Creed was enlarged by the incorporation with it of the Nicene phraseology concerning the nature of the pre-Incarnate Christ; and further, since in the course of the controversy new forms of heresy had emerged against which the Nicene formulary offered no protection, it was found necessary to introduce fresh clauses

[1] *Decline and Fall of the Roman Empire*, chap. xxi.

in some instances to guard against them. There was thus a revision on a tolerably wide scale of the existing Creeds in the latter part of the fourth century, which has left permanent traces on the expression of the Church's faith.

Three novel forms of heresy must here be mentioned, as having led to the expansion of the Creed.

(1) *The heresy of Marcellus of Ancyra in Galatia.* Marcellus had been one of the principal champions of the faith in our Lord's true Godhead at Nicæa. Unhappily, in the controversies that followed the Council, in endeavouring to refute the Arians he himself used language which laid him open to the charge of Sabellianism. What he really taught is not quite certain, but he appears to have drawn a distinction between 'the Word of God' and 'the Son,' and finally to have maintained a merely temporary connection between the two. The *Logos* (or Word) 'by a sort of " expansion " of the Divine unity became temporarily related to Jesus, Who, as the chosen organ for its manifestation, the man Whose being was filled with its presence, was called the "Son" and "Image" of God; but from Whom, in God's appointed time, the Logos would withdraw itself, and relapse by a movement of " contraction " into the bosom of Divinity.'[1] Such a view involved the denial of the eternity of Christ's reign, which, according to Marcellus, would come definitely to an end when the Son's distinct personality ceased, and the Logos was absorbed into the Godhead.

[1] Bright, *Age of the Fathers*, i. 157.

THE NICENE CREED

(2) *Apollinarianism*. It was not long before the denial of our Lord's *true* Godhead was followed by the denial of the *perfection* of His humanity. This is the essential feature of the heresy called after Apollinaris of Laodicæa, its author. Apollinaris appears to have been anxious to protect the true Divinity of the Son, and in the endeavour to do this, probably from fear of maintaining a sort of double personality in Him after His Incarnation, he fell into the error of a partial denial of His humanity. Adopting the threefold division of man's nature—body, soul, and spirit (cf. 1 Thess. v. 23)—he taught that though at the Incarnation Christ took body and soul (*i.e.* the lower nature with the appetites and desires common to man and the animal creation), yet He was without the rational 'spirit' or higher nature, the place of which was supplied by the Divine Word or *Logos*. Such a view protects the Divinity at the expense of the Humanity. It is destructive of the redemptive work of Christ, and is obviously inconsistent with the teaching of Scripture, which attributes to Christ a true and proper nature in all its parts—*spirit*,[1] as well as *soul* and *body*.

(3) *Macedonianism*. We have seen that the Creed of Nicæa ended abruptly with the words 'and in the Holy Ghost,' because at that time no question had been raised concerning the Spirit. But a denial of the Divinity of the Third Person of the Holy Trinity was logically involved in a denial of the Divinity of the Second Person.

---

[1] See especially S. Mark viii. 12 ; S. Luke xxiii. 46 ; S. John xi. 33, xiii. 21, xix. 30, in all of which the human *spirit* is definitely spoken of.

If Christ be not truly God, then certainly the Holy Spirit, Who is spoken of in Scripture as the Spirit of Christ, and as sent by Him, cannot be truly God. This inference was presently drawn in the course of the controversy, some teachers maintaining that the Spirit is a 'creature of a creature.' The name given to this heresy, Macedonianism, is taken from Macedonius, Bishop of Constantinople, who was deposed under Arian influence in 360. It is said that it was during his retirement that he elaborated the views with which his name is connected; but he is somewhat of a shadowy personage, and makes no figure in the controversy beyond giving his name to a form of heresy, of the rise of which there are clear indications at an earlier stage, and which was really a necessary inference (as Athanasius and others pointed out) from the Arian denial of the Consubstantiality of the Son with the Father.

Of these three heresies, that which is associated with the name of Marcellus was the first to cause anxiety; and shortly after the year 340 we find that Creeds and formularies of faith were being enlarged by the insertion of some words asserting the eternity of Christ's existence throughout all ages to come. The earliest of these are connected with the Council of Antioch in 341. Of the four forms of Creed which claim some sanction from this Council, the first adds to the clause on the judgment the words, 'and remaineth a king and God for ever,' the third has 'and remaineth for ever,' while the fourth has a longer form: 'Whose kingdom being unceasing will remain unto the boundless ages, for He will be sitting on the right hand of the Father not only in this world, but also in the world to come.' From Antioch such language spread elsewhere, and is found in several of the Creeds put forth under Arian auspices, and we find also from the Lectures of S. Cyril of Jerusalem, delivered in 348, that a similar clause had already been introduced by that date into the baptismal Creed of his Church, for the Creed on which he comments contains the words which have since been adopted into the enlarged form of the Nicene Creed familiar to us: 'Whose kingdom shall have no end,'—words which are (in the original Greek) a direct citation from the announcement of the angel Gabriel, 'and of His kingdom there shall be no end' (S. Luke i. 33); and the object of the insertion is clearly evidenced by S. Cyril's comment and exhortation:—

'And shouldest thou ever hear any say that the kingdom of Christ shall have an end, abhor the heresy; it is another head of the dragon, lately sprung up in Galatia. A certain one has dared to affirm that after the end of the world Christ shall reign no longer; he has also dared to say that the Word having come forth from the Father shall be again absorbed into the Father, and shall be no more.'[1]

Such language clearly indicates the object of the clause, which in the form in which we are familiar

[1] *Catech. Lectures*, xv. 27. The reference to the heresy having recently sprung up in Galatia points directly to Marcellus.

with it appears for the first time in the Creed of Jerusalem as given by S. Cyril. From this it appears from time to time in other formularies, as in the Creed in the *Apostolical Constitutions*,[1] and it will be shown presently how it probably made its way into the enlarged form of the Nicene Creed.

It is not till rather later (*c.* 360-400) that we find language inserted in various formularies of faith against both Apollinarianism and Macedonianism. A specimen of the manner in which Creeds were now enlarged for these purposes may be given from a work of Epiphanius, Bishop of Salamis, entitled the *Ancoratus*, put forth in 373 or 374. In this work he transcribes a lengthy and rather verbose formulary which begins with the language of the Nicene Creed on God the Father, and on the pre-Incarnate Christ, but, when it comes to the doctrine of the Incarnation, diverges in a remarkable manner as follows :—

> 'Who for us men and for our salvation came down and was incarnate, that is, was born perfectly of the holy Mary the ever-virgin, through the Holy Ghost, was made man, that is, took perfect manhood, soul and body and mind and all things, whatever belongs to manhood, without sin ... and was perfectly made man.'

Again, later on in the same formulary the expression of belief in the Holy Ghost is similarly amplified :—

> 'And we believe in the Holy Ghost, Who spake in the law, and proclaimed in the prophets, and came

[1] *Apost. Const.*, VII. xli.

THE NICENE CREED 145

down upon Jordan, speaking in apostles, dwelling in saints. And we thus believe in Him that He is the Holy Spirit, the Spirit of God, perfect Spirit, the Spirit the Comforter, uncreate, proceeding from the Father, and receiving of the Son, and believed on.'

This Creed has been referred to because it contains such obvious and laboured signs of having been enlarged for the express purpose of guarding against the two heresies referred to above. But the same object may be detected in other formularies, where the enlargement is less laboured and more natural. This is the case in a far more important formulary which also occurs in the same work of Epiphanius, and which must now be given in full :—

'We believe in one God, the Father Almighty, Maker *of heaven and earth, and* of all things visible and invisible.

And in one Lord Jesus Christ, the only begotten Son of God, *Begotten of His Father before all worlds*— that is of the substance of the Father—Light of Light, Very God of Very God, Begotten, not made, Being of one substance with the Father ; By Whom all things were made, both that are in heaven and that are in earth ; who for us men and for our salvation came down *from heaven,* and was incarnate *of the Holy Ghost and the Virgin Mary,* and was made man ; *and was crucified for us under Pontius Pilate,* and suffered, *and was buried,* and rose again the third day *according to the Scriptures,* and

K

ascended into heaven, *and sitteth at the right hand of the Father,* and is coming *again with glory* to judge the quick and dead; *Whose kingdom shall have no end.*

And in the Holy Ghost, *the Lord and Life Giver, Who proceedeth from the Father, Who with the Father and the Son together is worshipped and glorified, Who spake by the prophets: in one Holy Catholic and Apostolic Church. We acknowledge one baptism for the remission of sins. We look for the resurrection of the dead, and the life of the world to come. Amen.*'

This Creed the reader will at once recognise as being virtually identical with that with which he is familiar from its place in our Communion Service, and which is referred to in the eighth of the XXXIX Articles as the 'Nicene Creed,' a name which it has borne for many centuries. Those parts of it which are not found in the original Creed of Nicæa are here printed in italics in order that the reader may be able to see at a glance how much it differs from that Creed.

Of the new clauses some are comparatively unimportant, and are already found in other Creeds of the fourth century, from one or other of which they were probably taken by the compilers of the enlarged Creed. Others are more important, and require attention to be drawn to them.

(*a*) '[And was incarnate] of the Holy Ghost and the Virgin Mary.' These words, as was expressly asserted by Diogenes, Bishop of Cyzicus, at the Council of Chalcedon, were added in order to insist on

THE NICENE CREED 147

the reality of the Incarnation, and to guard against the heresy of Apollinaris.

(*b*) 'Whose kingdom shall have no end.' The object of these words has already been sufficiently explained.

(*c*) The additions after the words 'and in the Holy Ghost.' These afford a clear and emphatic assertion of the Church's faith in the Divinity of the Third Person of the Blessed Trinity. In the opening phrase the English reader requires to be on his guard against a possible misconception. The words are not 'the Lord and giver—of life,' but 'the Lord, and the Life-giver.' The first term, 'the Lord,' used absolutely, is intended to express the true Godhead of the Spirit, and the second, 'the Life-giver,' or, as we have it in our version, 'Giver of Life,' is adopted straight from Scripture (see S. John vi. 63, 2 Cor. iii. 6, with which should be compared Romans viii. 11, and such passages as 1 Cor. iii. 16, and others which speak of the indwelling Spirit). 'Who proceedeth from the Father.' Of this expression and of the way in which the words 'and the Son' have been added, more must be said later on. It is sufficient to notice here that it is entirely Scriptural (see S. John xv. 26), and is intended to describe (so far as can be described) the manner in which from all eternity the Holy Spirit derives His Godhead from the Father. 'Who with the Father and the Son together is worshipped and glorified.' These grand words proclaiming the Holy Spirit as the object of the doxologies and worship of the Church sound almost like a pæan of victory when the battle against Macedonianism was won. They contain as strong an assertion of His co-essential Deity with the Father and the Son as can be imagined, while the next phrase, 'Who spake by (*through*) the prophets,' identifies Him with 'the Lord' Whose 'word' came to the prophets of the Old Testament.[1]

(*d*) The remaining clauses of the third division of the Creed. These, as we have already seen, were wanting in the original Creed of Nicæa, as not being needed for the purpose for which that formulary was promulgated. We now find them in the enlarged Creed, to which they were probably appended from one of the baptismal Creeds already existing.

The Creed as it has now been placed before the reader was, according to Epiphanius, 'delivered by the holy apostles, and in the church of the holy city, by the holy bishops, above three hundred and ten in number.' This extraordinary account of its origin bears its own refutation on the face of it, if it is to be

---

[1] It has been sometimes thought that 'the prophets' are those of the New Testament who, as we now know, formed an important body in the primitive Church. This does not appear probable. In some other Creeds of the fourth century we find fuller phrases, as 'Who spake in the law and proclaimed in the prophets' in the longer form of Creed given by Epiphanius, quoted above, p. 144, or 'Who spake in the law and in the prophets and in the gospel' in a form of faith (probably erroneously) attributed to Athanasius, and the Creed of Armenia. (See Hahn, *Bibliothek der Symbole*, pp. 138, 153.) Since in these 'the prophets' can only mean those of the Old Testament, the phrase has almost certainly the same meaning here.

THE NICENE CREED 149

taken literally; and it is hard to know what its author means by it. His reference to the bishops as 'above three hundred and ten in number' implies that he identified it in some sense with the Creed of Nicæa, while the words 'in the holy city' seem to point to Jerusalem as its birthplace, and the statement that it was 'delivered by the holy apostles' is remarkably similar to language applied by contemporaries of Epiphanius in the West to the Apostles' Creed. Epiphanius is, however, so confused and inaccurate a writer that we need not pay much attention to his statements on such matters. What he is a valuable witness for is the fact of the existence about the year 373 of this Creed, which may rightly be called in a sense 'Nicene,' since it embodies the great Nicene clauses on the Eternal Godhead of the Son.

The question of the place where, and the circumstances under which, this enlarged Creed really came into existence, is a puzzling one. It was made the subject of careful investigation some years ago by the late Dr. Hort.[1] The conclusion at which he arrived was that it was framed about the year 360, and that its birthplace actually was Jerusalem, the place where Epiphanius locates it. He held that it was really not so much an enlarged Nicene Creed, as the local Creed of Jerusalem enlarged by the insertion of the great Nicene clauses on the pre-Incarnate Christ, and the expansion of other clauses to meet later heresies. His views have been generally accepted by subsequent

[1] *Two Dissertations* (1876).

writers, and more need not be said on them here.[1] For the present we may pass on to notice that the ascertained fact, to which Epiphanius is an unimpeachable witness, that the Creed in its full form was in existence in the year 373 or 374, is absolutely fatal to the view, which till comparatively recent days was generally accepted, that the additions were made at the Council of Constantinople in 381. Since the Creed was already well known at least seven or eight years before that Council was held, the additions cannot possibly have been made to it then. It is possible, of course, that the Council may have sanctioned or promulgated the Creed, but even this is uncertain. None of the early historians, Socrates, Sozomen, or Theodoret, mention any Creed save that of Nicæa as having been ratified by this Council. There is no mention of any such proceeding in the acts of the Council, and the first canon passed at it says expressly that 'the Creed of the three hundred and eighteen bishops assembled at Nicæa shall not be made void, but shall remain firm.' Moreover, though the full form appears in the *Ancoratus* of Epiphanius about 373, we find no subsequent use whatever made of it till the Council of Chalcedon in the year 451. The third General Council, that of Ephesus in 431, like the second (Constantinople) simply ratified the original Creed of Nicæa. At Chalcedon, however, *both* Creeds were read and confirmed, the authority of Constan-

[1] See the note at the end of the chapter, where fuller details are given, and some reasons are urged for doubting whether the last word has really been said on the subject.

tinople being directly claimed for the fuller form both in the discussions which took place and in the formal decree of the Council. That decree runs as follows:—

'We, therefore, declare that the exposition of the right and blameless faith by the three hundred and eighteen holy and blessed fathers who were assembled at Nicæa in the time of the then Emperor Constantine of pious memory, should have the first place; and that those things should also be maintained which were defined by the hundred and fifty holy fathers of Constantinople, for the taking away of the heresies which had then sprung up, and the confirmation of the same, our Catholic and Apostolic Faith.'

To the promulgation of this decree there followed the recital of *both* the Creeds, that of Nicæa in the first place, and then the fuller form of it supposed to have been sanctioned at Constantinople.

The form as recited at Chalcedon is given as follows:—

'We believe in one God, the Father Almighty, maker of heaven and earth, and of all things visible and invisible.

And in one Lord Jesus Christ the only begotten Son of God, begotten of His Father before all worlds, Light of Light, Very God of Very God, Begotten not made, Being of one substance with the Father, By Whom all things were made; Who for us men and for our salvation came down from heaven, and was incarnate of the Holy Ghost and the Virgin Mary, and was made man, and was crucified also for us under Pontius Pilate, and suffered, and was buried, and rose again the third day according to the Scriptures, and ascended into heaven, and sitteth on the right hand of the Father, and is coming again with glory to judge both the quick and the dead, Whose kingdom shall have no end.

And in the Holy Ghost, the Lord and Life-Giver, Who proceedeth from the Father, Who with the Father and the Son together is worshipped and glorified, Who spake by the prophets; in one holy Catholic and Apostolic Church; We acknowledge one baptism for the remission of sins, we look for the resurrection of the dead, and the life of the world to come. Amen.'

This form, it will be noticed, differs slightly from the form given by Epiphanius, and also lacks two phrases familiar to us. Attention must also be drawn to the fact that, as recited at Chalcedon it was without the anathemas which were appended to the original Nicene Creed, and which are also attached to the fuller form as given in Epiphanius. It is generally thought that it was a mistake on the part of Epiphanius to attach them to this longer Creed, and that they never really belonged in any way to it. Be this as it may, they have certainly never been appended to it since Chalcedon, which was the earliest occasion on which the Church really adopted the use of the Creed.

There is no doubt, then, that the bishops at Chalcedon were fully under the impression that the Creed had been previously sanctioned at Constantinople, and from their time onward we find it constantly referred to as the Creed of the 150 or 180 fathers of Constantinople.

What really happened at Constantinople it is, perhaps, impossible now to discover. The fuller form of the Creed *may* have received some sort of sanction then as an orthodox creed. Possibly, as has been suggested, it was proffered to the Council by S. Cyril of Jerusalem as the expression of his own faith. Cyril had in earlier days been associated with the semi-Arians, and there is some evidence that his orthodoxy was not allowed to pass without question at Constantinople. If so, he may possibly have submitted this Creed in proof of the soundness of his faith, and the Council may well have accepted it. Such a proceeding would account for the rise of the belief that the Council was in some way responsible for the Creed. But nothing certain is known of this. What is certain is that the Council of Constantinople never intended this fuller form to be substituted for the original Creed of Nicæa. The substitution only came about many years later. The fuller form was only gradually brought into general use after its promulgation at Chalcedon, and for some time yet in both East and West it was still regarded as distinct from the Creed of Nicæa, and given the second place ; nor was it till much later that the confusion between the two Creeds arose, and the name of the ' Nicene Creed ' was transferred to the later and fuller form.

§ 3

The Nicene Creed after Chalcedon

WITH the Council of Chalcedon the general promulgation of the fuller form of the Nicene Creed begins. But, as we have already seen, it had not even then received the final form which it has since taken in the Western Church. Before, however, proceeding to trace out its subsequent history, and to describe how the changes were made which have given it the form in which it is familiar to English churchmen, it will be well to say something on the doctrine of the procession of the Holy Spirit, in order that the reader may be better able to understand the questions raised in the controversy on the subject.

The term 'proceeding from' was used in the Church from very early days in order to express the eternal relation in which the Holy Spirit stands to the First Person of the Blessed Trinity. The Father is spoken of as the ἀρχή, or Fount of Deity, the source of the Godhead of both the Second and Third Persons of the Holy Trinity. But whereas the Second Person is spoken of in Holy Scripture as 'the Son,' and as 'begotten,' no such terms are used to describe the relation of the Third Person to the First. The Church, therefore, has been careful never to use them of the Holy Spirit, and she has confined herself to the term which she finds in Scripture, and which our Lord Himself uses: 'The Spirit of truth which proceedeth from the Father' (S. John xv. 26). It became necessary, however, in course of time, to express in some way what was believed to be the relation of the Spirit to the Son in the Blessed Trinity; and as soon as ever attention was drawn to the subject, it could not escape notice that in Scripture nearly all the same phrases are used to denote the relation of the Spirit to the Son as are used of the Spirit's relation to the Father. If He is spoken of as 'the Spirit of God,' or 'the Spirit of the Father,' so also is He spoken of as 'the Spirit of His Son,' or 'the Spirit of Christ.' If He is said to be 'sent' by the Father, he is also said to be 'sent' by the Son. Christ says of Him, He shall 'take' or 'receive of Mine'; and though the actual term 'proceeding from' is in strictness of speech only used of His relation to the Father, yet since the 'river of water of life' which S. John sees in the Revelation is spoken of as 'proceeding from the throne of God and of the Lamb,'[1] and since the river of water of life, in accordance with the symbolism of Scripture, must be identified with the Spirit, it would seem to follow almost of necessity that the Spirit must be conceived of as in some sort 'proceeding from the Father *and the Son*,' or 'from the Father *through* the Son,' an expression

[1] Rev. xxii. 1; cf. S. John vii. 38, 39.

which is free from any ambiguity, and does not lie open to the charge of suggesting the notion of two different sources of the Godhead of the Holy Spirit, a notion which must be carefully excluded from our thoughts when using the formula to which we are accustomed. Accordingly, we find that so soon as theological writers began to write with precision on the subject, the Spirit is spoken of by them as 'the Third,' and 'from God and the Son,' or 'from the Father through the Son,' or as 'proceeding from the Father and receiving of the Son'; and when during the Arian controversy the question of the relation of the Spirit to both Father and Son came prominently forward in discussion, such phrases passed into the general language of the Church, the term 'proceeding from the Father' being formally adopted, as we have seen, in the fuller form of the Nicene Creed as given by Epiphanius (in 373 or 374); while in the still longer Creed of the same period given by the same writer there is the yet ampler phrase 'Who proceedeth from the Father and receiveth of the Son.' About the same time the subject began to attract the attention of divines in the Western Church, which till the latter part of the fourth century had been comparatively free from controversy; and though writers like S. Hilary of Poictiers and S. Ambrose scarcely go beyond the use of the terms cited above in speaking of the relation of the Spirit to both Father and Son, yet towards the beginning of the fifth century S. Augustine, discussing the doctrine more fully than had been done by any previous writer, lays down definitely that, though there is but one Fount of Godhead, the Father, yet the Spirit may be said to proceed in strictest truth 'from the Father *and the Son*'; and from his time onward this became in the Western Church the traditional mode of expressing the Scriptural truth which the Easterns continued to express by the use of such expressions as 'proceeding from the Father through the Son,' or 'proceeding from the Father and receiving of the Son.'

We are now in a position to return to the history of the Creed after the Council of Chalcedon. Of its fortunes in the East there is little more that need be said. For some time after Chalcedon the true Nicene Creed and the fuller form of it were still regarded as distinct, but no general use was made of either of them until Peter the Fuller, patriarch of Antioch (476-488), introduced the use of the Creed into the Communion service of his church. Alexandria is believed to have followed the example of Antioch shortly afterwards, and in 511 Timothy, patriarch of Constantinople, ordered the regular use of the Creed in his church at the same service. In this latter case it was apparently the original Creed of Nicæa that was so used, and the probability is that it was so in Antioch and Alexandria as well. But about the year 565-6, by order of the Emperor Justin II., the fuller form was substituted for 'the Creed of the three hundred and eighteen'; and from this time onward it appears to have been generally adopted throughout the Greek Church, and somewhere about the same time to have appropriated the name as well as the place of the Nicene Creed.

Turning now to the West, it must be premised that, although Western bishops had been present at Nicæa, it was only very gradually that any general knowledge of the Nicene formulary spread throughout the Western or Latin-speaking Church. S. Hilary, the Athanasius of the West, one of the stoutest champions of the faith in our Lord's Eternal Godhead, was consecrated Bishop of Poictiers about the year 350, and was sent into exile in Asia Minor in 356, as a confessor for the faith's sake; and yet he tells us distinctly that 'though long ago regenerate in Baptism and for some time a bishop,' he had 'never heard the Nicene Creed until the eve of his exile';[1] and later Latin writers as well are strangely silent about it. Most remarkable of all, perhaps, is the very slight reference to it in the writings of S. Augustine, who died in A.D. 430. Even in his great work on the Trinity, written about the year 416, he never once mentions or alludes to it.[2] Nor does there appear to have been any notice taken of the fuller form of the Creed in the West until many years after Chalcedon. Indeed, the first clear occasion of use being made of it was at the third Council of Toledo in 589. Spain had been overrun by the barbarians and lost to the Empire in the course of the fifth cen-

[1] *De Synodis*, c. 91.

[2] Augustine refers to the Creed of Nicæa very occasionally in his work, *Against Maximin the Arian*, Bk. ii. chap. xiv. *seq.* (*Op.* vol. viii. pp. 704, 711, 717), but I do not know of any other reference to it in his works.

tury, and the kingdom of the Visigoths established there had for about a century professed an Arian Creed, the Catholics being subjected to severe persecution. King Reccared, however, who succeeded to the throne in the year 586, at once avowed himself a Catholic, and exerted himself to bring back his kingdom to the unity of the faith. Three years later he summoned a synod to meet at Toledo, at which seventy bishops were assembled, and there the Spanish Church formally embraced the Nicene faith. At this synod the bishops declared that they subscribed with their whole heart and soul and mind the constitutions of the holy councils of Nicæa, Constantinople, Ephesus, and Chalcedon, ' thinking that nothing can be more lucid for the knowledge of the truth than what the authorities of the aforesaid councils contain. Of the Trinity and the unity of Father, Son, and Holy Ghost, nothing can ever be shown to be clearer or more lucid than these.' They also repeated (1) ' the Creed published at the Council of Nicæa '; and (2) ' the holy faith which the hundred and fifty fathers of the Council of Constantinople explained, consonant with the great Council of Nicæa '; and for the future they enacted that ' for reverence of the most holy faith, and for the strengthening of the weak minds of men . . . through all the churches of Spain and Gallæcia the symbol of faith of the Council of Constantinople, *i.e.* of the hundred and fifty bishops, should be recited according to the form of the Eastern Church; so that, before the Lord's Prayer be said, it be sung with clear voice by the people; to the intent that the true faith should have a manifest testimony, and the hearts of the people approach, purified by faith, to taste the Body and Blood of Christ.' It is, however, a remarkable fact that the Creed, as recited by the assembled fathers, was not in all points in accordance with the form of the Eastern Church, for it contained two additions to the form as promulgated at Chalcedon, viz.: (1) 'God of God,' a clause which, though contained in the original Creed of Nicæa, had been omitted from the longer form as given by Epiphanius and subsequently; and (2) 'and the Son' (*et Filio* or *Filioque*) in the clause on the procession of the Holy Ghost.

In regard to the former of these additions no question has ever been raised. The insertion cannot have been made with any dogmatic intention, for the doctrine contained in it is fully expressed in the subsequent clause, 'Very God of very God.' It was probably purely accidental. And it is believed that the other insertion was also the result of accident. There was no controversy whatever on the subject at the time. Western writers had since the days of Augustine been accustomed to speak of the Holy Spirit as 'proceeding from the Father and the Son,'[1] and the addition may very naturally have been made in the process of translating the Creed into Latin, and either not have been noticed at all at the time, or, if noticed, have been

---

[1] It will be remembered that the words 'and of the Father and the Son' (*a Patre et Filio*) are contained in the *Quicunque vult*, which, as will be shown later, probably belongs to the fifth century.

believed to be a correction of a faulty Greek text.
Anyhow, there the clause appears in the Creed for the
first time, and with it the Creed was henceforth used in
the Communion service of the Church of Spain. Of the
circumstances and date of the introduction of the Creed
into the Communion service of the other Churches of the
West our knowledge is but scanty. It was apparently
in use in some part of the Frankish Church as early as
the latter part of the seventh or beginning of the
eighth century, as it is contained in the Vatican MS.
of the (so-called) Gelasian Sacramentary; and it is
noteworthy that in this MS. the text is correctly given
without either of the two additions noted above. But
before the eighth century had run its course the
Filioque clause had somehow made its way into the
Creed as used in the Frankish Church; and it was
stoutly defended by Charlemagne, as against a phrase
used at the Second Council of Nicæa in 787 by
Tarasius, patriarch of Constantinople, who had asserted
his belief in the Holy Ghost as 'proceeding from the
Father *through* the Son.' When the proceedings of
this Council were communicated to the West, exception was taken by Charlemagne to this phrase as not
being in agreement with 'the Nicene Creed.' By this
he obviously meant the fuller form of the Creed, with
which alone he was probably acquainted, as by this
time it had entirely superseded the original form;
and he evidently had no suspicion that the *Filioque*
clause was no part of its genuine text. About the
same time, and apparently under the influence of

Charlemagne himself, the devotional use of the Creed in the Communion service was generally adopted by the Frankish Church, and thus the knowledge of the clause spread; but for some time longer the more accurate text of the Creed was preserved elsewhere in the West. Early in the ninth century, however, a dispute arose on the subject at Jerusalem. Some Latin monks who had founded a convent on the Mount of Olives were charged with heresy on various grounds, the principal one being this, that in reciting the Creed they said, ' Who proceedeth from the Father and the Son.' Up till this time, though there had been a certain amount of controversy on the doctrine of the Procession, the fact of the interpolation of the Creed seems not to have been discovered by the Greeks. Now for the first time the fact was manifest, and a controversy was set on foot which was to end in the separation of the Eastern and Western Churches. The incriminated monks appealed to Pope Leo III. at Rome, stating in their defence that they were using the Creed as they had received it, and as they had heard it sung in the Emperor's chapel. They urged, moreover, that the clause in question was also contained in ' the faith of S. Athanasius.' Whether Leo directly answered this letter or not we have no information; but we know that he communicated with the Emperor, and that as a result the Council of Aachen (809) was summoned, when the cause of the Latin monks was strongly upheld, and an embassy was sent to Leo on the subject. Leo himself was entirely at one with the Frankish

Church in holding to the *doctrine* of the double procession, but having received the Creed in its uninterpolated form, he strongly objected to the unauthorised insertion of the word *Filioque* into it. To this it was replied that if the term was excised, it would appear to those who had hitherto been accustomed to use the Creed with it, that the *doctrine* was also condemned. Leo saw the danger of this, and as a way out of the difficulty suggested that the singing of the Creed at Mass might be discontinued in the Frankish Church. It was not so sung at Rome, and the use might therefore well be abandoned elsewhere. Moreover, in order to preserve the true text of the Creed inviolate, he is said to have caused two silver shields to be set up in S. Peter's with the Creed engraved upon them in Greek and Latin without the *Filioque* clause. This plan succeeded in preventing the interpolation from being received at Rome for two centuries, until in 1014 the Emperor Henry II. persuaded Pope Benedict VIII. to adopt the German use of chanting the Creed (evidently with the *Filioque*) in the Mass. But Leo was not successful in inducing the Frankish Church to drop the use of it. The Creed continued to be sung with the clause in question wherever the influence of the Emperor was powerful, and by degrees it spread to the other Churches of the West.[1] And when some

---

[1] It is interesting to find that in the 'Stowe Missal,' one of the earliest remaining service-books of the Irish Church, written in the ninth century, the Creed is given in its uninterpolated form, but that the word *Filioque* has been added by a later hand.

fifty years after the time of Leo III. disputes again broke out between the East and West, one of the charges urged with the greatest vehemence against the Western Church was the interpolation of the Creed, which was said not only to be wholly unauthorised, but to be suggestive of false doctrine; and from that time to this the Eastern and Western branches of the Church have preserved their different forms of the Nicene faith.

Such a divergence of use is a serious misfortune. But it will be clear to the reader from what has been said above that the Western Church is really free from any charge of wilfully making an interpolation in the Creed, and that the meaning of the formula familiar to us is entirely in accordance with the teaching of Holy Scripture, and is not and never has been intended to imply anything like two 'sources' of the Godhead of the Holy Ghost. It is the dread of such an interpretation of the clause that has led the Easterns to take such strong exception to it. They claim, and justly, that their own formula is free from all ambiguity, and that it emphasises the doctrine of the *Monarchia*—the doctrine, that is, that the Father is the sole ultimate source of the Godhead of both the Second and Third Persons of the Trinity. The Westerns, however, have always disclaimed the false interpretation that has been put upon their formula, and have steadily maintained that it means no more than what Eastern divines have again and again admitted, viz. that the Holy Spirit derives His Godhead from all eternity from the Father through the Son. They have also feared (and not without some reason) that any change in their words might endanger the faith. This being so, it was too much to expect the Western Church, when the interpolation was discovered, to alter the form in which it had been customary to use the Creed. Nor, on the other hand, could the Easterns have been expected to change their form of it. Little practical inconvenience would have arisen had both parties acquiesced in each retaining its own form. But unhappily passions were aroused, and the voice of reason was unable to make itself heard, and the result has been a divided Christendom. We can only hope and pray that in God's time a door to reunion may some day be opened, and that whenever it is, explanations may be offered by the Western Church of the meaning of her formula, and the recitation of the Nicene Creed, either with or without the *Filioque*, may be accepted as one of the first conditions on either side.

§ 4

On the use of the Nicene Creed in the Services of the Church

IN the Eastern Church the Nicene Creed, perhaps at first in its original form and later on in its 'enlarged' form, has, as has been mentioned above, been used in the Liturgy or Communion service since the fifth and sixth centuries. It is said that the direction of the Emperor Justin in 565-6 was that it should be sung before the Lord's Prayer, i.e. *after* the consecration of the elements. But there is, according to Mr. Brightman, no other trace of such a position for the Creed in an Eastern rite.[1] Either, then, the historian (John of Biclarum) was misinformed, or Justin must have unsuccessfully attempted a change, as the universal position which the Creed occupies in Eastern Liturgies is early in the Liturgy of the Faithful in connection with the kiss of peace, which it sometimes precedes, as in the Syrian and Egyptian Liturgies as well as in those of the Nestorian Church, and sometimes follows, as in

---

[1] The decree of the Council of Toledo, however, cited above on p. 159, may imply that it was from the Eastern Church that the position of the Creed in the Spanish Liturgy was adopted.

the Liturgy of Constantinople, and thus of the Greek Church generally. It also, in comparatively early times, took the place of the different local Creeds in the Baptismal service in the East, and has in later days been introduced into the Hour services, so that it has come to be the only Creed that is used by the orthodox Greek Church.[1] Local Creeds with Nicene language introduced into them have, however, lingered on among some of the separate bodies of Christians in the East, as *e.g.* the 'Jacobite' and Maronite Churches of Syria, the Nestorians, Armenians, and Abyssinians.

In the West the Nicene Creed has never been generally adopted as a baptismal Creed, though it was used in the *Traditio Symboli* at Rome and perhaps in some other places from about the sixth to the tenth centuries, being recited both in Greek and Latin. This use was, however, something quite exceptional, the Apostles' Creed being regularly connected with baptism elsewhere in the West, as at Rome both before and after the dates given above. When the Nicene Creed (in its enlarged form) was first introduced into the Communion service of the Church of Spain in 589, it was ordered to be sung before the Lord's Prayer, as in the direction said to have been given twenty years earlier by Justin; and this has remained the position given to it in the Mozarabic or Spanish Liturgy ever since. Elsewhere in the West, practically as far back as we can trace it, it occupies the position familiar to us immediately after the Gospel as being a summary of

[1] At the Council of Florence in 1438 the Greeks expressly disclaimed any knowledge of the Apostles' Creed.

evangelical doctrine.[1] But the Anglican Communion stands alone in the West in ordering its recitation at every celebration. In the Roman Church its use is confined to Sundays and greater festivals, and this was also the Pre-Reformation use in our own country. In the first Prayer Book of Edward VI. the direction in the rubric before the Creed apparently contemplates its recitation at every Communion, but in the course of the service there is a note to the effect that 'when the Holy Communion is celebrate on the workday or in private houses: Then may be omitted the Gloria in Excelsis, the Creed, the Homily, and the Exhortation,' and at the close of the book among 'Certain Notes for the more plain explication and decent ministration of things contained in this book' there stands the following: 'If there be a sermon, or for other great cause, the Curate by his discretion may leave out the Litany, Gloria in Excelsis, the Creed, the Homily, and the Exhortation to the Communion.' This was omitted at the revision of 1552, and since that date there has been no provision made by the rubric for any exceptions in the use of the Creed in the public service of the Church.

In the Hour services of the West the Nicene Creed has never been given a place, but it should be mentioned that the rubrics of the American Prayer Book have since 1790 permitted the alternative use of either the Apostles' or the Nicene Creed at Mattins and Evensong.

[1] Cf. S. Thomas Aquinas, *Summa*, p. iii. q. 83 art. 4. When the Gospel has been read, the Creed is sung, in which the people show that they give the assent of faith to the doctrine of Christ.

NOTE C

ON THE ORIGIN OF THE ENLARGED 'NICENE' CREED

THE theory which the late Dr. Hort set forth in his *Two Dissertations* (1876) as to the origin of the Enlarged Creed is this, viz. that the Creed familiar to us as the 'Nicene' is really 'not a revised form of the Nicene Creed at all, but of the Creed of Jerusalem' (p. 76), the revision being influenced by the Creeds of Antioch and the *Apostolic Constitutions*, or, it may be, lost Creeds of a similar type, and the Creed so revised containing a long insertion from the true Creed of Nicæa on the nature of the pre-Incarnate Christ. This theory has been generally accepted by scholars, but to the present writer it appears that there are weak points in it which have not received sufficient consideration, and that it may be well to draw attention to them. The theory involves not merely the addition of a certain number of clauses to the Jerusalem Creed, and the insertion of the 'Nicene' paragraph, but many substitutions and omissions, and even, in one instance, a change of the order of clauses so that it practically postulates an entire rewriting of the Creed, making the original Creed in one part at least wholly unrecognisable. This may easily be made plain by placing side by side the Creed of Jerusalem as given by S. Cyril, and the Enlarged Creed as given by Epiphanius.

THE CREED OF JERUSALEM.	THE ENLARGED CREED.
We believe in one God the Father Almighty,	We believe in one God the Father Almighty,
Maker of heaven and earth, and of all things visible and invisible :	Maker of heaven and earth and of all things visible and invisible:
And in one Lord Jesus Christ,	And in one Lord Jesus Christ,
the only begotten Son of God,	the only begotten Son of God,
Begotten of His Father, very God, before all worlds,	Begotten of His Father before all worlds,

	that is of the substance of the Father,
	Light of Light,
	Very God of very God,
	Begotten not made,
	Being of one substance with the Father.
By Whom all things were made	By Whom all things were made both that are in heaven and that are in earth,
	Who for us men and for our salvation
	Came down from heaven,
and was incarnate	and was incarnate of the Holy Ghost
	and the Virgin Mary,
and was made man,	and was made man,
was crucified	and was crucified for us under Pontius Pilate,
	and suffered,
and was buried,	and was buried,
and rose again the third day	and rose again the third day according to the Scriptures,
and ascended into heaven,	and ascended into heaven,
and sat at the right hand of the Father,	and sitteth at the right hand of the Father,
and is coming in glory	and is coming again with glory
to judge the quick and the dead,	to judge the quick and the dead,
Whose kingdom shall have no end.	Whose kingdom shall have no end.
And in one Holy Ghost,	And in the Holy Ghost,
the Paraclete,	the Lord and the Life Giver,
	Who proceedeth from the Father,
	Who with the Father and the Son together is worshipped and glorified,
Who spake in the prophets,	Who spake by the prophets,
and in one baptism of repentance for the remission of sins,	and in one holy Catholic and Apostolic Church.
and in one holy Catholic Church,	We acknowledge one baptism for the remission of sins,
and in the resurrection of the flesh,	We look for the resurrection of the dead,
and in the life everlasting.	and the life of the world to come.

THE NICENE CREED

There is no doubt that about the middle of the fourth century local Creeds were enlarged by the insertion of Nicene language on the nature of the pre-Incarnate Christ, as Hort thinks has been the case here; and in favour of this view he can point to the close correspondence between the Creed of Jerusalem as given by S. Cyril, and the Enlarged Creed in the opening clauses down to 'before all worlds.' Then comes what he holds to be the 'Nicene' insertion down to the words 'came down,' and he points out, as favourable to his theory, that from this point onwards down to the end of the second paragraph several of the clauses of the Enlarged Creed, which are wanting in the Creed of Nicæa, are contained (and, so far as we know, for the first time) in the Creed of Jerusalem. But attention must be directed to the fact that there is also in this part a considerable amount of material that is new both to the Creed of Nicæa and to the Creed of Jerusalem, so that even if the Creed of Jerusalem lies at the basis of the Enlarged Creed, it has been revised by the help of other Creeds, as those of the *Apostolic Constitutions* and the Church of Antioch. Thus the words 'from heaven,' 'of the Holy Ghost and the Virgin Mary,' 'also for us under Pontius Pilate,' 'according to the Scriptures,' and 'again,' must all come from some other source; while of the remaining phrases in this part of the Creed which are wanting in the Nicene, the words 'and was buried,' and 'Whose kingdom shall have no end,' are the only ones which can really be traced with reasonable certainty to Jerusalem. 'Was crucified' *may* come from it, but it is quite as likely that it was taken from the same source as the words that follow in the same clause, 'also for us under Pontius Pilate'—words which certainly do not come from the Creed of Jerusalem; and with regard to the two clauses, 'sitteth at the right hand of the Father,' and 'is coming again with glory to judge both the quick and the dead,' it must be noticed that though there are corresponding clauses in the Creed of Jerusalem, in neither case are they identical. Instead of 'sitteth' ($\kappa\alpha\theta\epsilon\zeta\acute{o}\mu\epsilon\nu o\nu$), that Creed has 'sat' ($\kappa\alpha\theta\acute{\iota}\sigma\alpha\nu\tau\alpha$), and instead of 'with glory' ($\mu\epsilon\tau\grave{\alpha}$ $\delta\acute{o}\xi\eta s$) it has 'in glory' ($\acute{\epsilon}\nu$ $\delta\acute{o}\xi\eta$). Now it seems improbable that these phrases would have been altered in a revision of the Creed. They are both Scriptural, and though it is easy to understand how Creeds would be enlarged by the *addition* of words and the insertion of new clauses, yet the minute *alteration* of phrases is another matter, and it can hardly be thought likely to have taken place. When once a phrase had become familiar, any change in it would be likely to be resented. But it is in regard to the third division of the Creed that Hort's theory seems completely to break down. If the Creed of Jerusalem really lies at the basis of the Enlarged Creed, then this part has been not revised, but *rewritten* from beginning to end. Not only has much been added, but 'Who spake *in* the prophets' (ἐν τοῖς προφήταις) has been changed to 'Who spake *by* the prophets' (διὰ τῶν προφητῶν). 'One' before 'Holy Ghost' has been struck out. 'The paraclete' disappears altogether; so does 'of repentance' after 'baptism.' The order of this clause and the following one on the Church has been reversed. For 'the resurrection of the flesh' the less definite 'resurrection of the dead' has been substituted, and for the 'life everlasting' the very remarkable and exceptional 'life of the world to come.' But this is just the part of the Creed where, if it be a revised Creed of Jerusalem, we should expect the correspondence with the original Creed to be closest. We can understand how the Nicene language on the pre-Incarnate Christ would come to be inserted, and how the clauses on the Incarnation and on the Holy Spirit might be enlarged. This would only be natural. But why a portion of the Creed on which there was no controversy whatever should be so completely altered as to efface its original characteristics, and substitute others, passes comprehension. It is really no answer to point out that, in the course of S. Cyril's lectures on the Creed, he employs phrases such as 'the resurrection of the dead,' which appear in the Enlarged Creed. In explaining and commenting on the words of the Creed he was bound to do this; for it is impossible to expound a formula without varying its phraseology and using equivalents for it. Anyhow, the differences between the Enlarged Creed and the Creed of Jerusalem in this section of the Creed are far greater than those between it and the Creed of Nicæa in other parts—so that on Hort's theory a more complete rewriting of the Creed of Jerusalem took place than any that has to be postulated in connection with the Nicene Creed, if *that*, as formerly held, be the basis of the Enlarged Creed. It must also be remarked that the correspondence between the Nicene and the Enlarged Creed is closer if the Epiphanian and not the Chalcedonian form of the latter be taken for purposes of comparison. Hort, in his tables, gives the Chalcedonian form as if it were the original, as he thinks that the clauses contained in the Epiphanian form and not in it are due to carelessness on the part of Epiphanius or his copyists. It seems, however, rather arbitrary to assume this. The *Ancoratus* of Epiphanius was written long before the Council of Chalcedon was held. There is no reason to suspect the text has been tampered with; and in considering the origin of the Creed we ought surely to go to it as our primary authority rather than to the acts of Chalcedon nearly eighty years later. The Creed of Nicæa, and the Enlarged Creed as given by Epiphanius, shall now be placed side by side, and the reader will be able to judge for himself whether it is not really more natural to suppose that the latter is formed on the basis of the former, than on the basis of the Creed of Jerusalem. That the Creed of Jerusalem was one of the contributory sources of the additional clauses is not denied. But it was only one of them. For many of the clauses, and for all the last section of the Creed, we must look elsewhere. To the present writer it appears clear that the Enlarged Creed must have been framed by a deliberate process of comparing local forms of the Creed such as those of Jerusalem, Antioch, and the *Apostolic Constitutions*, borrowing from any of them clauses that it was deemed desirable to insert into the original Nicene Creed, and completing that Creed by the addition of the concluding articles following the expression of belief in the Holy Spirit.

THE CREED OF NICÆA.	THE ENLARGED CREED.
We believe in one God the Father Almighty,	We believe in one God the Father Almighty,
Of all things visible and invisible Maker.	Maker of heaven and earth, and of all things visible and invisible.
And in one Lord Jesus Christ,	And in one Lord Jesus Christ,
The Son of God,	The Son of God, the only begotten,

Begotten of His Father,	Begotten of His Father before all worlds—
Only begotten—that is of the substance of the Father,	That is of the substance of the Father.
God of God,	
Light of Light,	Light of Light,
Very God of Very God,	Very God of very God,
Begotten not made,	Begotten not made,
Being of one substance with the Father,	Being of one substance with the Father,
By Whom all things were made both that are in heaven and that are in earth,	By Whom all things were made both that are in heaven and that are in earth,
Who for us men and for our salvation	Who for us men and for our salvation
Came down,	Came down from heaven,
and was incarnate,	and was incarnate of the Holy Ghost and the Virgin Mary,
was made man,	and was made man,
	and was crucified for us under Pontius Pilate,
suffered,	and suffered,
	and was buried,
and rose again the third day,	and rose again the third day according to the Scriptures,
ascended into heaven,	and ascended into heaven,
	and sitteth at the right hand of the Father,
and is coming to judge the quick and the dead,	and is coming again with glory to judge the quick and the dead,
	Whose kingdom shall have no end,
And in the Holy Ghost.	And in the Holy Ghost,
	The Lord and the Life Giver,
	Who proceedeth from the Father,
	Who with the Father and the Son together is worshipped and glorified,
	Who spake by the prophets,
	and in one holy Catholic and Apostolic Church.
	We acknowledge one baptism for the remission of sins,
	We look for the resurrection of the dead,
	And the life of the world to come.

THE NICENE CREED

NOTE D

ON THE ENGLISH TRANSLATION OF THE NICENE CREED

WHILE Anglo-Saxon and early English renderings of the Apostles' Creed are numerous, and translations of the Athanasian Creed are not unknown, the Nicene Creed does not appear to have been translated into English before the sixteenth century. The rendering which appears in the first Prayer Book of Edward VI. was apparently a new one made by Cranmer. It is found with the slightest verbal differences in one or two of his earlier Liturgical projects,[1] but was never published until it appeared in the Prayer Book of 1549. The form in which it is given in the Prayer Book of that year is practically identical with that which stands in the Prayer Book to-day, except in one particular. The clause 'Whose kingdom shall have no end' is wanting in all editions of the first Prayer Book. This has commonly been supposed to be due to an oversight or error of the printers, but the Bishop of Edinburgh has shown that it is probable that the omission was deliberate, and was due to critical inquiry.[2] If so, Cranmer soon discovered that there was no real authority for the omission, as the clause is restored in the Prayer Book of 1552 in the form 'Whose kingdom shall have none end,' for which 'no end' was substituted at the last revision in 1662. Variations from the correct text (both Greek and Latin) are found in the clause on the Church: 'I believe one Catholic and Apostolic Church.' Here there is nothing corresponding to 'I believe' in either the Greek or Latin text, but both of them have 'holy' between 'one' and 'Catholic.' 'I believe' was perhaps inserted by Cranmer in order to make a distinction between believing *in* the Holy Ghost, and believing the Catholic Church, *i.e.* believing *that there is* such a holy Catholic Church; for such a distinction between *credere in* and *credere* by itself was often drawn by Latin writers, and is actually made by Cranmer himself in his *Annotations upon the king's*

---
[1] See *The Journal of Theological Studies*, i. p. 232.
[2] *The Workmanship of the Prayer Book*, p. 106.

book, where he writes 'I believe in the Holy Ghost, and that there is an holy Catholic Church.'[1] The other change, viz. the omission of 'holy,' is almost certainly due to an attempt at criticism, for the Bishop of Edinburgh has pointed out that in several early editions of works on the Councils the Reformers would have found that the word was—wrongly, as we now know —omitted from the text of the Creed.[2] But though, as the Bishop truly remarks, 'if the Reformers were mistaken, they are not to be blamed for following the best lights of their day,' yet it is a misfortune that the mistake should have been allowed to remain uncorrected till the present day, as the result is the omission of one of the 'notes' of the Church from the Creed as recited in the Communion service.

NOTE E

ON 1 COR. XV. 24-28, AND THE CLAUSE 'WHOSE KINGDOM SHALL HAVE NO END'

DIFFICULTY is sometimes felt in reconciling the language of the Creed with that of S. Paul in the First Epistle to the Corinthians, where he says: 'Then cometh the end, when He shall have delivered up the kingdom to God, even the Father; when He shall have put down all rule and all authority and power. For He must reign, till He hath put all enemies under His feet. The last enemy that shall be destroyed is death. For He hath put all things under His feet. But when He saith all things are put under Him, it is manifest that He is excepted, which did put all things under Him. And when all things shall be subdued unto Him, then shall the Son also Himself be subject unto Him that put all things under Him, that God may be all in all.'[3] This passage is admittedly a difficult one; but it must be noticed that the whole context implies that S. Paul's

[1] Cranmer, *Remains*, p. 83, quoted in *The Workmanship*, etc., p. 108.
[2] *Op. cit.*, p. 104, and *Church Quarterly Review*, July 187
[3] 1 Cor. xv. 24-28.

THE NICENE CREED

reference throughout is to the Son in His mediatorial capacity. His exaltation was a *consequence* of His Incarnation and obedience unto death (cf. Phil. ii. 8-11). All authority was 'given' to Him in heaven and earth, and *therefore* He sent His Apostles to make disciples of all the nations (S. Matthew xxviii. 19). When, then, this mediatorial work is concluded and the eternal purposes of the Incarnation are fulfilled, this kingdom given for special purposes will be 'delivered up,' and the Son will become subject to Him to whom He shall have delivered it up, and God—the Eternal and Tri-personal—will be all in all. This appears to be the meaning of the Apostle in this passage which stands quite by itself. His words ought not to be pressed further, as if, contrary to all that we should gather from the rest of Scripture, the Son in His eternal Personality would be 'absorbed' and the Tri-personality of the Godhead cease. Indeed, such a notion is inconsistent with his words, which speak of the Son not as being absorbed, but as being subject. Yet this was the theory anciently deduced by some from his words and attributed to Marcellus of Ancyra, against whose views it is historically certain that the clause 'Whose kingdom shall have no end' was inserted into the Creeds of the Eastern Church in the fourth century. The clause is intended, then, to guard the doctrine of the eternal Personality of the Son; and the 'kingdom' of which it speaks being not the mediatorial kingdom, but that which belongs to Him in virtue of His eternal Godhead, must necessarily remain His throughout eternity, since His 'is the glory and the dominion for ever and ever'—1 Peter iv. 11; Rev. i. 5, 6; v. 12, 13; cf. Rom. ix. 5; Heb. i. 8; xiii. 22, and 2 Peter iii. 18, all of which passages clearly indicate the eternal nature of the Son's dominion. There is, then, no real contradiction between the teaching of the Creed (which, it may be repeated here, adopts the very words of S. Luke i. 33) and the teaching of S. Paul, for they speak of different kingdoms—S. Paul of what is called the mediatorial kingdom, which was given to our Lord for a special purpose, the Creed of that which belongs to Him from all eternity as being essentially God and one with the Father.

CHAPTER IV

THE ATHANASIAN CREED

CHAPTER IV

THE ATHANASIAN CREED

§ 1

The Date and Authorship of the Athanasian Creed

FROM the tenth century onwards the Athanasian Creed found a recognised place in psalters and service-books, and was commonly regarded as the work of the saint whose name it bears. Indeed, in manuscripts belonging to the tenth century it is sometimes said to be ascribed to him '*etiam in veteribus codicibus*,' and the traditional authorship of this Creed remained practically unquestioned till the seventeenth century. In the sixteenth, as we have seen, doubts were freely raised about the authorship of the Apostles' Creed, but little question was raised as to that of the Creed of S. Athanasius. In a formulary of faith known as 'The Ten Articles,' published in 1536, it was boldly said of the Three Creeds that 'one was made by the Apostles which is the common Creed which every man useth; the second was made by the Holy Council of

182   THE THREE CREEDS

Nice, and is said daily in the Mass; the third was made by Athanasius, and is comprehended in the psalm *Quicunque vult*.' But in the next few years Cranmer learned to speak with more caution of the authorship of the first of these, for in the XLII Articles of 1553 (the precursors of our own XXXIX) it is spoken of as 'that which is commonly called the Apostles' Creed'—a phrase that is evidently employed in order to avoid expressing a decided opinion of its authorship, while the *Quicunque vult* is still spoken of as 'Athanasius' Creed.' And, still later, Richard Hooker, writing towards the close of the sixteenth century, unhesitatingly follows Baronius in ascribing it to Athanasius, and assigning it to the year 340.[1] Nor does any indication of doubt as to its authorship appear in any of our formularies until the last revision of the Prayer Book after the Restoration (1661-2), when for the first time it was described in the rubric as 'this confession of our Christian faith commonly called the Creed of S. Athanasius.'

The reason for the change then made in the rubric, and for the guarded language then employed, is to be found in the work of a Dutch theologian, Gerard Voss, who had been given a prebend at Canterbury. Voss's work on the Three Creeds (*De Tribus Symbolis*) was published in 1642, being dedicated to Charles I. and

---

[1] *Eccl. Polity*, V. xlii. 6. It should be mentioned that in 1569 Jewel, in his *Defence of the Apology* (Parker Society's edition, p. 254), speaks of the Creed being written 'as some think by Athanasius; as some others by Eusebius Vercellensis.'

THE ATHANASIAN CREED 183

Henrietta Maria together with William of Orange. In this, if not quite for the first time, yet more forcibly than ever before, an attack was made on the received opinion of the Athanasian authorship of the Creed, on the following grounds: (*a*) it rarely occurs in any manuscript of Athanasius' works, and where it does it has not his name affixed to it; (*b*) neither Gregory Nazianzen, Basil, nor Chrysostom, nor others of the early Fathers allude to it; (*c*) had it been extant and owned for Athanasius' work during the controversy on the procession of the Holy Spirit, in the eighth century, it must have been referred to; (*d*) it is seldom mentioned for a thousand years after Christ. For these reasons Voss rejected the current tradition, and attributed the Creed to some Gallican writer of the ninth century. His work was written in the early days of criticism, and the case against the Athanasian authorship of the Creed is even stronger than Voss imagined. Still more conclusive than the reasons which he gives are the following: (1) Athanasius wrote in *Greek*, whereas the Creed is undoubtedly a *Latin* composition. The Greek copies which exist vary greatly from one another, and bear clear marks of being translations. This argument is of itself sufficient to disprove the traditional authorship. But it may be added (2) that Athanasius died in 373, whereas the Creed is largely dependent on the works of Augustine, which were not written till the early years of the fifth century. Moreover, Apollinarianism, which is very definitely condemned in the Creed, did not become a serious danger till the last years of Athanasius' life, and was not formally condemned till after his death.

The work of Voss immediately attracted the attention of scholars, and was from the first completely successful in breaking down the traditional opinion. Indeed, since his day there has scarcely been found a scholar of repute who, having made a study of the question, has ventured to defend the Athanasian authorship of the Creed. But though the belief of the mediæval Church was wrong, there is no reason whatever to think that the Creed was a forgery or that the title was given to it in order to enhance its authority by its ascription to so great a name. In like manner the *Te Deum* is in mediæval manuscripts widely ascribed either to S. Ambrose or to S. Augustine, or to the two together; yet no one imagines that it is a forgery. As a matter of fact, nothing is more common in ancient manuscripts than erroneous ascriptions of authorship. How they arose it is often impossible to say; but it is easy to understand how, when once they had been started, they would be perpetuated. There is no evidence that when the Creed was first published it was deliberately passed off as the work of Athanasius. In some way or other—possibly from a genuine, though mistaken, belief that it was his—his name was attached to it, and, when once attached, it was naturally continued, and we need seek for no other explanation of its prevalence in uncritical ages than the belief that it was the work of the great champion of the doctrine of

THE ATHANASIAN CREED 185

the Incarnation and the Godhead of our Blessed Lord, which the Creed so carefully expounds.

But although, as has been said, Voss's work was immediately successful in breaking down the mediæval belief as to the authorship of the Creed, his positive conclusions were not so readily accepted. Archbishop Ussher, writing only five years later (1647), was able to bring forward evidence to show that the Creed must have been in existence long before the date to which Voss had assigned it, and that it could not properly be regarded as a work of the ninth century. Other writers followed, and for some eighty years the questions of the date and authorship of the Creed were keenly debated, the prevailing view being that it was the work of some African or Gallican writer of the fifth or sixth century, either Vigilius Tapsensis, or Vincentius Lerinensis, or Venantius Fortunatus. In 1723 Daniel Waterland entered the lists with his masterly *Critical History of the Athanasian Creed*, an exhaustive treatise in which he reviewed the work of previous writers, and gathered together all the evidence then available on the questions under discussion. From a combination of external and internal evidence Waterland came to the conclusion that the Creed was a work of the fifth century and that its probable author was Hilary, Bishop of Arles. The external evidence on which he relied consisted of: (1) testimonies and allusions to the use of the Creed, which he thought dated back to the seventh century; (2) commentaries upon the Creed, one of which, that ascribed to Venantius Fortunatus, he placed at 570; (3) manuscripts of the Creed, the earliest of which (after Ussher) he dated at 600; and (4) versions or translations, some of which he thought belonged to the ninth century. These various branches of external evidence combined to show that the Creed could not be later than the sixth century; and then came in the internal evidence of the Creed itself, which seemed to him to carry it back to the fifth century, and to point to the years between 420 and 430 as the time to which it belonged. It could not be earlier than 420, so Waterland argued, partly because it combats so fully the Arian and Apollinarian heresies, and partly because it depends so largely on the work of S. Augustine on the Trinity, which was written about 416. On the other hand, it was argued that it could not well be later than 430, because it is wanting in those critical terms which were used against the heresies of Nestorius and Eutyches which were condemned at the General Councils of Ephesus (431) and Chalcedon (451). In this way Waterland arrived at the date 420-30, and as the earliest reception of the Creed could be shown to have been in Gaul, he looked for its author among the most considerable men and those best qualified for such a work at that time in Gaul, and fixed on Hilary, Bishop of Arles, 'a celebrated man of that time, and of chief repute in the Gallican Church,' as the writer to whom with most probability it might be assigned. Waterland's work was so thorough, and its conclusions were supported by such cogent arguments, that the controversy was practically closed by it, and for a century and a half it seemed as if the last word had been said upon it. The controversy was, however, reopened shortly after the year 1870 by the Rev. E. S. Ffoulkes, who put forth a theory that the Creed came from the closing years of the eighth century, being the composition of Paulinus, patriarch of Aquileia, who died in 804, and that it was deliberately palmed off upon the Church by Charlemagne, with the acquiescence both of Paulinus and Alcuin, as a genuine work of Athanasius.[1] The question, being thus reopened, was not allowed to rest. The work of Ffoulkes was followed by others, notably by those of Lumby (*History of the Creeds*, 1873) and Swainson (*The Nicene and Apostles' Creed: their Literary History, together with an Account of the Growth and Reception of the Sermon on the Faith commonly called the Creed of St. Athanasius*, 1875). The views of these three writers differed in detail, but all three agreed in maintaining that the Creed, as we know it, was a work of the Carolingian period. Swainson went so far as to hold that it was completed in the province of Rheims between the years 860 and 870, while Lumby put it in its present form a little earlier, some time between 813 and 850, and held that before that date two separate compositions existed which formed its groundwork, one of them—that which contains the statement of the doctrine of the Trinity—being considerably earlier than the other, and dating back perhaps to the fifth century.

These theories obviously depended upon their writers

[1] *The Athanasian Creed: by whom written and by whom published.* By the Rev. E. S. Ffoulkes, B.D. London, 1872.

being able to demonstrate that Waterland's estimate of the external evidence was erroneous; and it was certainly possible for them to show that some of the documents on which he relied were not necessarily so early as he had placed them. For example, the manuscript which Waterland had referred to as described by Ussher, and dated by him about the year 600, though it could not be found in Waterland's day, had since then been discovered and identified with a Psalter at Utrecht, and a fresh examination by experts had suggested that it was not really written so early as Ussher had thought, but that it probably belonged to the end of the eighth or even to the ninth century. It was also possible to throw a doubt on the relevancy of some of the testimonies and allusions which Waterland had urged. For a time it appeared as if the attack on the antiquity of the Creed was likely to be completely successful, and as if it might have to be regarded as something very like a forgery. Anyhow, for some years the weight of critical opinion among scholars seemed to be thrown into the scale in favour of a late date, and the connection of the author with the court of Charlemagne. Since then, however, the evidence previously available has been thoroughly sifted anew, and a good deal of fresh evidence has been discovered, and, as a result of the labours of the late Prebendary Ommanney and Dr. A. E. Burn,[1] with others, it may

---

[1] See especially *A Critical Dissertation on the Athanasian Creed*, by G. D. W. Ommanney, M.A., 1897; and *An Introduction to the Creeds and to the Te Deum*, by A. E. Burn, B.D., 1899.

now be set down as an ascertained fact that, whatever may be the actual date of the Creed, it cannot possibly be a work of the ninth, or even of the closing years of the eighth century. The external evidence is overwhelming for an earlier date than this. Nor is there really any ground for holding that it was made up by the combination of two originally distinct documents, or that it was formed by a process of accretion and (so to speak) grew up gradually into its present form. The evidence, as now known to us, not only is consistent with, but actually points to, the document being the work of a single hand, composed at a definite period; and that period may well be the one to which Waterland assigned it. The details of the proof of this are largely of a technical character, and are therefore reserved for a place in a note at the end of the chapter. It will be sufficient here to give a brief outline of the chief heads of the evidence.

(1) In the ninth century the Creed is freely cited *as the work of Athanasius* by representative writers such as Hincmar, Archbishop of Rheims (*c.* 857), to whom it was 'familiar as household words';[1] Agobert of Lyons (*c.* 820); Theodulf of Orleans (794-821), and (probably) Alcuin (who died in 804). It is also referred to by name by the monks of Mount Olivet in their appeal to Pope Leo III. in 809.[2]

(2) In the same century we meet with various canons, capitulars, and episcopal directions, charging the clergy to learn it by heart, so that they may be

[1] Ommanney, *op. cit.*, p. 24.   [2] See above, p. 162.

able to repeat it. Thus there are directions to this effect given by Hincmar, Theodulf, and Hatto, Bishop of Basle (806-36).

(3) Canons exist in various collections, which are apparently even of an earlier date, and which speak to the same effect. Of these the most important is a canon of Autun, generally assigned to the year 670 or thereabout, in which it is ordered that 'If any presbyter, deacon, sub-deacon, or clerk doth not, without mistake, recite the Creed which the Apostles delivered by the inspiration of the Holy Ghost, and also *the faith of the holy prelate Athanasius*, let him be censured by the bishop.'

(4) Manuscripts of the Creed are still in existence, which are definitely assigned by experts to the ninth, and even, in some cases, to the eighth century; some of them being Psalters, in which the Creed is given at the close of the Psalms, together with documents of such recognised authority and antiquity as the New Testament Canticles, the *Te Deum*, and the *Gloria in excelsis*.

(5) A large number of mediæval commentaries upon the Creed remain, some of the earlier of which are ascribed by good authorities to the eighth century, and one exists which is almost certainly as early as the seventh, and may belong to the closing years of the sixth.

Each of these branches of evidence is of great importance, and, taken together, their value is cumulative. They combine in throwing back the date of the Creed to a considerably earlier period than the age in which the earliest of them was written. A work would never have been admitted into Psalters or have been required to be learnt by heart by the clergy unless it had a long history behind it, and had come down from comparatively early days; nor would commentaries have been written on a new and unauthoritative work. We are therefore driven to postulate for the Creed a date many years before the eighth or even the seventh century; and when we find that there exist a number of coincidences of language between the Creed and a series of representative writers from the fifth to the eighth century (precisely similar in character to allusions made by later writers when the Creed was definitely regarded as an authoritative work), we can scarcely doubt that the writers in question were quoting from the Creed itself, even though they do not specify it by name.

Thus (6) it appears to be quoted by Denebert, Bishop of Worcester, in a profession of faith belonging to the year 798; by the Fathers assembled at the Council of Toledo in 633; by Cæsarius, Bishop of Arles (502-42); by Avitus, Bishop of Vienne (490-518); by Vincentius of Lerins (450). Indeed, so close are the coincidences between portions of the Creed and the works of Cæsarius and Vincentius, that it has been maintained in the case of the former by Dom Morin, and of the latter by Ommanney, that they point not so much to familiarity with the Creed as to actual authorship of it. Besides these coincidences with the works of well-known writers, there is also a remarkable fragment of a sermon on the Creed by an unknown writer, which remains in a manuscript of the eighth century, into which it was copied from a manuscript which the writer says that he found at Treves. The sermon itself is obviously much older than the manuscript in which the copy of a portion of it has come down to us, and is generally placed in the sixth or seventh century.

The greater number of these testimonies are valuable as showing not merely the great antiquity of the Creed, but also the respect with which it was regarded by churchmen, and the recognised position which it occupied long before the days of Charlemagne. Some of them, if they stood alone, might be regarded as inconclusive; but taken together they are absolutely inconsistent with a date so late as the eighth or even the seventh century, even if it be held that they fail to *prove* that the Creed is as early as the first half of the fifth century, to which Waterland assigned it. We are then left to the internal evidence, and here the matter stands very much where Waterland left it. The Creed is certainly later than Augustine, for had it been the case (as has been suggested) that Augustine borrowed from it, there would surely have been some definite allusion to it somewhere in his voluminous writings. It is, however, perhaps not conclusively established that it was written before the rise of the Nestorian heresy. Ommanney holds that it 'reproduces the terminology of the Nestorian epoch,'[1] and there

---

[1] *Critical Dissertation*, p. 361.

are clauses in it which may well be thought to be aimed at this heresy. On the other hand, it is difficult to think that it can be later than the rise of Eutychianism (which was condemned at Chalcedon in 451), for terms condemnatory of this heresy are entirely wanting in it. There is indeed one expression occurring in it which might plausibly be pressed into the service of Eutychianism: 'One not by conversion of the Godhead into flesh, but by taking of the manhood into God.' And it is probable that an author who wrote after the rise of the heresy of Eutyches, which taught the absorption of the manhood or human nature of Christ into the Godhead, would have avoided language which, though in itself perfectly orthodox, might readily lend itself to an Eutychian interpretation. On the whole, we can scarcely arrive at any more definite conclusion than this. The *Quicunque vult* cannot have been written before 420. It is very possibly earlier than 450. It cannot be later than the sixth century. Between these limits its author must be sought. Everything points to the south of Gaul as the place of its composition. Various names have been suggested: Cæsarius, Bishop of Arles (470-542), by Dom Morin;[1] Vincent of Lerins (450), by the late

---

[1] *Le Symbole d'Athanase et son premier témoin Saint Césaire d'Arles.* Revue Bénédictine, Oct. 1901. In this article Dom Morin certainly brings very strong arguments from *style* in favour of Cæsarius, to whom, if he was not the actual author, the Creed was evidently 'a houschold word.' It is also pointed out that Cæsarius was in the habit of placing at the head of his works the name of the author from whom he quoted, or whom he followed; and it is thought that in this

Mr. Ommanney;[1] and Honoratus, Bishop of Arles, and founder of the famous monastery and school of Lerins (d. 429), by Dr. Burn;[2] but the evidence does not appear to be sufficient to warrant us in arriving at a definite conclusion. We must rest content with knowing the quarter whence this venerable document comes, and the approximate date to which it belongs.

way the name of Athanasius may have become attached to the document. On the whole the case for Cæsarius appears to be stronger than that for either of the others mentioned above.

[1] *Critical Dissertation*, p. 378 *seq.*
[2] *Introduction to the Creeds*, p. 148.

§ 2

The Use made of the Athanasian Creed by the Church

THE *Quicunque vult* occupies a unique position among the formularies of the Church in that it is at once a Creed, a canticle, and an exposition of or sermon on the Creed. These different characters are all marked by the various titles which it bears in mediæval manuscripts of it. It is sometimes spoken of as *symbolum*, more often as *fides*, the faith, a term which is also frequently applied to the Nicene Creed, and which is practically the equivalent of our English word 'the Creed.' But, although it is a Creed, an expression of the Church's faith in the Trinity and Incarnation, it stands in no relation to the baptismal Creed. It does not begin in the usual way as a personal profession of faith, *I believe*; the first person rarely occurs in it; nor does it follow the ordinary structure of Creeds with their three paragraphs on the Father, the Son, and the Holy Spirit. In form it is a canticle rather than a Creed. Its balanced clauses and measured rhythm mark it out as something to be sung. It is sometimes styled 'the

Psalm *Quicunque vult*,' and it was a true instinct which suggested that its proper place would be in the Church's Psalters, together with the Canticles of the New Testament, and such hymns as the *Te Deum* and the *Gloria in excelsis*. But, again, it is not an ordinary canticle. It is didactic as well as devotional. It is an exposition as well as a confession. It is intended to teach and expound, as well as to supply material for meditation. So we find it sometimes spoken of as a *sermo*, or discourse, or as an *expositio fidei*; and in this character it has probably done more than any other single document to explain and bring home to Church people what is really meant by the doctrines of the Holy Trinity and the Incarnation. Of this more must be said later on. The object of the present section is to describe the position given to it in the Church, and the use made of it in her services.

The earliest notices that we have of it point to its use chiefly by the clergy. Early canons, as we have seen, direct that it should be learned by heart and committed to memory by them, obviously with the intention that they should use it in instructing their flocks in the mysteries of the faith. This accounts for the number of allusions to and quotations from it which we find in early sermons and expositions. There is abundant evidence that long before the ninth century the preachers of the Church were thoroughly familiar with it, and drew from its stores the phrases which they needed in order to establish their congregations in the true doctrine of the Church.

Rather later we find signs of the devotional use of the *Quicunque* in the Church's worship. Its position in Psalters of the eighth century implies that it was already in some way connected with the services of the Church; and we know from definite statements that in the early years of the ninth century it was beginning to be recited at Prime in monastic establishments. It was so used by the Benedictines at the Abbey of Fleury in the days of Theodulf at the beginning of the ninth century; and in the year 922 we are told that in the famous Church of S. Martin at Tours it was resolved, with the consent of the whole chapter, 'that the brethren should all sing' at the hour of Prime, as well on festivals as on ordinary days, 'the Catholic faith, which the holy Athanasius composed by the inspiration of the Holy Spirit, that is *Quicunque vult salvus esse*.' The Church of S. Martin at Tours, like that at Fleury, was monastic. But it was not long before the use of the Creed was extended to ordinary parochial churches as well; and at least from the tenth century onwards it appears to have occupied a recognised position in the service of Prime both in this country and on the Continent. There was, however, a good deal of diversity of use as to the frequency with which it was recited. In some places it was ordered to be said daily, in others on Sundays only; and finally, for some centuries before the Reformation, while according to the Roman use it was only ordered to be said on certain Sundays, the English use required its daily recitation between the Psalms and prayers at the office of Prime. This office was in its origin a purely monastic one, and even after it had become the rule for the clergy to recite the hour services from the breviary, there was no obligation on the part of the laity to attend them. They were intended for the clergy, though there is evidence that in the Middle Ages a considerable number of the laity did as a matter of fact attend some of them, and Prime in particular. Nor are there wanting in comparatively early days traces of attempts to familiarise the laity with the words as well as the substance of the Athanasian Creed, even though they were never required to learn it by heart, as they were the Apostles' Creed. For instance, the charge which Hincmar gives to the clergy that they should not merely learn it by heart, but also understand it and be able to 'enunciate it in common words,' *i.e.* in the vulgar tongue, clearly points to the fact that it was to be used for the purpose of instructing the laity in its tenets. For the same purpose versions were made in the vernacular. There still remain German translations of the tenth and twelfth centuries, the former of which was made by the well-known Notker, a monk of S. Gall; and there is a third German version for which an even earlier date is claimed, for it is thought to belong to the ninth century. In France translations into French of the twelfth and fourteenth centuries are still in existence, and the preface to the manuscript Psalter which contains the later of these says expressly that the translation of the book was made '*pour les gens laye.*' In our own country we find that in Psalters of the tenth and eleventh centuries Anglo-Saxon glosses are sometimes given, stating the meaning of the Latin words; and there are not only English translations belonging to the thirteenth and fourteenth centuries, but there are also French versions of an even earlier date, 'which were written in England, and were obviously intended to meet the devotional and religious requirements of the upper classes, who continued as late as the fourteenth century to speak the language of their French or Norman ancestors who had come to our shores with William the Conqueror.' Thus in the 'Eadwine Psalter' in the library of Trinity College, Cambridge, which belongs to the twelfth century, 'two versions of the Athanasian Creed appear in Saxon and French respectively, written between the lines of the text, one above the other, the former clearly being for the Saxon subjugated folk, the latter for the dominant classes of Norman descent.'[1]

Almost more significant of the desire to familiarise persons with the substance of the Creed is the fact that *metrical* versions were composed in the vernacular. These must have been intended for the use of the laity with the object of bringing home to them the teaching of the Creed, just as the well-known *Lay Folk's Mass Book* was designed not only to explain the order of the service of the Mass, but to familiarise the laity

[1] Ommanney, *Critical Dissertation*, p. 326. For a very large number of the details given in this section I am indebted to the fifth chapter of this book.

with the substance of the prayers and other parts of the service, and consequently includes a metrical version of the *Gloria in excelsis*. Of the *Quicunque* at least two such versions exist: an English one, found in a manuscript in the Bodleian Library (*MS. Bodl.* 425), which is said to date from 1240, and to come from the northernmost part of Lincolnshire, perhaps not far from Hull; and a French version contained in a Paris manuscript, also of the thirteenth century (*Bibl. Nat. Suppl. Franc.*, No. 5145). Of these the former is given in full in Hickes's *Thesaurus*, and the latter has been edited by F. Michel in his *Libri Psalmorum versio Gallica antiqua*; and as they are very curious and interesting, and some readers may be glad to have easy access to them, they are both printed here in an appendix to this chapter.

The evidence just summed up all goes to show that real efforts were made to ensure the acquaintance of the laity with the Creed. But, on the other hand, it should be stated that the most obvious and effective method of familiarising them with it was never taken, as up till the sixteenth century it was never given a place in what has been well called 'The Layman's Prayer Book,' viz. the Primer or book of devotions, in English as well as in Latin, for private use at home and at church. Besides the Hours of the Blessed Virgin Mary, this book contained such forms as the Lord's Prayer, the Hail Mary, and other devotions in English. It is surprising that we do not find the *Quicunque* in any edition of it until the doctrinal

THE ATHANASIAN CREED 201

changes of the sixteenth century were beginning. It is then placed in some editions of the Primer issued in the reign of Henry VIII., from 1536 to 1541, notably in that which is known as 'Bishop Hilsey's Primer' (published in 1539), but it is not contained in 'the King's Primer,' which superseded all earlier ones in 1545. A more successful and determined attempt was made in the following reign to accustom the laity to the use of it, when on the appearance of the first English Prayer Book in 1549 it was ordered to be said in English after *Benedictus* at Mattins on the six great festivals—Christmas, Epiphany, Easter, Ascension Day, Whitsunday, and Trinity Sunday. On the publication of the second Prayer Book of Edward VI. in 1552, seven saints' days were added to the list of days on which it was to be read, so that (roughly speaking) the people might hear it about once a month. To use it on these thirteen days has ever since been the rule of the Church of England; but apparently, when first it was placed in the Prayer Book to be used at Mattins, it was regarded rather as a kind of supplementary canticle, for it was to be followed by the recitation of the Apostles' Creed. Not till the last revision of the Prayer Book in 1661-2 was the order given that on the days appointed for its use the Athanasian Creed should be *substituted* for the Apostles'. It is perhaps scarcely necessary to add that the adherence of the Church of England to the three Creeds was emphatically stated in the seventh of the XLII Articles of 1553, which has continued to be enforced, with the slightest change, as the eighth of the XXXIX Articles of 1563 and 1571 :—

'The Three Creeds, Nicene Creed, Athanasius' Creed, and that which is commonly called the Apostles' Creed, ought thoroughly to be received and believed: for they may be proved by most certain warrants of Holy Scripture.'

On the Continent, in the course of the changes of the sixteenth century, the use of the *Quicunque vult* was generally discontinued in public worship by the various bodies which broke away from the Church of Rome, although in several of the confessions of faith put forward by them, their adherence to the Athanasian as well as the Apostles' and Nicene Creeds is expressly stated. This formal acknowledgment of it was, however, apparently insufficient to prevent disastrous consequences from following in some cases, which gave point to Hooker's memorable warning that the danger of Arianism was not so remote as the Puritans (who desired to see the Athanasian Creed removed from the Book of Common Prayer) seemed to imagine.

'Against which poison [*i.e.* the Arian heresy], if we think that the Church at this day needeth not those ancient preservatives which ages before us were so glad to use, we deceive ourselves greatly. The weeds of heresy being grown unto such ripeness as that was, do even in the very cutting down scatter oftentimes those seeds which for a while lie unseen and buried in the earth, but afterward freshly spring up again no less pernicious than at the first. Which thing they very well know and I doubt not will easily confess, who live to their great both toil and grief, where the blasphemies of Arians, Samosatenians, Tritheites, Eutychians, and Macedonians are renewed; renewed by them who to hatch their heresy have chosen those churches as fittest nests, where Athanasius' Creed is not heard; by them, I say, renewed, who following the course of extreme reformation, were wont in the pride of their own proceedings to glory, that whereas Luther did but blow away the roof, and Zwinglius batter but the walls of popish superstition, the last and hardest work of all remained, which was to raze up the very ground and foundation of popery, that doctrine concerning the deity of Christ which *Satanasius* (for so it pleased those impious forsaken miscreants to speak) hath in this memorable Creed explained. So manifestly true is that which one of the ancient hath concerning Arianism, "Mortuis auctoribus hujus veneni, scelerata tamen doctrina non moritur." The authors of this venom being dead and gone, their wicked doctrine notwithstanding continueth.'[1]

Some account will be given in a later section of the controversies which have arisen on the subject of the recitation of the Creed in the English Church. At present it will be sufficient to mention that ever since the severance of the United States from the mother country, the *Quicunque vult* has found no place in any edition of the Prayer Book of the

[1] Hooker, *Eccl. Polity*, V. xlii. 13.

'Protestant Episcopal Church in the United States of America'; and that at the revision of the Book of Common Prayer which took place in Ireland after the disestablishment of the Church (1869-70), although the text of the Creed was allowed to remain, the rubric preceding it was altogether omitted, as was the reference to it in the rubric before the Apostles' Creed in the order for Morning Prayer, while the following statement was made in the new preface which stands in 'the Book of Common Prayer . . . according to the use of the Church of Ireland':—

'With reference to the Athanasian Creed (commonly so called), we have removed the Rubric directing its use on certain days; but in so doing, this Church has not withdrawn its witness, as expressed in the articles of Religion, and here again renewed, to the truth of the articles of the Christian Faith therein contained.'

This chapter would be incomplete without a brief notice of the position which the *Quicunque* occupies in the Eastern Church. At least six different Greek versions of it exist, some of which may be fully as old as the thirteenth or fourteenth century. But they cannot be cited as proof that the Creed occupied any authoritative position in the Greek Church. Some of them were obviously written for Greek-speaking members of the Latin Church in Constantinople, or in South Italy or Sicily. Some recognition the Creed has, however, received, though, as might naturally be expected, with the omission of the words 'and the

Son' in verse 23, on the procession of the Holy Spirit. With these words omitted, it has since the last quarter of the eighteenth century been accorded a place in the *Horologion*, or office book of the Greek Church; but neither now nor at any previous time has it been recited in any of the services of that Church. It is regarded with respect, and individual teachers have expressed a high sense of its value, but that is all that can be said.

§ 3

Exposition of the Athanasian Creed

THE history of the *Quicunque vult* and of its use has now been traced, and we have seen that it is not only a Creed, but also an exposition of the faith. It remains to give some explanation of it; and the most convenient plan to follow appears to be this: first to consider briefly the exposition of the Catholic faith contained in it, and then in another section to deal separately with the monitory clauses, giving in connection with them a brief account of the controversies to which they have given rise, and the objections taken to the use of the Creed.

The Creed consists of two parts: Part i., verses 1-28, expounding the doctrine of the Holy Trinity; and Part ii., verses 29-42, expounding the doctrine of the Incarnation. The form which it takes throughout is conditioned by heresies that have actually arisen and had to be met by the Church. Each clause is a battle-field, and marks the spot where, often at the cost of much suffering, the faith had to be defended from attacks made against it. In Part i. the principal heresies in view are the Sabellian and the Arian. The latter of these has been sufficiently described in the chapter on the Nicene Creed, and there is no need to repeat here what was then said. Sabellianism has been but briefly touched upon, and it may be convenient to give a somewhat fuller notice of it here. Its characteristic feature is the denial of the reality and the permanency of the distinctions between the Father, the Son, and the Holy Spirit. So far back as the days of Justin Martyr (before A.D. 150) there were some who professed to be Christians who maintained that 'the Son is the Father,'[1] apparently making the distinction between them merely one of character or representation; and later on in the second century this form of teaching came into prominence under the name of Patripassianism, the inference drawn from the language of some of its teachers being that they actually held that it was the Father who suffered crucifixion in the character of the Son. The chief propagators of the heresy were Noetus and Praxeas and (rather later) Sabellius, from whom the heresy has taken its name. It was a formidable danger to the Church till well on in the third century, and there appears to have been a revival of it in the extreme west in the fifth century, which may possibly have given occasion for the composition of the Athanasian Creed. It was in the course of the controversy aroused by the teaching of the Sabellians that the Church was compelled to formulate more precisely her belief in the Father, Son, and Holy Ghost, and to say what she meant by direct-

[1] Justin Martyr, *Apol.*, I. lxiii.

ing worship to Each as God, and yet insisting that she believed in one God. In explaining this she was compelled, however reluctantly, to make use of expressions not contained in Scripture, and to adopt the technical terms which have since become so familiar to us, and which we find employed in the early verses of the Athanasian Creed, viz. the terms *Trinity*, *Person*, and *Substance*. Of these terms *Trinity* is the first to appear in ecclesiastical writings. The Greek form τριάς is found as early as A.D. 180 in the works of Theophilus, Bishop of Antioch. The Latin equivalent *Trinitas* occurs a little later in the works of Tertullian, almost, if not quite, the first of the Latin Fathers. While the Church believed emphatically in 'one God,' she had yet learned from the New Testament that there were distinctions of some sort within the Godhead, so that Father, Son, and Holy Ghost could be spoken of as in some sense Three, or a Trinity. But this was not enough. So long as the Church spoke only of a Trinity, or of 'the Three,' room was left for the teaching of Sabellius and his followers within her borders. 'The Three' might be only three aspects or characters. The Church was therefore compelled to take a further step, and to answer the question what was meant by speaking of the Father, the Son, and the Holy Ghost as Three? Three what? was the obvious question, and when once it was asked, after Sabellianism had proved itself a real danger, it could not remain unanswered. Thus the Church was driven to find some term to express what she understood the teaching of Scripture to be. She saw that our Lord spoke of 'the Father,' and 'My Father,' and that He called Himself 'the Son,' and such titles would be misleading if they merely described distinction of aspects or character. The distinction which they imply must be real and eternal, something that we can only describe as personal. So also with our Lord's teaching on the Holy Spirit: in the great revelation of the Upper Chamber in S. John xiii.-xvi., language is used which freely attributes personal actions to the Holy Spirit, and which clearly implies that He is personally distinct from both the Father and the Son, *e.g.* 'The Comforter whom I will send to you from the Father.' He shall 'teach,' 'guide you into all the truth,' 'convict the world of sin, of righteousness, and of judgment.' With her eye on such passages as these, the Church could only answer the question, 'Three what?' by saying 'Three *Persons*,' and thus adding another term to her ecclesiastical terminology.

But while Sabellianism was thus excluded, there was a danger on the other side to which the use of the term *Person* was exposed. It might lead men to think of the Three Persons as so separate as to be Three Gods, and thus endanger the great central truth of revelation, viz. the doctrine of the Divine Unity. The Church was consequently compelled to take yet one more step, and find some other term that would guard against this danger, and, saving her from the charge of worshipping three Gods, express her belief in the unity of God. For this purpose it was that the term *Substance* (*i.e.* essence or nature) was employed, it being said that the Son was 'of one substance with the Father,' and therefore, though personally distinct, not separated from Him so as to be a Second God. Both this word 'substance' and 'Person' appear for the first time in the writings of Tertullian about the close of the second century. But it was not without hesitation and obvious reluctance that they were employed; and it was only after prolonged controversy that experience taught the Church the absolute necessity of them, if the revealed truths of Scripture were to be faithfully taught, and protected from the perversions of heresy. Indeed, it was not till the latter part of the fourth century that, under the stress of the Arian controversy, these terms became generally accepted by the Church as the best ones for expressing the unity of the Godhead, and the distinctions within it as taught in Scripture; the Latin *Una Substantia, Tres Personæ*, being taken as the equivalents for the terms which, after much hesitation and some variety of usage, the Greeks had come to use, μία οὐσία, τρεῖς ὑποστάσεις, and hence we derive our English formula, 'Three Persons of one substance.'

This brief sketch of the growth of the Church's technical phraseology will enable the reader the better to understand the terms of the Athanasian Creed.

Verses 1 and 2 form the introduction. Their exact significance will be the subject of some remarks in the next section. The reader's attention may, however, be called here to the fact, which, obvious as it is, requires constant emphasis to be laid on it, viz. that 'will' in the English version is not the auxiliary verb, but means 'willeth to be.' The words, therefore, speak not of the man who *is going to be saved*, but of one who *desires to be saved*. It supposes a man who is anxious about his salvation, and says of such an one that ' before all things '—since faith must necessarily precede practice—' it is necessary that he hold' (i.e. *keep hold of*, rather than *lay hold of*) ' the Catholic Faith.' Were it thoroughly recognised that this is the meaning, there need be no controversy as to whether ' salvus ' means ' saved,' or ' in a state of salvation.' As a matter of fact the word is ambiguous, and instances of either meaning may be found in Latin writers of the fourth and fifth centuries. It probably here means saved, but undue importance has often been attached to the determination of its exact significance. It really matters very little which meaning be adopted, since that which the Creed speaks of is *the desire* for salvation.

1. Whosoever will be saved : before all things it is necessary that he hold the Catholick Faith.
2. Which Faith except every one do keep[1] whole and undefiled : without doubt he shall perish everlastingly.[2]

---

[1] 'Do keep,' better 'shall keep' or 'shall preserve': *servaverit*.

[2] 'Everlastingly.' A more exact rendering of *æternum* here and in verse 41 would be 'eternally' and 'eternal.'

Verses 3 and 4 introduce the exposition of the faith itself, stating in briefest terms the doctrine of the Holy Trinity, and pointing out in a remarkable manner the connection between faith and worship.

3. And the Catholick Faith is this : that we worship one God in Trinity, and Trinity in Unity.
4. Neither confounding the Persons : nor dividing the Substance.

The warnings, as will at once be seen, are directed specially against these two heresies, Sabellianism and Arianism, the former of which 'confounded the Persons,' *i.e.* confused them, by asserting that the distinction between Father and Son was merely one of character, and that they were personally to be identified; while the latter 'divided the substance' by the refusal to acknowledge that the son was *Homoousios*, or 'of one substance with the Father.' So, as against Sabellius, the Creed proceeds with its assertion :—

5. For there is one Person of the Father, another of the Son : and another of the Holy Ghost.

And, as against Arius :—

6. But the Godhead of the Father, of the Son, and of the Holy Ghost, is all one : the Glory equal, the Majesty co-eternal.

The following verses, 7-18, enforce the statements just made by emphasising the truth that while each of the Divine Persons possesses the Divine properties and attributes, each being uncreated, infinite, eternal,

THE ATHANASIAN CREED 213

almighty, God, and Lord, yet we are not to think of the Persons of the Holy Trinity as being so separate one from another as to be three uncreated, infinites, eternals, almighties, or as being three Gods or three Lords.

7. Such as the Father is, such is the Son : and such is the Holy Ghost.
8. The Father uncreate, the Son uncreate : and the Holy Ghost uncreate.
9. The Father incomprehensible, the Son incomprehensible : and the Holy Ghost incomprehensible.
10. The Father eternal, the Son eternal : and the Holy Ghost eternal.
11. And yet they are not three eternals : but one eternal.
12. As also there are not three incomprehensibles, nor three uncreated : but one uncreated, and one incomprehensible.
13. So likewise the Father is Almighty, the Son Almighty : and the Holy Ghost Almighty.
14. And yet they are not three Almighties : but one Almighty.
15. So the Father is God, the Son is God : and the Holy Ghost is God.
16. And yet they are not three Gods : but one God.
17. So likewise the Father is Lord, the Son Lord : and the Holy Ghost Lord.
18. And yet not three Lords : but one Lord.

In these verses there is one expression which needs a word of comment. In verse 9 we read in the English version, 'The Father *incomprehensible.*' This may give some readers a wrong impression, since by 'incomprehensible' we now denote that which cannot be understood. In its older sense, however, the word meant that which cannot be contained in space, i.e. *infinite*; and this is in reality its meaning here and in verse 12. The Latin is *immensus*, the same word that is translated *infinite* in the *Te Deum:* '*Patrem immensæ majestatis*' ('The Father of an infinite majesty').

Verses 19 and 20 sum up the foregoing:—

19. For like as we are compelled by the Christian verity: to acknowledge every Person by himself to be God and Lord;
20. So are we forbidden by the Catholick Religion: to say there be three Gods or three Lords.

The wording of verse 19 may perhaps raise a difficulty in some minds, as if it indicated that each Person of the Holy Trinity by Himself would constitute the entire Godhead, in which case it would necessarily follow that there would be three Gods. This, however, as the very next verse shows, cannot possibly be the meaning of the words. 'By Himself' represents the Latin *singillatim*, and would be better rendered by 'severally,' the object of the clause being to emphasise the fact that each Person of the Trinity is essentially God. As Bishop Harold Browne has said: 'We must not view God as we would a material being, as though the Godhead could be *divided* into three different parts, which three united together made up one whole;

and so imagine that the Father alone was not God, but required to have the Son and Spirit *added* to Him in order to make up the Godhead. No! The spiritual unity of the three Blessed Persons in the Trinity is far closer, more intimate, and more real, than the unity by which parts make up a whole. Each, by Himself, or considered alone [better 'severally'], must be confessed to be God; and yet all make not up three Gods, but are one in essence, and therefore but one God.'[1]

The Creed, having now set forth the unity of the Godhead and the distinction of Persons, proceeds to explain, so far as can be explained, what are the 'properties' of the Persons in the Godhead which distinguish each from the others. The Father alone is unoriginate, the Fount or Source of the Deity of both the Son and the Spirit, and we must be careful to guard against the thought of some abstract Godhead existing, as it were, prior to the Persons, and of which the Persons each partake. The Father is the essential Godhead with this property, *to be of none*, and is thus the first Person in the Holy Trinity. The very same nature or substance of God, which the Father has of Himself, is from all eternity communicated by Him to the Son; and this communication is in the language of theology (after Scripture) termed 'generation'; and thus the very selfsame substance or nature with this property, *to be of the Father*, makes the Person of the Son, the second Person in *order*, but

[1] *Exposition of the Thirty-Nine Articles*, p. 226.

not in *time*, seeing that the Divine nature is eternally communicated to Him. The same substance or nature of the Godhead is from all eternity received by the Holy Ghost from the Father through the Son—or, as the Western Church has always expressed it, 'from the Father and the Son'—after the manner which the Church, again following Scripture, has expressed by the term 'proceeding,' so that the same substance or nature with the property of *proceeding from the other two* makes the Person of the Holy Ghost, the third in *order*, but not in *time*, in the Blessed Trinity.[1] This it is which the Creed expresses so tersely in verses 21-24.

21. The Father is made of none: neither created nor begotten.
22. The Son is of the Father alone: not made, nor created, but begotten.
23. The Holy Ghost is of the Father and of the Son: neither made, nor created, nor begotten, but proceeding.
24. So there is one Father, not three Fathers; one Son, not three Sons: one Holy Ghost, not three Holy Ghosts.

The object of the last of these verses (24) is not at first sight obvious. But there is really ample evidence that in early days some such reminder as that which it contains was far from being needless. Thus one of the (so called) *Apostolical Canons* (probably belonging to the fourth century) runs as follows: 'If any bishop or

[1] Cf. Hooker, *Eccl. Polity*, V. li. 1.

presbyter does not baptize according to the Lord's institution into the Father, the Son, and the Holy Ghost, but into three Unoriginates, or into three Sons, or into three Paracletes, let him be deprived.'[1] Nor had the danger thus indicated entirely passed away even so late as the sixth century, for Pope Vigilius (537-54) found it necessary practically to repeat this canon, and say: 'If any bishop or presbyter does not baptize according to the Lord's institution in the name of the Father and of the Son, and of the Holy Ghost, but in one Person of the Trinity, or in two; or in three Fathers, or in three Sons, or in three Paracletes, let him be cast out of the Church';[2] and about the same period the Council of Bracara (Braga) in Spain (A.D. 563) passed a series of canons, the first two of which exactly illustrate the language of the Athanasian Creed and the need of the warnings which it contains.[3]

> 'If any one does not confess that the Father, the Son, and the Holy Ghost are three Persons of one substance, and power, and might, as the Catholic and Apostolic Church teaches, but recognises only a single Person, so that He who is the Son is also the Father and the Paraclete, as Sabellius and Priscillian teach, let him be Anathema.
>
> If any one introduces any names of the Godhead,

[1] Canon 49.
[2] *Ep. 2 ad Eutherium*, cap. 6. The letter, though so entitled, was really written to Profuturus, Bishop of Braga, in 538. Mansi, *Concilia*, ix. 32.
[3] Mansi, *Concilia*, ix. 774.

besides those of the Holy Trinity, maintaining that in the Godhead there is a Trinity of the Trinity, as the Gnostics and Priscillianists teach, let him be Anathema.'

It is clear from these citations that, remote as may now appear the danger of so misconceiving the faith as to believe in three Fathers, or three Sons, or three Holy Ghosts, yet in the age to which the composition of the Creed belongs, it was neither remote nor insignificant.

The next four verses, 25-8, emphasise the co-eternity and co-equality of the three Persons, and contain the conclusion of the first section of the Creed, viz. that which deals with the doctrine of the Trinity.

25. And in this Trinity none is afore, or after other: none is greater or less than another;
26. But the whole three Persons are co-eternal together: and co-equal.
27. So that in all things, as is aforesaid: the Unity in Trinity, and the Trinity in Unity is to be worshipped.
28. He therefore that will be saved: must thus think of the Trinity.

Of these, verse 25 would be more accurately rendered, 'there is nothing afore or after: nothing greater or less' (*nihil prius aut posterius: nihil majus aut minus*). The words 'afore or after' refer to time, 'greater or less' to power. Of verse 28 more will be said later on. It will be sufficient for the present to indicate that the

English rendering (as now understood) seriously misrepresents the original. For 'he therefore that will be saved: must thus think of the Trinity,' should be substituted 'He therefore that would [or *willeth to*] be saved: so let him think of the Trinity' (*Qui vult ergo salvus esse: ita de Trinitate sentiat*).[1]

Verse 29 forms the introduction to the second part of the Creed, viz. that on the Incarnation.

29. Furthermore, it is necessary to everlasting salvation: that he also believe rightly the Incarnation of our Lord Jesus Christ.

Here, again, attention must be called to an unfortunate mistranslation; the English 'believe rightly' is misleading. It suggests that what is necessary is *correctness* of belief, and thus implies that faith is a matter of the *head*, as we say, rather than of the *heart*.

---

[1] It is interesting to find that the inadequacy of the English rendering was beginning to attract attention in the early part of the seventeenth century; for in Charles I.'s copy of an English Prayer Book, with alterations and additions for the 'Scottish Liturgy' made in the king's own hand, we find that in this verse the king has struck out 'that will be saved, must' and has written 'that would be saved, so let him.' It appears further, from a letter of Archbishop Laud to the Bishop of Dunblane (April 20, 1636), that the Scottish bishops desired more changes of translation, for the archbishop says 'we can agree to no more emendations, no not according to our best Greek copies, than you shall find amended in this book.' Accordingly the only two changes made in the Creed in the published book (1637) are the one noted above and one in verse 37, also marked by the king, the second half of the verse being made to run as follows: 'So *He who is* God and man is one Christ.' See J. Cooper, *The Book of Common Prayer . . . for the use of the Church of Scotland, commonly known as Laud's Liturgy*. Introduction, pp. xxviii. *seq.*

The Latin is *fideliter*, which, of course, should be rendered 'faithfully.' If this were done, all danger of misapprehension would be removed, and it would be at once manifest that the Creed is not speaking of a mere intellectual belief, but of a living faith, such as that of which the Apostle speaks when he says: 'With the heart man believeth unto righteousness' (Rom. x. 10).

In the verses which follow, 30-3, the perfection of the two natures, the Divine and the human, in the one Person of the God-man is dwelt upon, the heresies that are principally in view being obviously the Arian and the Apollinarian, the former of which denied the truth of our Lord's Divine nature, while the latter impugned the perfection of His humanity. Sufficient has already been said on these heresies in the chapter on the Nicene Creed, and no further comment or explanation seems to be needed here.

30. For the right faith is that we believe and confess: that our Lord Jesus Christ, the Son of God, is God and Man;
31. God, of the Substance of the Father, begotten before the worlds: and Man, of the substance of His Mother, born in the world.
32. Perfect God, and perfect Man : of a reasonable soul and human flesh subsisting;
33. Equal to the Father, as touching his Godhead : and inferior to the Father, as touching his Manhood.[1]

[1] There are in these verses a few slight inexactnesses which may be here noted. In verse 30 the word 'equally' should perhaps be in-

In verses 34-7 the writer of the Creed passes on to insist on the *Unity of Person* in Christ. Here, again, there can be no doubt that the Apollinarian heresy was forcibly present to his mind, and he may have been concerned to deny the charge which the Apollinarians brought against the Catholics of making 'two Christs,' because it seemed to them that the acknowledgment of the existence of the human spirit in the Incarnate Christ as well as the Divine Logos, or Word, involved the recognition of a twofold personality. This inference from her teaching the Church has always repudiated. She holds, indeed, that in Christ are two whole and perfect *natures*, but that they are joined together in one *Person*. Spirit, as well as soul and body, is necessary to the perfection of humanity (see 1 Thess. v. 23), but it does not constitute a distinct person. Hence, perhaps, the language of the Creed in these verses. But it is possible that the writer may also have had in view the Nestorian heresy, for the distinction which Nestorius and his followers drew between the

serted : 'Our Lord Jesus Christ, the Son of God, is *equally* God and man,' many of the manuscripts of the Creed having the words, 'et Deus *pariter* et homo est' (see Burn, p. 187); verse 31 should begin 'He is God,' etc. (Deus *est* ex substantia), and the copula 'and' at the beginning of the second half of this verse should be deleted, as also in verse 32, where the Latin is ' perfectus Deus, perfectus homo.' In verse 31, again, there should be no copula at the beginning of the second half, and 'his' in both places where it occurs should be 'the.' The language is as broad and general as possible : ' Equal to the Father as touching the Godhead: inferior to the Father as touching the Manhood.' It may also be noted that the division of verse 32 may easily cause its full meaning to be overlooked. It should be 'Perfect God: perfect man of a reasonable soul and human flesh subsisting.'

Son of God and the Son of Mary was wholly destructive of the unity of Person, and actually *did* involve the belief that there were two Persons in Christ, the Son of God and *a* man, on whom the Son of God descended, and whom He left before the crucifixion, so that according to Nestorius it was not the Son of God Who was born or Who died, suffered and died; whereas the belief of the Church has ever been, that since there is but one Person in Christ, He Who was conceived and born, and suffered and died, was indeed the Son of God, Himself very God of very God. In any case, whether these clauses were directly aimed against the heresy of Nestorius or not, they obviously condemn it, and proclaim the truth as to Christ's Person which the Church was called on to defend in the controversy which arose in the fifth century on the subject.

34. Who although he be God and Man: yet he is not two but one Christ.
35. One; not by conversion of the Godhead into flesh: but by taking of the Manhood into God;
36. One altogether; not by confusion of substance: but by unity of Person.
37. For as the reasonable soul and flesh is one man: so God and Man is one Christ.

In the second of these verses the English version omits a particle, which is found in the original, and which shows that the verse is added to guard against a possible misunderstanding of what has gone before. It should be, 'One, *however*, not by conversion,' etc.

THE ATHANASIAN CREED 223

(Unus *autem*). 'Into flesh' and 'into God' should probably be 'in flesh' and 'in God,' as the weight of manuscript authority is in favour of the ablatives 'in carne . . . in Deo,' as against the accusatives 'in carnem . . . in Deum.' The phraseology 'the conversion of the Godhead *in* flesh' is, however, very harsh, and, whichever be the true reading, the clause is less happily worded than the remainder of the Creed ; and care is needed to guard against any erroneous influence from it. It is, as has already been indicated, in all probability prior to the time when the rise of the Eutychian heresy had taught divines the need of the utmost precision of language. Eutyches taught that after the Incarnation the human nature of Christ was absorbed into the Divine, and thus ceased to have any distinct existence. Such a notion is entirely excluded by verse 36 of the Creed, and of course cannot, therefore, be intended to be expressed by verse 35, though the words 'taking of the manhood in (or *into*) God,' if they stood alone, might be interpreted in accordance with it. What is really meant by this verse is the truth that the Godhead lost nothing by its conjunction with flesh in the Person of Christ, while the manhood, though losing none of its essential properties, was infinitely exalted by its union with the Divine nature in the same one Person of Christ.

Verses 38-41 complete the summary of the faith by describing the work of the Incarnate Christ in close adherence to the statements of the Apostles' Creed. It should be noticed that only one article of this Creed is enlarged upon and elaborated, and very remarkable is the elaboration. It consists of an emphatic assertion that the rule of judgment at the last day will be in accordance with men's *works*. 'They that have *done* good,' not they that have 'thought correctly,' or even 'believed rightly,' but they that have 'done good shall go into life everlasting, and they that have done evil' (not 'thought wrongly,' or 'failed to believe rightly') 'into everlasting fire.' This is the only one of the three Creeds to assert so clearly the rule of judgment by works; and it is very noteworthy that it should be so. It should also be added that the account which it gives of the reward and doom in store for those that have done good and evil respectively is wholly scriptural, being stated in the terms of S. Matthew xxv. 41, 'Depart from me, ye cursed, into everlasting fire, prepared for the devil and his angels'; and verse 46, 'These shall go away into everlasting punishment: but the righteous into life eternal.'

38. Who suffered for our salvation: descended into hell, rose again the third day from the dead.
39. He ascended into heaven, he sitteth on the right hand of the Father, God Almighty: from whence he shall come to judge the quick and the dead.
40. At whose coming all men shall rise again with their bodies: and shall give account for their own works.
41. And they that have done good shall go into life everlasting: and they that have done evil into everlasting fire.

The text of verses 38 and 39, as given above, has apparently suffered from two insertions being made in it in order to make it correspond more closely with that of the Apostles' Creed. In verse 38 the words 'the third day' should certainly be omitted, and similarly in verse 39 the words 'God Almighty.' Manuscript authority in each case is conclusive against the insertion.[1]

Verse 42 forms the conclusion of the whole document, corresponding to the introduction in verses 1 and 2.

> 42. This is the Catholick Faith: which except a man believe faithfully he cannot be saved.

In this the Latin has 'fideliter, firmiterque,' and the English version should, therefore, be made to correspond more closely with it by the insertion of the words 'and firmly' after 'faithfully.'

[1] The Latin of verse 40 is curious. It is not the simple future 'resurgent,' but 'resurgere habent,' *i.e.* 'are to rise,' or 'must rise.'

§ 4

The Monitory Clauses, and the Controversies raised on the use of the Athanasian Creed

IT is proposed in this section to give a brief account of the objections taken and controversies raised from time to time with regard to the use of the Creed; and, after some consideration of the force of the objections, and an explanation of the monitory clauses, to conclude with a notice of the chief modifications as to the use of the Creed by the Church of England that have been recently suggested.

The earliest objections of which we hear, raised to the language or use of the Creed, are in the sixteenth century. Its use in public worship was apparently dropped by most, if not all, of the Protestant and Reformed bodies on the Continent, and in some quarters dislike was expressed of its language, especially by the Socinians and Arians, some of whom delighted to call it the Creed, not of Athanasius, but of Sathanasius. So Valentinus Gentilis, an Arian from Naples, who settled at Genoa about the middle of the century, is said to have termed it; and the silly nickname was caught up by others, as Gregorius Paulus in

THE ATHANASIAN CREED 227

Poland, and many Arian sectaries in Lithuania. In England no exception appears to have been taken to the position given to it in the Book of Common Prayer until well on in the century, when we hear of objections raised by Thomas Cartwright, the Puritan leader, and others. Cartwright objected to its recitation in church, not apparently on grounds of dissatisfaction with the substance of it, but simply because he said that Arianism was dead, and therefore the Creed was no longer needed. He was answered by Hooker, whose words have been cited above,[1] and still earlier by Whitgift, who pointed out that 'Athanasius' Creed is not only an excellent confutation of Arius' heresy, but a plain declaration of the mystery of the Trinity, such as is necessary for all Christian men to learn and know.'[2] Isolated objections also begin to be raised about this time. Thus we hear of Bishop Aylmer being compelled to silence a minister in his diocese who was accused, among other offences, of being 'a busy disputer against Athanasius' Creed.'[3] But the exceptions taken to its use were evidently not regarded as serious, nor can they have been widely spread, or we should have heard much more of them. Nothing was said against its use at the Hampton Court Conference (1604), or at that held at the Savoy (1661). Indeed Baxter, the leader of the Presbyterian party at that conference, is reported to have said : 'In a word, the damnatory sentences excepted or modestly expounded,

[1] See above, p. 202.   [2] Whitgift, *Works*, ii. 481.
[3] Strype's *Aylmer*, p. 71 (cap. vii.).

I embrace the Creed called Athanasius' as the best explication of the Trinity.' Somewhat earlier, however, there appear to be traces of the disuse of the Creed in some churches, for in Visitation Articles of 1636 and later, a question is sometimes asked whether the minister reads the Athanasian Creed on all those days for which it is appointed.[1] To the same period belong the objections of such men as Chillingworth and Jeremy Taylor. The former of these felt himself at one time unable to accept the Creed, but he overcame his scruples later, when he was appointed Chancellor of Salisbury in 1638, and signed the three articles of the Canon. Jeremy Taylor, in his *Liberty of Prophesying*, speaks at some length on the Creed, and says: 'I confess I cannot see the moderate sentence and gentleness of charity in his preface and conclusion, as there was in the Nicene Creed. Nothing there but damnation and perishing everlastingly, unless the article of the Trinity be believed as it is there with curiosity and minute particularities explained.' He further points out that what he calls 'the censure in the preface and end . . . are extrinsical and accidental to the articles, and might as well have been spared.'[2]

So far we have seen little more than the objections of individuals. Not till 1689 does any suggestion for some change in its use appear to have been seriously

---

[1] See Bishop Wren's Articles in the *Report of the Ritual Commission of* 1867, p. 559.

[2] *Liberty of Prophesying*, § ii. c. 36.

brought before the Church. In that year there was an attempt made to revise the Prayer Book, and the Commissioners appointed for this purpose appear to have had before them several of the proposals for dealing with the Athanasian Creed which have been revived in later days. The total disuse of the Creed was suggested, but only to be rejected as likely to endanger the faith. The *optional* use of it was considered; as well as the excision of the monitory clauses, and, lastly, the addition of an explanatory note. This last course, which was proposed by Stillingfleet, Bishop-elect of Worcester, found most favour, and finally the Commissioners agreed to enlarge the rubric so as to make it state that 'the articles of [the Creed] ought to be received and believed as being agreeable to the Holy Scripture. And the Condemning clauses are to be understood as relating only to those who obstinately deny the substance of the Christian Faith.' It was also contemplated that the Creed should only be read on the five great festivals (omitting the Epiphany) and on All Saints' Day. Nothing, however, came of this. Archbishop Tillotson said: 'The account given of Athanasius' Creed appears to me nowise satisfactory. I wish we were well rid of it.' But the temper of Convocation was such that it was felt to be useless to submit the proposals of the Commissioners to it, and the whole scheme was quietly dropped.

During the revival of Arianism within the Church in the eighteenth century, we hear that the Creed was disused by many of the Arian clergy, and Dr. Samuel

Clarke wrote vehemently against it. His attack was the occasion which called forth Waterland's masterly defence of it, which had the effect of putting an end to all active controversy on the subject for many years. But the dislike of the Creed remained in many quarters, and the directions for its recitation shared the fate of many other rubrics in the general neglect of the eighteenth century. There were probably many churches where it was never heard, including the Royal chapels, in which George III. would never allow it to be recited.

The omission of the Creed from the American Prayer Book (1785-1789), though acquiesced in with great reluctance by Bishop Seabury, attracted but little attention in this country. When the proposed changes in the Prayer Book were submitted to the English Bishops, from whom the American Church hoped for consecration of its Bishops, the faintest possible exception was taken to the alteration, the Bishops mildly adding at the end of their remarks: 'Nor can we help adding, that we hope you will think it a decent proof of the attachment you profess to the services of our Liturgy to give the other two Creeds [as well as the Apostles'] a place in your Book of Common Prayer, even though the use of them should be made optional.' Not much attention was paid to this, though in the (American) Convention of 1789 the House of Bishops actually did propose to retain the Creed with a rubric *permitting* its use. This was, however, negatived in the other House, and

THE ATHANASIAN CREED 231

the Creed has never found a place in the American Prayer Book.[1]

In the early part of the nineteenth century, as in the eighteenth, the rubrics generally were treated with scant respect, and the disuse of the Creed was very common. The Tractarian movement (1833) brought a change. By degrees the directions of the rubrics came to be more strictly observed, and, among others, that which directs the recitation of the Athanasian Creed on certain days was far more generally regarded, and the revival of the use of the Creed was very marked. It was, perhaps, not altogether unnatural that this increased use of it should be regarded with dislike and disfavour in some quarters; the voices of individuals were from time to time raised against it, but no serious attack upon its position was made until the latter part of the century.[2] It was in the course of the labours of the Royal Commission on Ritual (appointed in 1867) that the controversy sprang up. Occasion was taken to present to the Commissioners a memorial against the use of the Creed, and the opposition to it was strengthened by the works of Ffoulkes and (later on) Swainson and Lumby, as well as Dean Stanley, who took the foremost place in the attacks upon it. The Commissioners themselves were very doubtful whether the consideration of the use of the Creed came within

[1] See W. McGarvey, *Liturgiæ Americanæ*, Introd. pp. xiv-xxix.

[2] It is remarkable that to judge from the Records of the Convocation of Canterbury there was no petition presented, or discussion raised on the subject until 1869.

the terms of their Commission. No reference to it was made in the first three of their reports, but when the fourth and last report was issued in 1870 it was found to contain, in a complete scheme for the revision of the rubrics attached as a schedule to it, the following note, to be appended to the rubric preceding the Creed :—

> '*Note that the condemnations in this Confession of Faith are to be no otherwise understood than as a solemn warning of the peril of those who wilfully reject the Catholic Faith.*'

The report was signed by the twenty-seven Commissioners, but out of this number no fewer than *seventeen* dissented from this recommendation, headed by the Archbishop of Canterbury (Tait), who made no secret of his desire that the Creed should not retain its place in the public service of the Church.

The matter obviously could not be allowed to rest where it was left by the Commissioners, and an agitated controversy on the whole subject at once broke out. Books and pamphlets were published by the score. It was soon manifest that the strength of feeling was not all on one side. If men like Bishop Thirlwall and Dean Stanley were fierce in their opposition to the use of the Creed, the former actually declaring that 'we now know it to be a wicked forgery,' there was no lack of strong speech on the other side, in protest against what its defenders termed the 'mutilation' or 'degradation' of the Creed. The Divinity Professors of the Universities of Oxford and Cambridge were ranged on opposite sides in the controversy. The promoters of memorials either for or against the retention of the Creed had no difficulty in securing thousands of signatures to their petitions and protests. The subject could not be kept out of the debates in Parliament, and in Convocation it was constantly before both Houses in some form or other in the years 1871-72-73. There is no need to tell the story at length here.[1] The Archbishop was at last convinced that no proposal for altering the rubric or revising the Creed could be carried through without a disruption in the Church. Drs. Pusey and Liddon not only protested in the strongest terms against any alteration, but allowed it to be generally known that if any change whatever was made in the rubric they would resign their preferments and retire into lay communion; and the great meeting held in St. James's Hall on January 31, 1873, showed what an extraordinarily strong feeling among churchmen had been evoked in support of their position. Finally it was agreed by a large Committee of Convocation appointed to consider the subject that the only possible course was to draw up a synodical declaration, which it was hoped might ultimately take its place as an explanatory rubric in the Book of Common Prayer. The declaration as ultimately adopted in 1873, and synodically reaffirmed in 1879, ran as given below; but it must be noted that no attempt was made on either of these occasions or at

[1] A full account of the whole controversy is given in the *Life of Archbishop Tait*, vol. ii. chap. xxii.

any other time to incorporate it in the Book of Common Prayer:—

'For the removal of doubts, and to prevent disquietude in the use of the Creed commonly called the Creed of S. Athanasius, this Synod doth solemnly declare:—

'1. That the Confession of our Christian Faith, commonly called the Creed of S. Athanasius, doth not make any addition to the faith as contained in Holy Scripture, but warneth against errors which from time to time have arisen in the Church of Christ.

'2. That as Holy Scripture in divers places doth promise life to them that believe, and declare the condemnation of them that believe not, so doth the Church in this Confession declare the necessity for all who would be in a state of salvation of holding fast the Catholic faith, and the great peril of rejecting the same. Wherefore the warnings in this Confession of Faith are to be understood no otherwise than the like warnings in Holy Scripture, for we must receive God's threatenings even as His promises, in such wise as they are generally set forth in Holy Writ. Moreover, the Church doth not herein pronounce judgment on any particular person or persons, God alone being the Judge of all.'

Little has been heard of controversy on the subject of the Creed until quite recently, since the agitation against its use died down in the course of the year 1873. It is remarkable, however, that in 1888 a

THE ATHANASIAN CREED 235

resolution was passed by the Bishops assembled at the Lambeth Conference asking for a new translation of the Creed, and—nothing apparently having been done in the interval—at the next Conference in 1897 a still more definite resolution was passed:—

'That the Archbishop of Canterbury be requested to take such steps as may be necessary for the retranslation of the *Quicunque vult.*'

But nothing has been heard of any action being taken on this resolution either by Archbishop Temple or by the present Archbishop.

The discussions on the use of the Creed which have been reopened during the last few years are so recent that it is not proposed to notice them here. We may therefore pass on to consider the nature of the objections raised to its use.

The objections taken to the use of the Creed have varied considerably at different times. But in the main the only serious ones may be grouped round these two heads: (1) The positive statements of the faith are said to be unintelligible, and to go into needless particulars; (2) the monitory clauses are sometimes objected to as 'anathemas,' as condemning the heathen, and even the Greek Church, and every one who does not accept the Church's faith in the Trinity and Incarnation; it is also freely said that they go beyond the teaching of Scripture and are untrue.

Other objections have sometimes been raised, as that the use of the Creed is contrary to the 7th Canon of the Council of Ephesus, which forbade any person to bring forth or compose a different Creed (ἑτέραν πίστιν) from that promulgated at Nicæa. This, which was vehemently urged at one time, has, it is hoped, been finally disposed of by a more accurate study of the history and true meaning of the Canon of Ephesus, which has really no bearing whatsoever on the use of the Athanasian Creed by the Church of England.[1] But the two objections stated above require full consideration.

(1) To the statement that the Creed is unintelligible and goes into needless particulars, the best answer is given by a study of the controversies which arose in the early Church, and led to the composition of the Creed. The general statement of the Church's faith in the Trinity is given in verses 3 (positively) and 4 (negatively), and in the Incarnation in verse 28. The remainder is really an exposition *per modum doctrinæ* of what is implicitly contained in the acknowledgment made in the above verses. In previous sections of this volume on the history of the *Quicunque vult* and of the Nicene Creed, it has been shown how the various definitions have been forced upon the Church, and how intensely practical the statements of the Creeds are as against false teaching which experience has shown to be fatal to any real grasp of the true faith. The statements made in the *Quicunque vult* are as essential to-day as when they were first made, and the 'particularities' of the Creed are very far from being

---

[1] Reference on this subject may perhaps be permitted to my volume on *The XXXIX Articles*, p. 225.

needless, if the Church's faith in the great central doctrines of the Trinity and Incarnation is to be retained as a living thing. The experience of missionaries has often borne witness to the great value of the Creed as an exposition of Christian doctrine. Bishop Cotton of Calcutta went out to India with a prejudice against the Creed, but had not been long there before he was convinced of its value, and in his last charge, delivered in 1863, he wrote of it as follows:—

'As in the case of the Baptismal service, so in that of the Athanasian Creed, there is much to be learned from coming to India. One who resides in the midst of a heathen nation begins to realise the state of things in which the Apostles wrote those passages of which the Baptismal service is a faithful echo, and in which the primitive bishops and fathers of the Church drew up their Confessions of Faith. For the errors rebuked in the Athanasian Creed result from tendencies common to the human mind everywhere, and especially prevalent in this country. We cannot too thoroughly impress on those who recoil from its definitions and distinctions that its object was, not to limit but to widen the pale of the Church, which various heretical sects were attempting to contract. It contains no theory of the Divine nature, but contradicts certain false opinions about it, and states the revealed truths of the Trinity and Incarnation without any attempt to explain them. It especially censures four errors: the heresy of Arius, who "divided the substance" of the

Godhead by teaching that the Father was the supreme and the Son an inferior Deity; of Sabellius, who "confounded the Persons," by supposing that the Father took our nature as the Man Christ Jesus, and after dying for our salvation operates on our hearts as the Holy Ghost; of Nestorius, who so completely separated our Lord's Divinity and humanity as to teach that He is not one but two Christs; and of Apollinaris, who asserted that He was not perfect Man, with a reasonable (or rational) soul, but a Being in whom the Godhead supplied the place of the human intellect. Now, these four tendencies correspond to four forms of error which are in full activity among us here. The chief cause of the horror with which Arianism was regarded by the Fathers of Nicæa was that it led directly back to the polytheism from which Constantine had just delivered the Roman Empire. Had it prevailed, Christianity would have been degraded into the worship of three Gods, the Father, the Son, and the Holy Ghost, with the Father as the Lord and Ruler of the other two. Arianism, therefore, so far as it was polytheistic, resembled the religion of the common people of this country. The theory of Sabellius, fatal to the truths of Christ's Mediation and Atonement, arose from that bare and unsympathising monotheism, which has since been erected by Mahomet into a kind of rival and hindrance to the Gospel. The foremost of Indian sects in public spirit and intelligence inherit from their Persian ancestors the doctrine of two co-ordinate independent principles, Ormuz and Ahriman, Good and

THE ATHANASIAN CREED 239

Evil, with the first of which Spirit, and with the other Matter, is immediately connected. From a tendency to this very same error, Nestorius separated altogether Christ's Divine from His human nature, although such a view leads to the denial that this world is redeemed from evil, and that man's body, as well as his soul and spirit, must be consecrated to God's service. The creed of many among the educated classes in India, and of not a few, I fear, in Europe, is the theory of Pantheism, which quenches in us the love of God, since we cannot feel affection for One who has no personal attributes, and which is at least fatal to morality, by teaching that evil is only an inferior stage of good, "good in the making," as some one has expressed it, so that the two are in fact identical, each having alike its origin in God. From Pantheistic sympathies Apollinaris, the precursor of Eutyches, was led to merge Christ's manhood in His Godhead, and to deny that He had a human soul. Now, if we remember that all these heresies sprang from tendencies which have given birth to separate religions of widely extended influence, in the midst of which we in India are living, we may surely pause before we expunge from the records of our Church an ancient protest against the application of these tendencies to Christianity, since, whenever the educated classes of this country embrace the Gospel, there will be need of watchfulness, lest its simplicity be perverted by the revival of errors which all had their origin in Eastern philosophy.'

Again: 'The Creed, then, so far from confining

itself to mere dogma, insists, even more distinctly than the Nicene or Apostles' Creeds, on the paramount necessity of a good life; so that if we view its doctrinal clauses in connection with certain prevalent and often recurring heresies; if we put a reasonable construction on those parts of it which seem harshly worded, or, as Baxter said, "expound them modestly"; if, above all, each of us employs them, not to condemn Socinians or unbelievers, but to condemn himself, for the small use which he makes of the Catholic faith as the appointed means of growing in Christian holiness, we need not regard it as obsolete or unedifying, still less as a snare to conscience and hindrance to ordination.'[1]

Not less striking is the evidence to the value of the Creed borne by the late Bishop M'Dougall of Labuan, who in a speech delivered in the Lower House of Convocation in 1872 spoke as follows:—

'In 1849 there was an emigration of Chinese [into Borneo], and some three thousand of them came with their teacher, a man of considerable learning, of an exercised mind, and acute intellect. That man began to inquire after Christianity: he became my catechumen, and I baptized him when sufficiently instructed. He became the catechist to his fellow-countrymen, was my able assistant for fourteen years, and at length I said to him: "I think the time has come; you know enough to be ordained, and I must teach you those things you have not yet learnt—the Athanasian Creed

[1] Bishop Cotton, *Charge to the Clergy of the Diocese and Province of Calcutta* (1863), pp. 37-42.

THE ATHANASIAN CREED 241

and the Articles of our Church;—we must go through them." We did so, and when I had gone through the Athanasian Creed with him, he said: "Why did you not teach me this before? I have had the greatest difficulty in understanding your doctrine of the Trinity; but now I understand it in a way I never understood it before. This is the thing to teach the Chinese."'[1]

One more testimony may be given to the practical value of the Creed, and to the fact that it does not go into needless particulars. The present Dean of Westminster, in a sermon preached before the University of Cambridge in the year 1904, used these striking words :—

'The Creed was not the fine-spun product of a mind which was snared by the delusion of systematic completeness; it is a simple recitation of the results reached by the great Christian thinkers from Athanasius to Augustine. . . . When we have done our best to think out the doctrine of the Incarnation, and to express it in terms which correspond with the present tenor of our thinking, we feel satisfied that no statement can so fully guard the mystery as the great clause, "Perfect God and perfect man," and we are more than ever thankful that these simple words are current coin. Again, while we fancy that the new philosophical conception of personality helps us to understand that in God personality is found in its highest realisation, in which distinction does not involve separation, we rejoice anew in the simple greatness of the antithesis which

[1] *Chronicle of Convocation*, Session April-May 1872, p. 412.

declares: "So the Father is God, the Son is God, and the Holy Ghost is God: and yet they are not three Gods, but one God." And we feel that, so long as these words ring out in English ears, we are safeguarded at once from tritheism and from a Sabellian view which contradicts what we have learnt of the inner life of love within the being of God. It is for these and other great phrases of the Athanasian Creed that I value its public recitation in our congregations, and that I should deplore a change which would thrust it into a corner out of common knowledge. If it still stood in the Prayer Book, but with no rubric for its use, it would soon be as unfamiliar to most of us as the prayers for use at sea.'

With such testimonies as these to its value it is idle to assert that it goes into needless particularities; nor is there really any reason why this Creed should be regarded as more unintelligible to any fairly educated person than the Nicene Creed, some expressions in which require quite as much explanation as any in the longer formulary. Indeed, great as is the value of the Nicene Creed, it must be remembered that while it is full in its statements of our Lord's eternal Godhead, yet its statement on the Incarnation is less completely developed, and there is but little on the relation between the Three Persons in the Godhead. It leaves almost unreconciled the opening assertion of belief in 'One God,' and the subsequent declarations on the Godhead of the Son and the Holy Spirit; so that it is hard to see how any intelligent faith in the doctrine of the Trinity in Unity could be propagated without the help of some such formulary as the *Quicunque vult*.

(2) There remain the objections to the monitory clauses.

(*a*) These are sometimes spoken of, and consequently objected to, as being *anathemas*. But to give them such a name is an abuse of terms, which is calculated to raise an unfair prejudice against them. An anathema is properly a curse, or *wish that evil may fall on some one*, and there is not one single word in the whole of the Creed that can by any ingenuity be twisted into a wish that evil may fall on the head of any one. The monitory clauses are simply warnings, not of what we wish to happen to any one, but of what, if God's Word be true, will happen to those who reject or let go the faith; and they are uttered in the spirit of the truest charity in order that those who hear them may take heed and, by holding fast that which they have, may avoid the doom that is here pronounced.

(*b*) But we are told that these clauses condemn the heathen, and even the Greek Church, and every one who does not accept the Church's faith in the Trinity and Incarnation as here declared.

Once more we must ask the objectors to consider the words which are actually employed, remembering that the original Latin must obviously be our guide to the meaning of the English rendering. The opening phrase, 'Whosoever will be saved,' i.e. *whosoever wishes to be saved*, shows us at once the kind of case contemplated. A person does not 'wish to be saved,' *i.e.* is not anxious about his salvation, unless he knows something of what is meant by salvation, and by the wrath to come: in other words, it is the case of a Christian and not of a heathen that is contemplated. This is made even clearer by what follows: 'Before all things it is necessary that he hold (*teneat*) the Catholic Faith, which faith except every one do keep (*servaverit*, shall have preserved) whole and undefiled, without doubt he shall perish everlastingly' (or eternally, *in æternum*). Now it is clear that 'hold' here means not 'take hold of' in the first instance, but 'hold fast,' as the same verb *teneo* so often means in the Vulgate; for instance, in S. Paul's words in 1 Thessalonians v. 21, 'Prove all things: *hold fast* that which is good,' the Latin is 'quod bonum est *tenete*.' In Hebrews iv. 14, 'Let us hold fast our profession,' and x. 23, 'Let us hold fast the profession of our faith without wavering,' the same verb is used in each case—*teneamus*. Again, in 2 Thessalonians ii. 15, where the Thessalonians are charged to 'stand fast and hold the traditions which ye have been taught, whether by word or by our Epistle,' it is *tenete*. So also in Rev. ii. 13, 'Thou holdest fast My name and hast not denied My faith,' and verse 25, 'That which ye have already, hold fast till I come,' the very same word is used, '*tenes* nomen meum, et non negasti fidem meam,' and '*tene* quod habes.' These passages exactly illustrate the use of the word in the Creed. In each case it is perfectly clear that what is warned against is the danger of letting go that which is already possessed. It is the very same with the Creed, and since the

Revisers of 1881, with their almost pedantic desire for exactness, have left 'hold fast' wherever it occurs in the Authorised Version in the passages cited above, we may fairly ask that if there is ever to be a revised translation of the Athanasian Creed, the meaning may be made clear from any possibility of misconception by rendering the word where it occurs in it by 'hold fast.' The verb in the latter half of the verse is perhaps even clearer: *servaverit*, 'shall have preserved,' for everybody can understand that it is impossible to preserve what has not been received, and what the person charged to preserve anything is not in possession of at the time when the charge is given. It would be an abuse of terms to tell an impure person to preserve his chastity. It is as great an abuse of terms when it is said that the warnings of the Athanasian Creed apply to any but those who are actually in possession of the faith. If persons would pay more attention to what is actually said than to what they imagine is said, we should hear far less of this objection, for they would understand that the warnings of the Creed are directed against apostasy from the Christian faith, and that they do not in any sense concern the heathen, or those who have been brought up in hereditary error, for these have never received the Catholic faith and cannot therefore be said to be in possession of it. With regard again to the Greek Church, it is an entire mistake to suppose that it is condemned by the warning clauses of the Creed. The Greek Church has, it is true, never accepted the Western formula in speaking of the Holy Spirit as 'proceeding from the Father and the Son,' *ex Patre Filioque procedens*; and it might therefore fairly be said that not having received it, it cannot be spoken of here. But more important is it to notice that this formula does not occur in the Athanasian Creed. All that is said is 'The Holy Ghost is of the Father and of the Son: not made nor begotten, but proceeding.' The doctrine is really stated in the form which would be least offensive to the Greeks, and to which it is believed that, if properly explained, they would even now take no exception. The crucial preposition *ex* (ἐκ), 'out of,' which has seemed to them to indicate a belief that the Spirit proceeds 'out of' the Son as a source or fount of Deity, is strikingly absent, and in its place the less definite '*a*' is used. It is a remarkable fact that the late George Williams tells us that the first time he visited Palestine he found a copy of the Athanasian Creed 'suspended in the Divan of the Greek Archbishop of Bethlehem, near the church which was erected by S. Helena, over what is supposed to be the place of our Lord's Nativity. What is more,' he proceeds to say, 'the copy which I saw there actually contained the double procession.'[1] Such a fact is very significant, and shows that the Greeks do not consider themselves to be condemned by the warning clauses of this Creed; and if a fair and reasonable construction is put upon the words of the Creed there is no sort of ground why any one else should imagine such a thing.

[1] *Report of Meetings in defence of the Athanasian Creed on Jan. 31, 1873* (reprint, 1904), p. 63.

THE ATHANASIAN CREED 247

(c) It is said, lastly, that the statements of the Creed go beyond the teaching of Scripture, and that they are untrue. If, indeed, they go beyond Scripture, then we have no right to make them, for in such a matter it is to Scripture that the Church must make her appeal as the ground of her teaching. But do they go beyond Scripture? Let us remind ourselves again of what it is that they really state, viz. the penalty of apostasy, of letting go what has been received, and that the only doctrines with which they deal are the doctrines of the Trinity and Incarnation, without which a man cannot be a Christian. Let us remember also what is the nature of the faith of which the Creed speaks. It is no mere barren orthodoxy, an affair of the intellect, but a matter of the *heart*: 'It is necessary . . . that he believe *faithfully* (fideliter) the Incarnation of our Lord Jesus Christ'—it is a faith that issues in good works and leads to action, 'for they that have *done good* shall go into life everlasting (or *eternal*) and they that have *done evil* into everlasting (or *eternal*) fire.' 'The condemnations,' says Bishop Dowden of Edinburgh, 'apply not to intellectual error, but to moral cowardice; . . . the emphasis is not on orthodoxy but fidelity. Everything points to the conclusion that it was loyalty, constancy, firmness in holding fast, and preserving despite temptations the faith as they had received it, that is the paramount thought of the *Quicunque*.'[1] Let us remember further that, as the

[1] *Helps from History to the true sense of the Minatory Clauses of the Athanasian Creed.*

late Dean Church has forcibly pointed out, 'The New Testament is a very severe book, as well as a very hopeful one. It takes a very severe view of the world, and of the ways and conduct of men. And certainly our Lord's own teaching is not the least stern part of it. Look at it carefully and you will find how large a proportion the language of rebuke and warning bears to the language of consolation and promise : the one is as grave, as anxious, as alarming, as the other is gracious beyond all our hopes.'[1] Bearing these things in mind, and remembering also that wherever the Creed adopts the words of Scripture we are justified in putting upon them precisely the same interpretation which we place upon them where they occur in Scripture,[2] let us ask ourselves whether the statements of the Creed taken together really go beyond the words of our Lord and His Apostles in such passages as these :—

S. John iii. 36. 'He that believeth on the Son hath everlasting life : and he that believeth not the Son shall not see life ; but the wrath of God abideth on him.'[3]

[1] *Human Life and its Conditions*, p. 102.

[2] 'Where the language of a doctrinal formulary and the language of the Bible are the same, whatever explanation we give, in case there is a difficulty, of the language of the Bible is applicable to the language of the formulary as well ; and therefore, in such a case, the statement in the formulary is no fresh difficulty, but only one which we have already surmounted in accepting the same statement in the Bible.'— Mozley, *Lectures and Theological Papers*, p. 220. This, of course, emphatically applies to such a term as 'everlasting (or *eternal*) fire.'

[3] Should it be urged that the R.V. has substituted 'disobeyeth' for 'believeth not,' Bishop Westcott's words supply the answer, '*Disbelief is regarded in its activity*.' Exactly so is it in the Creed as verse 39 shows.

THE ATHANASIAN CREED

[S. Mark] xvi. 16. 'He that believeth and is baptized shall be saved; but he that believeth not shall be damned.'

S. Matthew xxv. 41, 46. 'Then shall He say also unto them on the left hand, Depart from Me, ye cursed, into everlasting fire, prepared for the devil and his angels; . . . and these shall go away into everlasting punishment: but the righteous into life eternal.'

Heb. vi. 4-6. 'For it is impossible for those who were once enlightened, and have tasted of the heavenly gift, and were made partakers of the Holy Ghost, and have tasted the good word of God, and the powers of the world to come, if they shall fall away, to renew them again unto repentance: seeing they crucify to themselves the Son of God afresh, and put Him to an open shame.'

Heb. x. 26-31. 'For if we sin wilfully after that we have received the knowledge of the truth, there remaineth no more sacrifice for sins, but a certain fearful looking for of judgment and fiery indignation, which shall devour the adversaries. He that despised Moses' law died without mercy under two or three witnesses. Of how much sorer punishment, *suppose ye*, shall he be thought worthy, who hath trodden under foot the Son of God, and hath counted the blood of the covenant, wherewith He was sanctified, an unholy thing, and hath done despite unto the Spirit of grace? For we know Him that hath said, Vengeance belongeth unto me, I will recompense, saith the Lord. And again, the Lord shall judge His people. It is a fearful thing to fall into the hands of the living God.'

2 Thess. i. 7-9. 'The Lord Jesus shall be revealed from heaven with His mighty angels, in flaming fire taking vengeance on them that know not God, and that obey not the gospel of our Lord Jesus Christ: who shall be punished with everlasting destruction from the presence of the Lord, and from the glory of His power.'

Rev. xxi. 8. 'The fearful, and unbelieving (ἄπιστοι), and the abominable, and murderers, and whoremongers, and sorcerers, and idolaters, and all liars, shall have their part in the lake which burneth with fire and brimstone: which is the second death.'

These are passages which every one who accepts the teaching of Scripture is bound to face; and I cannot but think that they justify the warnings of the Athanasian Creed, for in view of the errors that have arisen, maiming and paring away from the faith, I see not how, if Jesus Christ be God, and if the Gospel teaches that God died for man, faith in Him and a belief in the Gospel can in any true sense remain, if men have let go the doctrine of the Trinity and the Incarnation; and if this is so, then it is surely the truest charity for the Church to repeat the warnings. She is bound to declare the whole counsel of God, and to proclaim in terms that men can understand the severe warnings as well as the gracious promises of Scripture; but in repeating and setting them forth she is careful to do so by way of proclamation, stating the law, as she finds it in Scripture, but not endeavouring to apply it to the case of any individual. This she dare not do, because to attempt it would be to claim to exercise the office of Him to Whom all judgment is committed, and to Whom alone the secrets of all hearts are open, and Who is, therefore, alone able to say in what cases there has really been deliberate and wilful rejection of the faith, deserving of the doom pronounced on such. Whatever qualifications or limitations common sense and an equitable consideration of the drift of words applies to our Lord's sayings in the passages cited above, or in such others as these: 'Except a man be born of water and the spirit, he cannot enter into the kingdom of God'; 'Except ye eat the flesh of the Son of Man, and drink His blood, ye have no life in you'; the very same ones should be applied to the language of the Creed. To do this is not to play fast and loose with language. It is simply to give it its ordinary interpretation, and not to take it in the worst sense possible. If it is to be understanded of the people, a proclamation must be made in general terms. If every conceivable exception be stated, or a *caveat* be put in against every possible misinterpretation, it not only loses its force, but it becomes hopelessly unintelligible to those for whom it is intended. The only documents into which such exceptions and *caveats* are introduced are legal ones, and any layman who has ever endeavoured to construe such knows how bewildering and puzzling they are. Let only such fair and equitable consideration be given to the words of the Athanasian Creed as is given by everybody to the statements of our Lord and His Apostles, and it is believed that much, if not all, of the difficulty that is widely felt about them will be removed.

Since, however, there have been various plans proposed for altering the status of the Creed and the use made of it in public worship of the Church of England, it will be well to conclude with a few remarks on the chief proposals made.

(1) It has been suggested that the use of it might be made optional instead of compulsory, by inserting *may* in the place of *shall* in the rubric.

The objections to such a plan are obvious. If there is irritation felt at the use of the Creed now, it would be increased a hundredfold were such a plan adopted. It would set clergy and congregations against each other, and would introduce strife and ill-feeling in many cases. Moreover, to make its use optional would completely alter the status of the Creed. It would be no longer the voice of the Church. 'The moment a clergyman may or may not use it, that moment the Creed ceases to be a part of the belief of the Church of which he is a minister. Its words become merely his own words; and when it is left to his discretion whether he may employ them or not, their whole force and weight are at once necessarily lowered. We have lost the Creed unless it speaks the voice of the Church—unless it is accepted as the solemn declaration of truth which Christ has revealed, and which the Church has accepted, and authoritatively placed before us.'[1]

[1] Dean Gregory, *Speech at meeting in defence of the Athanasian Creed*, 1873.

THE ATHANASIAN CREED

(2) A second suggestion is that it might be repeated without the monitory clauses.

The anathemas, we are told, have been dropped from the Nicene Creed. Why then, it is asked, should these clauses not be excised from the Athanasian? The answer is that the cases are in no way parallel. To begin with, it is doubtful whether the anathemas were ever properly appended to the Enlarged Creed, and anyhow, there is no evidence that the Church has ever used it with them. True, they are found in the Creed as given in the text of Epiphanius, but they are not found in the Creed as recited at Chalcedon in 451, the first occasion on which, so far as we know, any public use of it was made by the Church. Then, further, the anathemas of the Nicene Creed are simply appended to it: they form no part of it, and are easily separable from it, whereas the warning clauses of the Athanasian Creed are bound up with it, and cannot be excised without what amounts to a serious mutilation of the document. Would the advocates of this plan be contented with the removal of clauses 1, 2, and 42? Most surely not; they would require also the removal of verses 28 and 29, in which case the two halves of the document would fall asunder, and its unity would be destroyed. But further, to allow the competence of one branch of the Church thus to deal with a document which comes down from such venerable antiquity, as a confession of faith of (to put it at the lowest) the whole Western Church, is to introduce a principle that is of very wide application, and may lead to disastrous results in the future. Where is such dealing with the text to stop? As is well known, this plan was at one time adopted by the authority of the Dean in Westminster Abbey, where not only were verses 1, 2, 28, and 42 excised, but the text of verse 29 was deliberately altered, so that it was no longer said that 'it is necessary to everlasting salvation that he also believe rightly the Incarnation of our Lord Jesus Christ'; and what is almost more extraordinary, verses 40 and 41 were also excised, and the words 'at whose coming all men shall rise again with their bodies; and shall give account for their own works. And they that have done good shall go into life everlasting: and they that have done evil into everlasting fire,' were not allowed to be recited in the Abbey. This plan of dealing with the Creed has now happily been discarded. But it is mentioned here because it indicates a grave danger. If one positive doctrinal statement may legitimately be expunged, who can reasonably object to the excision of another, to which exception may be taken? Moreover, if it be admitted that it is within the competence of one branch of the Church thus to deal with the text of one of the three Creeds, why should it not deal in the same way with the text of the others? Admit the principle, and a demand may any day be made for the removal from the Apostles' Creed (which also comes to us on the authority of the Western Church) of the articles in which we express our belief in our Lord Jesus Christ as 'born of the Virgin Mary' and as having 'risen again the third day from the dead.'[1] The document has come down to us as an integral whole, and as such it ought to be treated. It has, indeed, been contended that anathemas are not for public worship or for the use of the laity, and on this ground the use made of the Creed has been deprecated.[2] To this the fact that has already been emphasised, that the clauses in question are not anathemas, supplies the real answer. It must be repeated once more that to warn the faithful of the danger of letting go what they have received is not to anathematise them ; and it is not, therefore, fair to speak as if the recitation of the Creed in full involved the 'exaltation of anathemas into an integral and permanent part of Christian worship.'[3] Moreover, the evidence adduced above of the attempts made in early days to familiarise the laity with the Creed indicates that, whatever may have been the exact intention of its unknown author, the Church was not slow to grasp the value of the Creed for lay folk as well as for clergy, and the existence of the warning clauses formed no obstacle to its use not only as an instruction for them, but also devotionally in public worship.

[1] The precedent of the American Church, which in 1790 allowed 'any churches' to 'omit the words, *He descended into hell*' in reciting the Apostles' Creed, is surely not one to be followed. The American Church has herself recognised the unwisdom of the act, and has removed the permission from her Prayer Book. All that is allowed now is the substitution of '*He went into the place of departed spirits*,' which are considered as words of the same meaning in the Creed.

[2] *The History and Use of Creeds and Anathemas in the Early Centuries of the Church*, by C. H. Turner, p. 82 *seq.*

[3] *Ibid.*, p. 88.

(3) A third proposal is that the rubric before the Creed should be removed, as has been done by the Church of Ireland, so that the Creed while remaining in the Prayer Book should be no longer used in public worship.

This suggestion does not raise so important a question of principle as the previous one. It cannot be denied that it is within the competence of the Church so to act. Changes have been made on previous occasions as to the rules governing the use of the Creed, and if necessary they may be made again. It is a question of wisdom and advisability rather than of principle. But the public recitation of this Creed acts as a solemn reminder of the responsibility of the intellect in matters of faith, with which we can ill afford to dispense; and, looking at the importance of maintaining a firm faith in the doctrines of the Trinity and Incarnation, and having regard to the immense value of the Creed as expounding these doctrines, it would, in the belief of the present writer, be an incalculable loss, and one which would render the Church's task immeasurably greater than it is at present, if the Creed was to be no longer publicly recited in our churches. The Dean of Westminster was surely right when, in words that have been already cited, he said, 'If it still stood in the Prayer Book, but with no rubric for its use, it would soon be as unfamiliar to most of us as the prayers for use at sea.'[1] That is a contingency which

[1] See above, p. 242.

THE ATHANASIAN CREED 257

in days when indefiniteness of belief is only too common, the Church cannot lightly contemplate.

(4 and 5) There remain the suggestions of a synodical declaration, or rubrical note, and of a new translation.

It is widely said at present that neither of these would be sufficient to satisfy the objectors; and possibly neither of them would by itself. But it is believed that in combination they might go far to do so. It has been already shown how much less harsh the original Latin is than the English, and that there is need of a change of rendering in several of the clauses. And if a new translation were accompanied by an explanatory note introduced with it into the text of the Prayer Book, such as those which stand after the order of the Holy Communion, and the Public Baptism of Infants, it is very possible that in a short time the common misunderstanding of the meaning of the Creed would disappear, and that we should hear less of the objections now raised to its recitation. It must be remembered that this course has never yet been tried. Twice over the Lambeth Conference has asked for a new translation. Its request has never been granted. Twice over Convocation has made a synodical declaration on the meaning of the Creed, but it has remained buried in the records of that body, and its existence is not known to one in a thousand among churchmen. All that is wanted is that the request of the Lambeth Conferences of 1888 and 1897 should be granted, and that the Synodical Declaration of 1873 and 1879 should be somehow introduced together with the new translation into the text of the Prayer Book, or (if it be found ultimately that there are insuperable difficulties in the way of this being done) that they should be together printed at the end of the book as a kind of appendix to it. If this were done constant reference could be made to them by preachers, and congregations could be properly instructed in the meaning of the Creed. If more pains were taken by clergy in expounding it, and more study devoted to its language and meaning by congregations, the result might in many cases be the removal of objections which have been somewhat hastily taken up, and have been thought to be serious because an immediate answer did not seem to be forthcoming. The experience of the great Duke of Wellington is worth recording, and may serve to conclude this defence of the use of the Creed. On one occasion at a party at which the Duke was present, a person was expressing his dislike for and objection to the Athanasian Creed. The Duke declined to discuss the subject at dinner, but said he would speak to him about it afterwards. When dinner was ended he took the man aside, and said: 'After the war was over, I thought it my duty to inquire why I was a member of the Church of England, and I examined the Prayer Book, the Articles, and especially the Athanasian Creed, and after doing this, and reading that famous treatise of Waterland's, I came to the conclusion that every word of it is borne out by Holy Scripture.'[1]

[1] Quoted in a speech by the late Sir George Prevost in the Lower House of Convocation. See *Chronicle of Convocation*, Sessions April and May 1872, p. 447.

Note F

EARLY AUTHORITIES FOR THE ATHANASIAN CREED

In the following note are given as briefly as possible specimens of the detailed evidence for the early date of the Athanasian Creed, arranged under the various headings given in the text.

(1) *Writers of the Ninth Century who cite the Creed as the work of Athanasius.*

(*a*) Hincmar of Rheims (*c.* 857).—*De una et non trina Deitate.*—'Sic crede et confitere sicut credit confitetur et prædicat sancta Catholica et Apostolica ecclesia, dicens ; Fides Catholica hæc est ut unum Deum in Trinitate personarum et Trinitatem personarum in Unitate Deitatis veneremur, neque confundentes personas sicut Sabellius ut tres non sint, neque ut Arius substantiam separantes ut trina sint. Quia alia non aliud est persona Patris, alia non aliud est persona Filii, alia non aliud est persona Spiritus Sancti. Sed Patris et Filii et Spiritus Sancti una est Divinitas, æqualis gloria, coæterna majestas. Et in hac Sancta et inseparabili Trinitate nihil est prius aut posterius, nihil majus vel minus, sed totæ tres personæ Pater et Filius et Spiritus Sanctus coæternæ sibi sunt et æquales. Ita ut per omnia, sicut jam supradictum est, et Trinitas personarum in unitate Deitatis, et Unitas Deitatis in Trinitate personarum veneranda sit.'—Migne, cxxv. p. 616. In this passage Hincmar directly refers to verses 3, 4, 5, 6, 24 and 25. Elsewhere he clearly refers to other verses ; and in his *Explanatio in ferculum Salomonis* he appears to refer to the portion of the Creed which deals with the Incarnation, while in the second of his treatises on Predestination he directly quotes verse 38 :—' Ad cujus

259

adventum secundum fidem Catholicam omnes homines resurgere habent cum corporibus suis.'—*De Prædest.*, Epil. c. 6.—Migne, cxxv. 464. For his references to the Creed as the work of Athanasius see *De una et non trina Deitate* (Migne, cxxv. p. 531), and cf. below under (2)*a*.

(*b*) Agobard of Lyons (*c*. 820).—*Adversus Felicem.*—' Beatus Athanasius ait Fidem Catholicam nisi quis integram inviolatamque servaverit, absque dubio in æternum peribit.'—Migne, civ. p. 35.

(*c*) Theodulf of Orleans (794-821).—*De Processione Sancti Spiritus.*—' Pater a nullo est factus, nec creatus, nec genitus. Filius a Patre solo est, non factus, nec creatus, sed genitus. Spiritus Sanctus a Patre et Filio, non factus, nec creatus, nec genitus, sed procedens. Unus ergo Pater, non tres Patres; unus Filius, non tres Filii; unus Spiritus Sanctus, non tres Spiritus Sancti. Et in hac Trinitate nihil prius aut posterius, nihil majus aut minus, sed totæ tres personæ coæternæ sibi sunt et coæquales. Ita ut per omnia, sicut jam supradictum est, et Trinitas in Unitate et Unitas in Trinitate veneranda sit. Qui vult ergo salvus esse, ita de Trinitate sentiat.'—Migne, cv. 247.

It is also said of Theodulf in a very early Life of him that he wrote a Commentary on this Creed. ' Explanationem edidit symboli Sancti Athanasii, quod a monachis post tres regulares psalmos ad primam cotidie canitur.'—See Ommanney, *Critical Dissertation*, etc., p. 19.

(*d*) Alcuin (804).—*Libellus de Processione Sancti Spiritus.*— ' Beatus igitur Athanasius reverendissimus Alexandriæ urbis Episcopus, qui summo ejusdem urbis pontifici Alexandro, suo etiam præceptori devotus adjutor in Nicæno fuit concilio, in *Expositione Catholicæ fidei*, quam ipse egregius doctor conscripsit, et quam universalis confitetur ecclesia, processionem Spiritus Sancti a Patre et Filio declarat, ita dicens: Pater a nullo est factus, nec creatus, nec genitus; Filius a Patre solo est, non factus, nec creatus, sed genitus; Spiritus Sanctus a Patre et Filio, non factus, nec creatus, nec genitus, sed procedens.'—Migne, ci. 73.

'Qualis enim Pater, et beatus Athanasius Alexandriæ urbis Episcopus testatur, talis et Filius, talis et Spiritus Sanctus; in hac enim Trinitate nihil prius aut posterius, nihil majus aut minus, sed totæ tres personæ coæternæ sibi sunt et coæquales. Ita ut per omnia, sicut jam supradictum est, et Unitas in Trinitate, et Trinitas in Unitate veneranda sit. Qui vult ergo salvus esse ita de Trinitate sentiat.'—Migne, ci. 82.

(*e*) The Monks of Mount Olivet (809).—*Epistola peregrinorum monachorum.*—' In regula Sancti Benedicti, quam nobis dedit filius vester domnus Karolus, quæ habet fidem scriptam de sancta et inseparabili Trinitate, dicit: Credo Spiritum Sanctum Deum verum ex Patre procedentem et Filio. Et in dialogo, quem nobis vestra sanctitas dare dignata est, similiter dicit. Et in fide sancti Athanasii eodem modo dicit.'—Migne, cxxix. 1257 *seq.*

(2) *Canons, Capitulars, and Episcopal directions of the Ninth Century charging the Clergy to learn the* QUICUNQUE VULT *by heart.*

(*a*) Hincmar.—' Necnon et sermonem Athanasii de fide, cujus initium est: *Quicunque vult salvus esse,* memoriæ quisque commendet, et sensum illius intelligat, et verbis communibus enuntiare queat.' *Capitula Synodica.*—Migne, cxxv. p. 773.

(*b*) Theodulf.—'Itaque vos, o Sacerdotes Domini, admonemus ut fidem Catholicam et memoriter teneatis et corde intelligatis, hoc est *Credo,* et *Quicunque vult salvus esse,* ante omnia opus est ut teneat *Catholicam fidem.*'—Migne, cv. p. 209.

(*c*) Hatto of Basle (806-836).—' Quarto ut fides Sancti Athanasii a sacerdotibus discatur et ex corde die Dominico ad horam primam recitetur.'—Labbe, *Concilia,* xiv. p. 391.

(3) *Canons of earlier date to the same effect.*

Ommanney cites two Canons which are almost certainly earlier than the ninth century, one of which certainly, and the other probably, refers to the *Quicunque vult.*

(*a*) *Epistola Canonica.* 'An Episcopal charge, containing a

262   THE THREE CREEDS

series of canons or capitula with reference to the duties of the clergy.' This begins as follows: 'Primum omnium Fidem Catholicam omnes presbyteri, diaconi, seu subdiaconi memoriter teneant, et si quis hoc faciendum prætermittat, xl. diebus a vino abstineat; et si post abstinentiam neglexerit commendandum, replicetur in eo sententia.' Good reasons are given for thinking that this Canon, which is found in several collections, is an early one — it has even been assigned to the sixth century—and that the *fides Catholica* can only have been the Athanasian Creed. See Ommanney, *Critical Dissertation*, etc., p. 47 *seq.*

(*b*) A canon of Autun. 'Si quis presbyter, diaconus, subdiaconus vel clericus symbolum quod Sancto inspirante Spiritu apostoli tradiderunt, et fidem Sancti Athanasii præsulis irreprehensibiliter non recensuerit, ab episcopo condamnetur.'

This Canon is found in several MSS. of the ninth century, and in one of the eighth or ninth, and there is no reason to doubt that it was framed at the Synod of Autun held under S. Leger in 670, or that the fides Sancti Athanasii was the *Quicunque vult* and not some other document. See Ommanney, *op. cit.* p. 52, and Burn, *Introduction to the Creeds*, p. 156.

(4) *MSS. of the Creed of the Ninth Century or earlier.*

MSS. of the ninth century containing the Creed are tolerably numerous. There is no necessity to give a complete list of them. The following Psalters are, however, specially worthy of notice, at least one of them being even earlier than the ninth century.

(*a*) Psalter of Lothaire (about 834). Fides sancti Athanasii Episcopi. This MS. is now in private hands. It is described by Ommanney, *Critical Dissertation*, etc., p. 118.

(*b*) Vienna, 1861. Fides Sci Athanasii Episcopi Alexandrini. This Psalter was presented by 'Charles' to Pope Hadrian, and if, as is commonly thought, 'Charles' is to be identified with Charlemagne, and Hadrian with Hadrian I., this MS. must be dated as early as 772. It has been suggested that it may be a century later, Charles being identified with Charles the Bald,

THE ATHANASIAN CREED   263

and Hadrian with the second of that name ; but the earlier date is now generally accepted.

(c) The Psalter of Count Henry, at Troyes, in the Treasury of the Cathedral. Ninth century. No title.

(d) Brit. Mus. Galba. A. xviii. Generally known as Athelstan's Psalter. Fides Sancti Athanasii Alexandrini. This MS., which was dated by Waterland A.D. 703, is now universally assigned to the ninth century.

(e) The Utrecht Psalter. Fides Catholica. Ninth century, but a copy of an earlier MS.

(f) Würtzburg, University Library, *Cod. Mp. th.* f. 109. Ninth century. No title.

(g) Rheims, Town Library, *Cod.* 20. Ninth century. No title.

(h) Paris, Bibl. Nat. 13159. In this the *Quicunque* has no title. The date of the MS. is fixed by internal evidence to the latter years of the eighth century between 795 and 800. See Ommanney, p. 107.

Other MSS. of a different character containing the Creed, and belonging to the early part of the ninth or to the eighth century, are the following :—

(i) Vatican, *Palat.* 540. Incipit fides Catholica beati Athanasii Episcopi. This is a collection of Canons assigned to the sixth century, followed by some other documents which include the Creed. The MS. itself is assigned to the ninth century.

(k) Karlsruhe, *Cod. Augiensis,* ccxxix. A miscellaneous volume, dated some time before 821 A.D. See Burn, *Introd.,* etc., p. 185. No title.

(l) Karlsruhe, *Cod. Augiensis,* xviii. A collection of Creeds and Commentaries, assigned to the ninth century. No title.

(m) Munich, Royal Libr., *Cod. lat.* 6330. A collection of *Doctrinae diversorum Patrum,* of the eighth or ninth century. Fides Sancti Ath[an]asii. Epi.

(n) Munich, Royal Libr., *Cod. lat.* 6298. A miscellaneous collection, assigned to the eighth century. No title.

(o) Paris, Bibl. Nat. 1451. Incipit exemplar fidei C̅h̅t̅. S̅c̅i Atanasii Epi Alexandrine ecclesie. A collection of Canons, together with the full text of the *Quicunque*, probably written before the death of Leo III. in 816.

(*p*) Paris, Bibl. Nat. 3848. Fides Sanct. Athanasii Episcopi. A collection of Canons, together with a series of testimonies to the faith, and among them the *Quicunque*. Early ninth century.

(*q*) Paris, Bibl. Nat. 4858. No title. The *Chronicon* of Eusebius, to which is appended the *Quicunque*. The volume is mutilated, and only the first eleven verses of the Creed are given, the remainder being torn off. The volume is assigned to the latter part of the eighth century.

(*r*) Lyons MS., containing a collection of Creeds, including the *Quicunque* (no title). The MS. contains an autograph inscription stating that it was given to the Altar of S. Stephen at Lyons by Leidrad, who was Archbishop of Lyons from 798 to 814. It cannot therefore be later than the early years of the ninth century. See Burn, p. 173.

(*s*) St. Petersburg, Imp. Libr. *Cod.* Q OTΠ. i. 15. This is now identified as the lost MS. St. Germains, 257, described by Waterland and Ommanney (p. 97) after Montfaucon (= Mabillon's *Corbiensis*, 267). Fides Sancti Athanasii Episcopi Alexandriæ. Assigned to the eighth century.

(*t*) Milan, Ambr. O. 212 *sup.* No title. A miscellaneous volume containing the Creed entire. Certainly not later than the eighth century, and possibly as early as 700. See Burn, p. 186. No title.

The above list furnishes complete evidence (1) that the Creed had obtained such recognition in the ninth century as to be freely included in the Psalters of the Church; and (2) that unless all the experts in palæography are wrong, it is an absolute impossibility that it can have been composed or put together from previously existing documents in the age of Charlemagne.

(5) *Mediæval Commentaries.*

A full account of these is given by Ommanney (cap. iv.), who made the subject peculiarly his own and added greatly to our knowledge. The earliest appear to be the following :—

THE ATHANASIAN CREED 265

(*a*) The Bouhier Commentary, assigned by Ommanney on internal evidence to the eighth century (p. 195 *seq.*), by Dr. Burn to the beginning of the ninth (*Introd.* p. 164).

(*b*) The Oratorian Commentary, compiled, according to Ommanney, 'some time between A.D. 681, when the sixth General Council was held, and the close of the Monothelite controversy at the end of the seventh or the commencement of the eighth century' (p. 189). But see Burn, p. 166, where it is placed later, and suggested that it might be the lost Commentary of Theodulf of Orleans. It should be noticed that in both this and the Bouhier Commentary the *Quicunque* is said to be ascribed to Athanasius *etiam in veteribus codicibus*.

(*c*) The Troyes Commentary, dating according to Ommanney from the middle of the seventh century during the height of the Monothelite controversy (p. 187), but assigned by Dr. Burn to the period when Adoptianism was an active heresy, *c.* 780-820 (*Introd.* p. 168).

(*d*) The Commentary of 'Fortunatus.' This has been long known, and was formerly believed to be the work of Venantius Fortunatus, Bishop of Poictiers about 570. It is, however, only ascribed to 'Fortunatus' in one comparatively late MS., and the view that it was the work of the Bishop of Poictiers is now generally abandoned, though it is certainly a very early work, and may have been written 'not later than the early part of the seventh century, possibly at the close of the sixth' (see the reasons for this in Ommanney, p. 166 *seq.*), but cf. Burn (*Introd.* p. 171), who puts it later, saying that 'we may fairly conclude that he [the author] wrote at least a century before the date 799.'

(6) *Coincidences with, and apparent allusions to, the* QUICUNQUE *in writers before the Ninth Century.*

(*a*) Profession of faith by Deuebert, Bishop of Worcester in 798 :—

'Insuper et orthodoxam Catholicam Apostolicamque fidem sicut didici paucis exponam verbis, quia scriptum est quicunque vult salvus esse ante omnia opus est illi ut teneat

Catholicam fidem. Fides autem Catholica hæc est ut unum Deum in Trinitate et Trinitatem in Unitate veneremur; neque confundentes personas neque substantiam separantes; alia est enim persona Patris, alia Filii, alia Spiritus Sancti; sed Patris et Filii et Spiritus Sancti una est Divinitas, æqualis gloria, coæterna majestas; Pater a nullo factus est, nec creatus nec genitus; Filius a Patre solo est; non factus, nec creatus, sed genitus; Spiritus Sanctus a Patre et Filio, non factus, nec creatus, nec genitus, sed procedens. In hac Trinitate nihil prius aut posterius, nihil majus aut minus, sed totæ tres personæ coæternæ sibi sunt et coæquales; ita ut per omnia, sicut supradictum est, et Trinitas in Unitate et Unitas in Trinitate veneranda sit. Suscipio etiam decreta Pontificum, et sex Synodos Catholicas antiquorum heroicorum virorum et præfixam ab eis regulam sincera devotione conservo. Hæc est fides nostra, etc.'
—Haddan and Stubbs, *Councils and Eccl. Documents*, iii. 526.

(*b*) Confession of faith promulgated by the fourth Council of Toledo, 633:—

'Secundum divinas scripturas et doctrinam, quam a sanctis patribus accepimus, Patrem et Filium et Spiritum Sanctum unius Deitatis atque substantiæ confitemur, in personarum diversitate Trinitatem credentes, in Divinitate Unitatem prædicantes, nec personas confundimus nec substantiam separamus. Patrem a nullo factum vel genitum dicimus, Filium a Patre non factum sed genitum asserimus, Spiritum vero Sanctum nec creatum, nec genitum, sed procedentem ex Patre et Filio profitemur, ipsum autem dominum nostrum Jesum Christum Filium Dei et Creatorem omnium, ex substantia Patris ante sæcula genitum . . . æqualis Patri secundum Divinitatem, minor Patre secundum humanitatem . . . perferens passionem et mortem pro nostra salute, non in virtute Divinitatis sed in infirmitate humanitatis, descendit ad inferos, ut sanctos, qui ibidem tenebantur, erueret, devictoque mortis imperio resurrexit; assumptus deinde in cælos venturus est in futuro ad judicium vivorum et mortuorum; cujus morte et sanguine mundati remissionem peccatorum consecuti sumus, resuscitandi ab Eo in die novissima in ea, qua nunc vivimus in carne et in ea qua resurrexit idem Dominus,

forma, percepturi ab ipso, alii pro justitiæ meritis vitam æternam, alii pro peccatis supplicii æterni sententiam. Hæc est catholica fides, hanc confessionem conservamus atque tenemus, quam quisquis firmissime custodierit perpetuam salutem habebit.'
—Hahn, *Bibliothek der Symbole*, p. 235.

It will be noticed that there are remarkable coincidences of language between this document and *both* parts of the Quicunque, and that they are so close as to imply almost certain dependence of one formulary on the other. The only reasonable question is as to the side on which is the dependence; and since on other grounds the *Quicunque* must be dated before the seventh century, we may fairly conclude that this formulary of Toledo is indebted to it for its phraseology.

(c) Cæsarius of Arles (502-542) :—

'Rogo et admoneo vos, fratres carissimi, ut quicunque vult salvus esse, fidem rectam ac catholicam discat, firmiter teneat, inviolatamque conservet. Ita ergo oportet unicuique observare ut credat Patrem, credat Filium, et credat Spiritum Sanctum. Deus Pater, Deus Filius, Deus et Spiritus Sanctus; sed tamen non tres Dii, sed unus Deus. Qualis Pater, talis Filius, talis et Spiritus Sanctus. Attamen credat unusquisque fidelis quod Filius æqualis est Patri secundum Divinitatem, et minor est Patre secundum humanitatem carnis, quam de nostro assumpsit; Spiritus vero Sanctus ab utroque procedens. Credite, ergo, carissimi,' etc. : August., *Opera*, vol. v.; Appendix, Serm. ccxliv.

The sermon is assigned by the Benedictine editors of S. Augustine to Cæsarius, and their conclusion is confidently adopted by modern writers, as Caspari, Kattenbusch, G. F. Arnold, and Malnory, as well as by Ommanney and Burn. Once more it should be noticed that the coincidences extend to *both* parts alike of the Quicunque.

(d) Avitus, Bishop of Vienne, 490-523. *De Divinitate Spiritus Sancti* :—

'Quem nec factum legimus nec genitum nec creatum. . . . Sicut est proprium Spiritui Sancto a Patre Filioque procedere istud fides Catholica etiamsi renuentibus non persuaserit, in suæ tamen disciplinæ regula non excedit.'—Migne, lix. 385, 386. See Ommanney, p. 2, where attention is drawn to the fact that Avitus is definitely quoting from some written work, as is shown by his use of the word *legimus*. It should also be noted that *Fides Catholica* is one of the earliest titles given to the *Quicunque*.

(*e*) Vincent of Lerins, *c*. 450.   *Commonitorium*, cap. xiii. :—

'Ecclesia vero catholica . . . et unam Divinitatem in Trinitatis plenitudine, et Trinitatis æqualitatem in una atque eadem majestate veneratur, et unum Christum Jesum, non duos, eundemque Deum pariter atque hominem confitetur . . . Alia est persona Patris, alia Filii, alia Spiritus Sancti. . . . Altera substantia Divinitatis, altera humanitatis ; sed tamen Deitas et humanitas non alter et alter, sed unus idemque Christus, unus idemque Filius Dei, et unius ejusdemque Christi et Filii Dei una eademque persona ; sicut in homine aliud caro, et aliud anima ; sed unus idemque homo, anima et caro . . . unus idemque Christus Deus et homo . . . idem Patri æqualis et minor ; idem ex Patre ante sæcula genitus, item in sæculo ex matre generatus ; perfectus Deus, perfectus homo ; in Deo summa Divinitas, in homine plena humanitas . . . Unus, autem, non corruptibili nescio qua Divinitatis et humanitatis confusione, sed integra et singulari quadem unitate personæ.'— Migne, l. 655.

(*f*) Besides these allusions in well-known writers there is the so-called 'Trèves' or 'Colbertine' fragment, known to us from a Paris MS. (Bibl. Nat. 3836), generally dated about 730. It has often been wrongly described as a MS. of the Creed. This it certainly is not ; it is a fragment of a sermon on the Creed, which, the writer says, he had discovered at Trèves. 'In it the author of the sermon adapts and modifies several verses of the Athanasian Creed, for the purpose of instructing his hearers in the doctrine of the Incarnation. It begins abruptly with the words of the 29th verse : " Domini nostri Ihesu Christi fideliter credat," and all the verses following, down to the 39th inclusive, are thus dealt with. The text of the Creed is not followed literally and exactly. No verse is reproduced without some variation, and in some places the divergence is very great.

THE ATHANASIAN CREED 269

The 35th verse is almost passed over. Still, the resemblance between the two documents is sufficiently obvious to show beyond a possibility of doubt the close relationship between them.'—Ommanney, p. 5. The date of the Trèves MS., from which the writer copied, must have been considerably older than that of the Paris MS., in which alone it is now known to us; and it is thought that the sermon itself may belong even to the fifth century, though so early a date cannot be postulated with certainty. The following is the full text of the fragment:—

'Haec invini Treveris in uno libro scriptum. sic incipiente Domini nostri Ihesu Christi. et reliqua Domini Nostri Ihesu Christi fideliter credat. Est ergo fides recta ut credamus et confitemur quia dominus ihesus christus dei filius. Deus pariter et homo est. Deus est de substancia patris ante saecula genitus, et homo de substancia matris in saeculo natus. perfectus deus, perfectus homo ex anima rationabili et humana carne subsistens aequalis patri saecundum divinitatem minor patri saecundum humanitatem. qui licet deus sit homo non duo tamen sed unus est christus. unus autem non ex eo quod sit in carne conversa divinitas. sed quia est in deo adsumpta dignanter humanitas. unus christus est non confusione substanciae sed unitatem personae qui secundum fidem nostram passus et mortuus ad inferna discendens. et die tertia resurrexit adque ad celos ascendit. ad dexteram dei patris sedet sicut vobis in simbulo tradutum est. Inde ad judicandos vivos et mortuos credimus et speramus eum esse venturum. Ad cuius adventum erunt omnes homines sine dubio in suis corporibus resurrecturi et reddituri de factis propriis rationem ut qui bona egerunt eant in vitam aeternam qui mala in ignem aeternum. Haec est fides sancta et catholica. quam omnis homo qui ad vitam æternam pervenire desiderat scire integræ debet. et fideliter custodire.'

(*g*) Dom Morin has recently called attention to another document which he compares with this. It is in the Library at Colmar, MS. 39, and is apparently part of a sermon, which cites language from both parts of the Creed. Its date is the eighth century. See the *Revue Bénédictine*, October 1905.

Note G

EARLY ENGLISH AND FRENCH METRICAL VERSIONS OF THE ATHANASIAN CREED

THE following Old English metrical version comes from the Bodleian MS. 425, and was first printed by Hickes in his *Linguarum Veterum Septentrionalium Thesaurus*, vol. i. p. 233. The date is said to be of the thirteenth century, *c.* 1240.

> Who so wil be sauf to blis
> Before alle thinges nede to is
> That he hald with alle his miht
> The heli trauthe and leve it riht
> Whilk bot ilken to queme
> Hole and wemles it yheme.
> Withouten drede bes thet forn
> Fro Godes sight in ai forlorn
> Sothelic the heli trauht this isse
> That o God inne thrinnesse
> And thrinness in onnesse
> Wurchip we the more and lesse
> Ne the hodes oht mengande
> Ne the stayelnes sondrande
> For other hode of Father other of Son
> Other of heli Gost wil with am wun.
> Bot of Fadir and Son and heli Goste
> On is Godes toningue that is moste
> Heven blis is til am thre
> Bi on in mikelhede to be
> Whilk the Fader whilk the Son
> Whilk heli Gost wil with am wun
> Unshapen Fader unshapen Son is
> Unshapen heli Goste in blis
> Mikel Father mikel Son ai
> Mekel heli Goste niht and dai.
> Ai lastand Fadir ai lastand Son
> Ai lastand heli be uton

THE ATHANASIAN CREED

And thow be ther noht thre ai lastand
But on ai lastand over al land
Als noht thre unmade ne mikel thre
But on unmade and on mickel is he.
Als so almihtand Fader almihtand Son
Almihtand heli Goste to wun
And thowhether noht almihtand
Bot on almihtand is licand
Als so God Fader God Sone isse
God hali Gost with am in blis
And thowhether noht Godes thre
Bon on is God and ai sal be
For als sengellic hode God oure louerd to be
Thurght christen sothenes lette sal be
So thre Godes or louerdes to kall
Thurght heli festnes forboden ar all
The Fadir of non made is he
Ne shapen ne kumed to be
The Son of only Fader blis
Noht shapen ne made but kumed is
The heli Goste of Fadir and Son mihtand
Noht shapen ne made but forth comand
Then o Fader noht Fadres thre
O Son noht thre Sones to be
O heli Gost and no mo
Of tham comand ne thre no two
And this thrinnes thet with inne
Noght first or latter noht more or minne
Bot al thre persones lastand ai
To tham and evenmette are thai
So that bi alle als bifore saide is
And thrinnenes in onnes
And onnesse in thrinnes ai
We to wurschip niht and dai
Who that then wil berihed be
So of the thrinness levo he
And nede at hele that last ai sal
That the flesshede ai with al

Of oure louerd Jhu Christ forthi
That he trowe it trewli
Then is ever trault right
That we leve withalle oure miht
That oure louerd Jhu Christ in blis
Godes Sone and man he his
Gode of kinde of Fadir kumed werld biforn
Man of kinde of moder into werld born
Fulli God fulli man livand
Of schilful saule and mannes flesshe beand
Even to the Fadir thurght God hede
Lesse then Fadir thurght man hede
That thof he be God and man
Noght two thrwthæther is bot Christ an
On noht thurght wendinge of Godhed in flesshe
Bot thurght takynge of manhede in Godnesshe
On al noht be menginge of stayelnes
Bot thurht onhede of hode that is
That yholed for oure hele doun went til helle
The thred dai ros fro dede so felle
Upstegh til heven sittes on right hand
Of God Fadir alle mightand
And yhit for to come is he
To deme the quik and dede that be
Ate whos come alle men that are
Sal rise with thaire bodies thare
And thelde sal thai nil thai ne wil
Of thair awen dedes il
And that wel haf doun that dai
Sal go to lif that lastes ai
And ivel haf doun sal wende
In fire lastend withouten ende
This is the trauht that heli isse
Whilk bot ilkon with miht hisse
Trewlic and fastlic trowe he
Saufe ne mai he never be.

THE ATHANASIAN CREED

(2)

The French metrical version which here follows is from a manuscript in the Bibliothèque Nationale at Paris (*Suppl. Franç.* 5145), apparently of the thirteenth century. The version was evidently composed, as its editor says, *ad usum Vulgi*. See *Libri Psalmorum versio antiqua Gallica* (Oxon. 1860), ed. F. Michel, Phil. D., p. 361.

SANCTI ATHANASII CREDO.

1. Qui voura estre saus,
   Si doit estre loiaulz
   Et la foi meintenir ;
   Ce li covenra faire
   Eins que nule autre afaire,
   S'à Deu wet parvenir.

2. La foi que nous creons,
   C'est ce qu' avoir devons
   i Deu en Trinité ;
   Et les parsones iii.
   Sunt, ce dist nostre lois
   Uns Deu et unité.

3. Ne devons, pour errer,
   Les persones mesler,
   Et la sainte substance
   Ne devons departir ;
   Qui en porroit isser
   Uns tems de mescreance.

4. Persone devisée
   Est au Pere donée
   Est au Fiz autresi ;
   Cele de Sains Espri
   Est autres, sens mentir,
   Qui cele que je di.

5. Mais une déités,
   Une divinités,

Sicum nous di la lois,
Une puissance autisme,
Une glorie méismes,
Est as persones iii.

6. L'une à l'autre est semblans ;
   Car li Peires est grans,
   Li Fiz od l'Esperit,
   Le Peire nun Criés
   Et li Fiz autretés,
   Le Saint-Espir ausi.

7. Li Peires si est grans,
   Et li Fiz ensement,
   [Li Sains-Espris ausi ;]
   Li Peires est durables,
   Li Fiz est permenables,
   Sains-Espris tout tens vit.

8. Ne sunt iii permenable
   Ne ne sunt iii durable,
   Mais i sols permegnans ;
   Ne ne sunt iii crié
   Ne ne sunt essaucé,
   Ains est i sous Deu grans.

9. Li Peires est puissans bien,
   Li Fiz puet toute riens,
   Li Sains-Espris tout puet ;
   Ne ne sunt iii puissant,
   Mais i Diex senglement :
   Ensi croire l'estuet.

10. Diex est Peire, Deu Fiz,
    Deu est Sains-Esperis,
    Sicum je l'a trové ;
    Mais iii deu nequedent
    Ne sunt, sicum je sent,
    Mais i Deu par vertés.

11. Li Peires est sire et rois
    Sire est li Fiz des lois,
    Li Sains-Espir est sire.
    Deus on ne doit nomer,
    Trois signour n'apeler,
    Mais i sol signour dire.

12. Sicum vertés commune
    Mostre person chaiscune
    Persone Deu clamer,
    Ensi deffant la lois
    Ices persones iii
    iii deu dire et nomer.

13. Li Peires n'est d'autrui
    N'est criés de nelui,
    Ne fais n'est ne formés ;
    Et li Filz del Peire est
    Ne fais ne formés n'est,
    Mais del Peire engendrés.

14. Seins-Espiris n'est criés
    Ne fais ne engenrés,
    Del Peire et de Fiz vient.
    Un Pere, non iii, croi ;
    i Fiz est non iii ;
    i Sains-Espris, non iii.

15. En ceste Trinité
    N'a nulle riens osté
    Ne avant ne après ;
    Mais les persones iii,
    Dist ensemble la lois,
    Permenables adès.

16. Aorés l'unitez,
    Vraie Trinité ;
    Vostre fois ités soit.
    Qui voura estre saus,
    Si doit estre loiaus
    Ensi croire le doit.

17. Mais qui virō et requiert
   Salus qui durable iert,
   A croire li estuet
   Que Dame-Deu a prise
   Char ; en nulle autre guize
   Salus avoir ne puet.

18. La foi qu'avoir devons,
   Est ce que nous creons
   Jhesu estre home et Dé ;
   Deu est de par la Peire
   Et hom de par la meire,
   Dont prist humanitez.

19. Parfais Deu, parfais hom,
   D'arme qui a raison
   Et de char d'onme esta ;
   En ce que il est Dieus
   Est-il au Peire niés,
   En char meins pooir a.

20. Il est Deu voirement,
   Deu et hom ensement,
   Verais Deus, verais hom ;
   Mais la lois nous aprent
   Qu'uns Deu est solement,
   Et non Diu par raisons.

21. Uns en l'umanité,
   Prins en sa deitez,
   Et uns en la sustance
   Que moller ne devom ;
   Mais uns en l'union
   Est de sa personance.

22. Par itele raison
   Qu'arme et chars est uns hons
   Per droiture apelés,
   Tous ensi faitement
   Deu et hom ensement
   Est i sols Cris només ;

23. Qui por nous mort souffri,
    En enfer descendi,
    Au tiers jor suscita ;
    A la destre del Pere,
    Le glorions sauvere,
    En ses sains cieus montait.

24. Dusqu'al jour de Juis
    Sera en paradis,
    Puis nous venrait jugier,
    Mors et vis jugerait :
    Qui en bien pris sera,
    S'aura riche louier.

25. A son avenement
    Venront communement
    Li home, et resordront,
    Et de tous lor bien fais,
    Ausi cum des meffait,
    Lor raison renderont.

26. Cil qui bien fait auront,
    Et ciel s'en iront
    En vie perdurable ;
    Cil qui auront mal fait
    En cest siecle entresait,
    Iront el feu durable.

27. Veiz ci toute la fois,
    Veis ci toute la lois ;
    Et qui ne le croira,
    S'il n'a ceste creance,
    Sachiés-vous sans doutance
    Que jai sans ne sera.

                      Amen.

The same manuscript contains a French metrical version of the Apostles' Creed ; see Michel, *op. cit.*, p. 361.

278 · THE THREE CREEDS

NOTE H

ON THE ENGLISH VERSION OF THE ATHANASIAN CREED

IT has been mentioned in the text that, although a few early English translations of the Athanasian Creed exist in MSS., it never found a place in the Primer before the sixteenth century. It was then included in the contents of several editions of that known as Hilsey's Primer (1539), where it was entitled 'The Symbole or Crede of the great Doctour Athanasius, dayley red in the Church'; but the translation there given differs widely from that with which we are familiar. That made for the English Prayer Book of 1549—which has remained in the Prayer Book ever since, with the slightest verbal alterations—was practically new; and interesting questions arise as to the sources from which it was drawn. It is clear that it was not made directly and simply from the Latin text of the Breviary, for it departs from this in various particulars of more or less importance. Waterland was the first to point out that these variations may be accounted for by the supposition that Cranmer, or whoever was responsible for the translation, had a Greek text before him; and it is now practically certain that this is the true explanation of some at least of the variations and peculiarities of translation. Four instances may be mentioned here.

(1) In verse 9, 'Immensus Pater, immensus Filius: immensus Spiritus Sanctus.' Hilsey's Primer rendered *immensus* by 'without measure,' as had an older Wicliffite version; whereas the rendering 'incomprehensible,' which has stood in our Prayer Book here and in verse 12 since 1549, was obviously suggested by a Greek version, which, as Waterland and Ommanney have shown, must have been accessible to the Reformers,[1] and which has the rendering ἀκατάληπτος.

[1] This Greek version was published, as Waterland shows, by Nicholas Bryling about the year 1540; but Ommanney has traced it back earlier, and finds it in several editions of a small book of Hours first edited by Aldus at Venice in 1497, as well as in a Greek Psalter printed at Strasburg in 1524, and Antwerp in 1533. See *Critical Dissertation*, p. 310.

(2) In verse 12 the Latin is 'Sicut non tres increati nec tres immensi: sed unus increatus et unus immensus.' In the English the order of the terms is reversed: 'As also there are not three incomprehensibles, nor three uncreated: but one uncreated and one incomprehensible.' Here, again, the Greek text has the same order as the English; οὐδὲ τρεῖς ἀκατάληπτοι οὐδὲ τρεῖς ἄκτιστοι.

(3) In verse 29 the Latin 'fideliter credat,' where Hilsey had 'believe faithfully' the Prayer Book version has 'believe rightly,' which obviously comes from the Greek ὀρθῶς πιστεύσῃ.

(4) In verse 42 the Latin is 'fideliter, firmiterque' (Hilsey, 'faithfully and stedfastlye'), where the Prayer Book has but the one word 'faithfully.' This also is accounted for by the Greek πιστῶς.

Other minor coincidences between the Greek and the English, where there is a departure from the Latin, might be mentioned, but these four are sufficient to make certain that the Greek has influenced our translation. It does not appear, however, that it was followed throughout, as there are several instances in which the English agrees with the Latin as against the Greek. Probably, then, the Latin text of the Breviary was taken as the basis of the translation, and this was corrected in various places by reference to what Cranmer may well have supposed to be the original, if, as is probable, he held the then wellnigh universal belief that the Creed was the work of Athanasius. Why, however, he did not allow the name of Athanasius to stand in the title it is impossible to say. It was called *Symbolum Athanasii* in the Breviary. Hilsey's Primer attributed it to 'the great Doctour Athanasius.' Cranmer himself in the Forty-two Articles of 1553 calls it 'Athanasius' Creed,' and no satisfactory explanation has ever been offered of the fact that in the Prayer Book he spoke of it simply as 'this confession of our Christian Faith.'[1]

[1] See Bishop Dowden, *The Workmanship of the Prayer Book*, p. 113.

INDEX

AACHEN, Council of, 162.
Ælfric, Canons of, 81.
Alcuin, 189, 260.
Agobard of Lyons, 189, 260.
Alexander, Bishop of Alexandria, 116.
Almighty, meaning of the term, 91.
American Prayer Book, the, 168, 203, 230, 255.
Apollinarianism, 70, 141, 239.
Apollinaris of Laodicæa, 141.
Apostles' Creed, the, traditional origin of, 40; origin of the name of, 46; history of, 49 *seq.*; later additions to, 60, 108; use of, in the Church, 80 *seq.*; doctrine of, 86 *seq.*; early English metrical translation of, 110.
Apostolical Canons, 216.
Apostolical Constitutions, 144.
Aquileia, Creed of, 69.
Arianism, rise of, 115.
Arius, 115.
Armenia, Creed of, 148.
Artemon, 134.
Aristides, Apology of, 61, 94.
Athanasian Creed, the, origin and growth of doubts as to its authorship, 181 *seq.*; question of date of, 185 *seq.*; theories of Ffoulkes, Swainson, and Lumby, as to, 187; evidence of early date of, 189 *seq.*; use of, 196; versions of, 198 *seq.*; position of, in the Greek Church, 204; exposition of, 206 *seq.*; history of objections to, 226 *seq.*; omitted from American Prayer Book, 230; Synodical Declaration on, 234; objections to, considered, 235 *seq.*; Bp. Cotton on, 237; Bp. M'Dougall on, 240; Dean Robinson on, 241; monitory clauses in, meaning of, 243; proposals for changing the use of, 252; request of Lambeth Conference for a new translation of, 257; early authorities for, 259 *seq.*; Canons referring to, 261; early MSS. of, 262; commentaries on, 264; early allusions to, 265; English and French metrical versions of, 270 *seq.*; origin of the English translation of, 278.
Athanasius, S., 119.
Augustine, S., 14, 23, 64, 77, 100, 110, 158, 186, 192.
Autun, Canon of, 262.
Avitus, Bishop of Vienne, 191, 267.
Aylmer, Bishop, 227.

BAIN, Professor, 9.
Balfour, the Right Hon. A. J., 103-4.
Bangor Antiphonary, the, 108, 110.
Baptismal formula, the, 20.
Baptismal Service, Creed of the, 57.
Basil, S., 132.
Baxter, R., 227.
Bede, Letter of, to Egbert, 80.
Benedict VIII., Pope, 163.
Bracara, Council of, 217.
Bright, Dr. W., 140.
Brightman, the Rev. F. E., 166.
Browne, Bishop Harold, 214.
Burn, Dr. A. E., 55, 110, 189, 196.

CÆSARIUS OF ARLES, 108, 109, 110, 191, 193, 267.
Carlyle, T., 9.
Cartwright, T., 22.

281

THE THREE CREEDS

Caspari, 42.
Catholic, meaning of the term, 62.
Chalcedon, Council of, 150.
Charlemagne, 56, 161.
Chase, Bishop, 88.
Chillingworth, 228.
Church, Dean, 248.
Clarke, Dr. S., 230.
Clement of Alexandria, 63.
Clifford, Professor, 9.
Clovesho, Council of, 81.
Communion of Saints, 72 seq.
Confession of Faith, required in Scripture, 13 ; value of it, 14.
Constantinople, Council of, 153.
Constantine, the Emperor, 118.
Convocation, Synodical Declaration of, 234.
Cotton, Bishop, 237.
Cranmer, Archbishop, 45, 175, 182, 278.
Creeds, traces of, in Scripture, 17 ; use of, in Baptism, 18 ; Interrogatory, 23 ; causes of development of, 26 ; Eastern and Western, 31.
Cyril of Jerusalem, 24, 54, 71, 143, 153, 171.
Cyprian, S., 53, 77, 109.
Cyprian of Toulon, 108.

DENEBERT, Bishop, 191, 265.
Descent into hell, the, 60 seq.
Development, how far found in the Creeds, 102.
Diogenes, Bishop of Cyzicus, 146.
Dionysius, Bishop of Rome, 50.
Docetism, 27.
Donatism, 76.
Dowden, Bishop, 175, 247, 279.
Durandus, 82.

EAST, turning to the, at the recitation of the Creed, 84.
Emerson, 9.
Epiphanius, 49, 144.
Erasmus, 44.
Eusebius of Cæsarea, 119 ; Creed of, 120 ; why insufficient, 121.
Eusebius of Nicomedia, 119.
Eusebius of Vercellæ, 182.
Eutychianism, 223.

FAITH, requirement of, in Scripture, 1 seq. ; meaning of, 6 ; reason for requirement of, 8 seq.
Faustus of Riez, 75, 108, 109, 110.
Felix, Bishop of Rome, 50.
Ffoulkes, the Rev. E. S., 187.
Filioque clause, introduction of the, into the Creed, 160 seq.
Firmilian of Cæsarea, 77.
Fleury, Abbey of, 197.
Frere, the Rev. W. H., 84.
Fulgentius of Ruspe, 108, 109, 110.

GALLICAN Creeds, 59.
Gelasian Sacramentary, 24, 161.
Gnostics, the, 29.
Gregorius Paulus, 226.
Gregory, Dean, 252.

Hades, 66.
Hahn, 58 *et passim*.
Hare, Archdeacon, 105.
Harnack, 50, 70, 87, 97.
Hatto of Basle, 190, 261.
Hell, meaning of the word, 65.
Henry II., the Emperor, 163.
Hieronymi Fides, 54, 69, 108, 109, 110.
Hilary of Arles, 185.
Hilary of Poictiers, 158.
Hilsey's Primer, 201, 278.
Hincmar of Rheims, 189, 198, 259, 261.
Hippolytus, Canons of, 24.
Holy Ghost, the, personality of, 95 ; procession of, 154.
Homoousios, meaning of the term, 123 ; necessity for its insertion in the Creed, 124 ; objections to, 125.
Honoratus of Arles, 194.
Hooker, R., 182, 202, 216, 227.
Hort, Dr., 149, 169 seq.
Hosius of Cordova, 119.

IGNATIUS of Antioch, 28, 63, 68, 94, 133.
Ildefonsus of Toledo, 109, 110.
Inferi, Inferna, 66.
Irenæus, 20, 51, 61, 68, 108.
Irish Prayer Book, the, 203.

INDEX

JEROME, S., 3, 54.
Jewel, Bishop, 182.
John of Biclarum, 166.
Justin II., 157, 167.
Justin Martyr, 61, 62, 68, 94, 207.

KATTENBUSCH, 50.

Lay Folk s Mass Book, 73, 110.
Leo III., Pope, 162, 189.
Lerins, 55.
Liddon, Dr., 136, 233.
Lightfoot, Bishop, 63.
Lumby, Professor, 187.

MACEDONIANISM, 95, 141.
Marcellus of Ancyra, 49, 119, 140.
Marcion, 50.
Martin of Bracara, 109, 110.
M'Dougall, Bishop, 240.
M'Giffert, A. C., 87.
Mediatorial Kingdom, Christ's, 176 *seq.*
Monarchia, the, 164.
Montanism, 77.
Morin, Dom, 55, 77, 191, 193.
Mozley, Professor, 248.
Muratorian Fragment, the, 63.

NESTORIANISM, 186, 238.
Nicæa, Council of, 118 *seq.*
Nicæa, Second Council of, 161.
Nicæa, Creed of, 127 *seq.*; in what sense a development, 136; enlarged form of, 145 *seq.*; sanctioned at Chalcedon, 151; introduced into the services of the Church, 157, 167 *seq.*; used at the *Traditio Symboli*, 167; English translation of the, 175.
Niceta of Remesiana, 54, 78, 108, 109, 110.
Nicodemus, Gospel of, 88.
Noetus of Smyrna, 207.
Notker of St. Gall, 198.
Novatian, 62.
Novatianists, the, 77.

OLIVET, monks of Mount, 162, 189.
Ommanney, Prebendary, 188, 191, 194.

Only Son, His, meaning of the term, 92.
Origen, 116.

PACIAN, Bishop of Barcelona, 63.
Paulinus of Aquileia, 187.
Pelagius, 109, 110.
Person, use of the term, 208 *seq.*
Peter, Gospel of, 68.
Peter the Fuller, 157.
Phæbadius of Agen, 108, 109.
Pionius, 63.
Pirminius, 56, 108.
Pliny, Letter to Trajan, of, 133.
Polycarp, of Smyrna, 52.
Praxeas, 207.
Priscillian, 109.
Psalters, early, containing the Athanasian Creed, 262.
Pusey, Dr., 233.

RECCARED, King, 159.
Ritual, Royal Commission on, 231.
Robinson, Dean, 19, 241, 256.
Rome, Creed of, in the fourth century, 47; traced to second century, 50; when and where enlarged, 52.
Rufinus of Aquileia, 39, 53, 69, 109.

SABELLIANISM, 115 *seq.*; 207, 238.
St. James's Hall, Meeting at, 233.
Sanday, Professor, 70, 71, 97.
Schopenhauer, 10.
Scotland, Prayer Book for, 219.
Seabury, Bishop, 230.
Sheol, 66.
Stanley, Dean, 231, 232.
Stillingfleet, Bishop, 229.
Stowe Missal, the, 163.
Substance, use of the term, 210.
Swainson, Professor, 82, 187.
Swete, Professor, 64, 65, 70, 92, 96.
Symboli Traditio et Redditio, 22.
Symbolum, meaning of the term, 40, 44.

TAIT, Archbishop, 232.
Tarasius, 161.
Taylor, Bishop Jeremy, 228.

Teaching of the Twelve Apostles, the, 89.
Tertullian, 21, 52, 208.
Theodulf of Orleans, 189, 197, 260.
Theophilus of Antioch, 208.
Thirlwall, Bishop, 232.
Tillotson, Archbishop, 229.
Timothy of Constantinople, 157.
Toledo, Council of, 159.
Toledo, Second Council of, 191.
Tours, Church of S. Martin at, 197.
Trent, Council of, 44.
Trinity, use of the term, 208.
Turner, C. H., 255.

Unicus and *Unigenitus*, 92.
Ussher, Archbishop, 185.

VALENTINUS GENTILIS, 226.
Valla, Laurentius, 44.

Venantius Fortunatus, 109, 185, 265.
Victorinus, 14.
Victricius of Rouen, 109.
Vigilantius, 75.
Vigilius, Pope, 217.
Vigilius Tapsensis, 185.
Vicentius Lirinensis, 185, 191, 193, 268.
Visitation of the Sick, the, 78.
Voss, Gerard, 182.

WATERLAND, DANIEL, 107, 185, 230, 258, 278.
Wellington, Duke of, 258.
Westcott, Bishop, 18, 92, 105, 248.
Whitgift, Archbishop, 227.
Whose Kingdom shall have no end, origin and meaning of the clause, 142, 176.
Williams, Dr. G., 246.

www.ingramcontent.com/pod-product-compliance
Lightning Source LLC
Chambersburg PA
CBHW050840230426
43667CB00012B/2081